Lt. SPALDING in
CIVIL WAR LOUISIANA

Lt. SPALDING in CIVIL WAR LOUISIANA

A Union Officer's Humor, Privilege, and Ambition

MICHAEL D. PIERSON

Louisiana State University Press

Baton Rouge

Published by Louisiana State University Press
Copyright © 2016 by Louisiana State University Press
All rights reserved
Manufactured in the United States of America
First printing

Designer: Laura Roubique Gleason
Typeface: Miller Text
Printer: McNaughton & Gunn
Binder: Dekker Bookbinding

Library of Congress Cataloging-in-Publication Data

Names: Pierson, Michael D., author.
Title: Lt. Spalding in Civil War Louisiana : a union officer's humor, privilege, and ambition / Michael D. Pierson
Other titles: Lieutenant Spalding in Civil War Louisiana
Description: Baton Rouge : Louisiana State University Press, 2016. | Includes bibliographical references and index.
Identifiers: LCCN 2016027017 | ISBN 978-0-8071-6439-6 (cloth : alk. paper) | ISBN 978-0-8071-6440-2 (pdf) | ISBN 978-0-8071-6441-9 (epub) | ISBN 978-0-8071-6442-6 (mobi)
Subjects: LCSH: Spalding, Stephen F., 1840–1863. | United States. Army. Vermont Infantry Regiment, 8th (1861–1865) | United States—History—Civil War, 1861–1865—Campaigns. | Louisiana—History—Civil War, 1861–1865—Campaigns. | Port Hudson (La.)—History—Siege, 1863. | Soldiers—Vermont—Biography.
Classification: LCC E533.5 8th .P54 2017 | DDC 973.7/32—dc23
LC record available at https://lccn.loc.gov/2016027017

To Jeremy S. Abramson, MD,
Brianne McGree, NP,
and the rest of the people at the
Center for Lymphoma at Massachusetts General Hospital,
in appreciation of their knowledge, talent, and compassion

CONTENTS

PREFACE
Entering the Archive

What is it that confers the noblest delight? What is that which
swells a man's breast with pride above that which any other experience can bring him? Discovery!

—Mark Twain, *The Innocents Abroad,* 1869

Walking into an archive is a wonderful thing to be able to do, a strange
blend of vacation and work. Very exciting work. Some of that excitement comes from the disconcerting act of walking into a new institution, one with its own customs and hierarchies. There are librarians to
meet and talk with about your project and their rules. Some libraries,
like the Historic New Orleans Collection or the American Antiquarian
Society, hit a perfect balance between helping you find what you are
looking for and making sure that their holdings are not damaged or
stolen. But no matter how friendly the staff may be, on that first morning all of this is just an infuriating delay keeping me from the letters,
diaries, and records that I'm there to see.

There's just no doubt about it—the moment of diving into the archives is the best of all professional worlds. You never know what you
might find. Who knows what's stored away somewhere, unseen for who
knows how many years? Even our popular culture toys with the idea
that at this moment even scholars who read old books can be exciting.
Consider the opening of two popular novels, both of which have
aroused Hollywood's interest. A. S. Byatt's novel *Possession* starts when
a down-on-his-luck graduate student named Roland Mitchell stum-
bles upon an old book that will launch the novel's action and change
his life. Deborah Harkness's *All Souls Trilogy* begins at the same moment, with researcher Diana Bishop picking up a book from a librarian
who tells her that it has not been taken out in ages. This kind of re-

search seems romantic and mysterious. Clearly, whatever Roland and Diana find will be theirs and theirs alone; no one else will know about it. It will be *new* knowledge.

And when knowledge is *new,* it gains a special appeal. It is hard otherwise to explain the appeal of archaeology, which is (or so I've heard) usually a dirty and physically taxing way to spend the day. But clearly people don't think of it that way—indeed, I don't think of it that way. What could be better than to unearth something that has not been seen for ages and that can tell you something that no one has known before? Accounts of archaeological finds can keep readers glued to the pages of *National Geographic* or David Winfred Noble's reports in Tuesday's "Science" section of the *New York Times.* Like many others, I've read Ivor Noël Hume's accounts of excavating Virginia's colonial past and wanted to join his next expedition, whatever it may be. Consider the way he starts his book, *Martin's Hundred,* which is about a series of digs in Virginia. Despite his New World focus, Hume starts in Egypt: "When, on November 26, 1922, Howard Carter knocked a small hole through the blocked doorway leading to Tutankhamun's tomb, his sponsor, Lord Carnarvon, asked: 'Can you see anything?' Peering into the shadows beyond the light from his flickering candle, Carter answered, 'Yes, wonderful things.'" Hume then elaborates on all of the "wonderful things" archaeologists can uncover, and his list does not include gold and silver. Rather, he says, he wants to have "the opportunity to peer into the past and to see wonderful things that no one has seen before. What keeps us going is the hope that it might happen."[1] The lure of new knowledge trumps the misery of lugging dirt in the heat and humidity of Tidewater Virginia. The thrill of the find is so great that cagey guides at Pompeii in the 1700s knew enough to arrange "discoveries" for their wealthiest clients.[2]

My own research adventures have been less dramatic—at least in their physical dimensions. I have never whisked dirt off of a long-buried skull (thank heavens!), let alone an entire buried colonial settlement. Sitting in a climate-controlled library with manuscripts is just not the same as sifting through Egyptian dust or Virginian clay. And unlike the characters in *Possession,* I have only rarely found things in archives that the librarians did not know were there. When I have "discovered" things, they have been minor, to say the least. I once bought a copy of a first edition of Alexander S. Webb's *The Peninsula: Mc-Clellan's Campaign of 1862,* printed in 1881, and quickly noticed that it had been annotated by a Union veteran. His notes, though, are brief. The most remarkable one is on the margin of page 113, which discusses the capture of Confederate general J. J. Pettigrew at the Battle of Fair Oaks. The sentence is underlined, and next to it is written: "Gave him my rubber blanket. N. P. H."[3] I am tempted to make much of this, to highlight (as an optimist) the decency of human nature, or to point (as an academic) to the postwar sectional reconciliation that sometimes played upon the trope of camaraderie between white Union and Confederate soldiers.[4] But I know that I only want to think this marginalia matters because it is, in a way, mine. I found it.

But really I have never found anything significant in an archive that was unknown to the librarians. Archived collections of letters from the Civil War have been read by too many people to contain secret stashes of documents. All of my discoveries have been, therefore, hiding in plain sight. This book is about the Stephen F. Spalding Letter, held by the Vermont Historical Society. Its existence has long been known; it is even listed on the Society's website for all to see. The Society's notation for it even reads like advertising copy, as if to draw in even the remotely curious: "Letter, July 8, 1862, from Stephen F. Spaulding [*sic*] to James S. Peck giving a candid and unusual account of life in the 8th Vermont Regiment and New Orleans."[5] But still, no one seems to have made too much of the letter, even though reading it has caused me to embark on what seemed at first to be a foolhardy project: to write an entire book about one letter. But the Spalding Letter sheds light on so many different aspects of Civil War America that I began to imagine, chapter by chapter, the outline of a book: humor; death; men and women; ambition; race; fear; premonitions. Later research trips to other places fleshed out the picture of Spalding's life and the meanings of his letter, and my conviction that this document has a lot to tell us only grew stronger. My discoveries would not be physical ones; I could not spot doubloons or yell "Eureka!" But all of us can find new knowledge by thinking longer about something than perhaps others have done. Whether that "something" is a historical source or a personal situation, giving a matter intense thought can turn up new ideas, new avenues of thought and action. Having spent several years with the

Stephen Spalding Letter, I can perhaps see into the writer's world and discover things about Civil War soldiers, or at least some of them, that have long been hidden, right where we can see them.

Civil War Letters and Their Place in Modern Culture

Before the house lights dim and the curtain goes up on Stephen Spalding's world, we need to look at the elevated place of Civil War letters in modern culture. Examining why such letters have become valued will tell us why, among all of the war correspondence that has filled our culture, the Spalding Letter can still strike us as arrestingly fresh. Americans (and others) have become almost reverential in the face of soldiers' letters. The Legacy Project, for example, gathers letters by American soldiers from all wars. Andrew Carroll, who has edited a collection of these letters, explains that "these letters are the first, unfiltered drafts of history. They are eyewitness accounts that record not only the minute details of war but the personal insight and perspective no photograph or film reel can replicate. And each one represents another page in our national autobiography." With Abigail Van Buren helping to spread the word through her column, the Legacy Project has received more than fifty thousand letters.[6] Clearly the rhetoric surrounding the Legacy Project has struck a collective nerve. The Civil War has a firm grasp on much of this literary market. Editions of Civil War soldiers' letters fill the catalogues of university presses and commercial publishers alike. I have had a good number of students ask me what their families should do with collections of World War II or Civil War letters; no one has ever asked me what they should do with peacetime letters, diaries, or documents.

Almost certainly Ken Burns's documentary film *The Civil War* fueled people's desire to seek out and read Civil War letters. By the end of its first run on the Public Broadcasting Service (PBS) in 1990, about 40 million people had seen at least part of the show, and I still meet people at Civil War Round Tables who first became fascinated with the war through the film.[7] Letters are one of the most moving parts of the program; the ones selected by Burns carry strong emotional appeals, especially love of family and of country. That the soldiers expressed themselves so well about love and sacrifice, family and patriotism, when they were on the verge of battle wins for them an authenticity that can seem lacking from public (or private) life now. The ideas and emotions of these writers seem to call through the decades to our often cynical age with a sincerity missing from our culture. It is not hard for a person who has just watched Ken Burns's film to walk away imagining the Civil War era, even with its bloodshed and violence, as a far, far better time.

The proximity of Civil War correspondents to death can make their letters too sad, too horrible to forget. Sullivan Ballou's letter to his wife, Mary, which Ken Burns included in *The Civil War*, stands in this class. But there are others. There is simply nothing that one can write after reading Lt. Col. Wilder Dwight's letter, written at Antietam and now housed at the Massachusetts Historical Society, that does not sound trivial by comparison.

> Near Sharpsburg September 17th
> 1862
> On the field.
>
> Dear Mother,
> It is a misty moisty morning. We are engaging the enemy and are drawn up in support of Hooker who is now banging away most briskly. I write in the saddle to send you my love and to say that I am very well so far.

Having written this much, Wilder Dwight entered the battle and was mortally wounded. He picked up his pen again, however, and finished what became his last letter. His penmanship is now much altered.

> Dearest Mother,
> I am wounded so as to be helpless. Good bye if so it must be.
>
> I think I die in victory. God defend our country. I trust in God & love you all to the last Dearest love to father & all my dear brothers Our troops have left the part of the field where I lay.
>
> Mother yrs
>
> Wilder
>
> All is well with those that have faith.[8]

The Massachusetts Historical Society chose this letter as one of the anchors of its 2011 Civil War exhibit, *The Purchase by Blood: Massachusetts in the Civil War*. They displayed the original letter but also reproduced it in a much larger format and placed it at eye level for people to read. In the midst of a visually rich exhibit, Dwight's letter was so moving as to almost erase everything else on display. It may even have driven the message of the entire exhibit, which centered on the sacrifices endured by Massachusetts soldiers and their families. Now, at the distance of a few years, I remember almost nothing else in the show.[9]

Other writers are just as moving, even if they were less schooled. The wartime letters of Melvyn Tibbetts create a memorable and sympathetic picture of this Maine soldier. Tibbetts had an eye for detail, and the sincerity of his letters home make reading his papers at the Historic New Orleans Collection a rich treat. He shows his readers details, charming and otherwise, as he writes his weekly letter home on Sunday mornings. On June 8, 1862, he describes himself to his family back in Maine: "this letter is writen on my knees and I am sitting flat on the ground. we have no seets here. So you cant expect to see anything much better than this from me especially." Nor was he content to merely describe himself. He placed himself "under the shade of a Fig tree. it is a large and handsome tree. it looks some like a Moosewood tree. the figs on them are as large as robins eggs." He then catalogues the trees around him, finding beauty even in a cedar tree that is not "like them in the north."[10] So we learn to like the young man from rural Maine and fancy that we can see through his eyes and live in his world, even knowing his family and his worries. Mercifully, he survives the Battle of Mansfield, in Louisiana, but his letter to his brother afterward conveys the extent to which the fighting unsettled him. His letter closes with:

> O Martin you can form some kind of an idear of course about battle but at the same time know nothing about the horrors of battle and the feelings of a man in a battle like that when we advanced on the rebs the ground was covered with men dead and dying but I felt just cool as I should driving the same amount of cattle. . . .—Martin while I was in the heavy of the fight I was loading and a ball came and struck my gun, nocked the tube of[f] and I lay it down and

picked up another springfield rifle and went in again. Martin the field for ½ mile was covered with guns [illegible words] and died and dying rebs and our men. oh what a sitein the eve after the battle. you could here in the woods men hollaring for some one to come and get them in the night. . . . Brother when I write this I am alive but when you get it I may not be but don't let that worry you at least.

from *Van*

Happily, Melvan lived a long life, long enough to fill his pension file in the National Archives almost to bursting.[11] In Melvan's case, it is the death of his brother Martin, presumed safe at home, that casts a pall over the collection:

Saturday May 27th [1864]

Oh can it bee possible that I should reed such news on opening a letter that came to me this morning. Oh can it bee that Dear Brother Martin is dead. what news will come. oh how can I believe that all this is real. well I suppose I must. but oh a harder thing I never was made to believe before. oh why should such a man as him die and leave such mortals as I on earth to lieve—but there I suppose it is all for the best. Mother I dont want you to worry a bit about me for I am real healthy and rugged and you have got enough to think of besides worrying about me for this cam pain is over for this summer and we are soon to go to N. O. Where we six months men are probably to quater for the summer. but there I cant write any more now. I will try and write again soon. now keep up good courage at home all of you and I will do the same here for it is a thing we can not help. tell mother to [illegible] good courage, write often and I will do the same when I am where I can.

Van[12]

Many people believe that Civil War–era Americans enjoyed a simpler, better time. Melvan Tibbetts seems, indeed, to be a better person than most. That many of the most famous war letters speak so eloquently of family, religion, and patriotism cannot help but inspire a conviction that the people who wrote them were somehow more virtuous than ourselves. The openly expressed emotions of the writers can be as winning as they seem foreign. Lt. Stephen F. Spalding, I might as well add, is a useful antidote to this two-dimensional vision of our Civil War past. Nostalgia is not always good history.

Civil War letters serve other purposes in our culture, though these are less well known to the general public. Letters (and diaries) written at the time have become crucial sources for any historian who seeks to find out what happened, either in battles or campaigns. The Melvan Tibbetts letter above, for example, gives a lengthy and detailed description of troop movements at the Battle of Mansfield. Letters written on the spot are invaluable because they are more accurate records of what happened than are soldiers' memoirs and autobiographies, written at a remove from the events they describe. The later sources often tell different stories from those written when everything was fresh in people's minds. Two examples can highlight the perils of relying on later recollections, especially of events that have come to assume mythic proportions. Historian William Marvel has found that soldiers' accounts written just after Robert E. Lee's surrender at Appomattox lack descriptions of camaraderie between Union and Confederate soldiers, whereas later writers, influenced by a culture of reconciliation, emphasize (or perhaps make up) stories of former enemies sharing food and memories of past campaigns. In my own research, I have found that Union soldiers who landed in New Orleans in 1862 wrote letters that describe their arrival as a peaceful event; recollections written in the 1880s, however, after New Orleans had built up a myth about itself as a hotbed of Confederate sympathy, depicted landing on the city's docks as a tense, loud confrontation against a hostile mob.[13] Letters and diaries, in other words, give Civil War historians a means to get at what happened without the grimy veneer that builds up even between people and their own experiences. The Stephen Spalding Letter sparkles in its immediacy, stripping away the mythology that makes all Union soldiers patriotic, virtuous, unselfish emancipationists, and all white Louisianans proud rebels. For his part, Spalding mocks these ideals, and he centers his world around more personal concerns: promotion, friendship, sex, alcohol, death, and jokes.

Discovering Stephen Spalding

Doing archival research with Civil War letters, then, offers emotional and intellectual rewards. It is a quiet experience, usually, and almost never generates the media frenzy that can accompany, say, the discovery of the Amesbury Archer skeleton near Stonehenge. And that is too bad, because there are plenty of historical discoveries to be made in the seclusion of libraries and reading rooms. As Mike Parker Pearson says of his archaeological work around Stonehenge, digs lure in television cameras, while the necessary lab work afterward has "none of the glamour and immediacy of discoveries made during excavations."[14] And yet, they are at least as important for determining what happened, when, and why. My own experience with the Spalding Letter has shown me that it can take years of quiet "digging" in archives to get to a point where I think I can understand Spalding and his letter. The amount of time I have spent working on Spalding's letter is a tribute to its unusual complexity and richness. Its depth, its humor, and its particular voice have prompted me to return to it again and again, whether I am sitting at my computer or walking on Cape Cod.

I can still remember the day eight years ago when I walked into the Vermont Historical Society in Barre with a list of the letters and diaries that I wanted to read for a book about a Civil War mutiny. Time is always of the essence in these situations, since researchers need to get through material before their time and research budget disappear. So I started my first day at the Vermont Historical Society with the Spalding Letter, figuring that a collection with only one letter in it would be easily read, duly noted, and then dispatched with a brisk check mark before I went on to the meatier collections. But it did not happen that way. There I was with my first letter of the day, already taking an enormous number of notes before finally giving up and asking for permission to photocopy the letter. And I'm glad I did, because the more time I spent on it, the more interesting it became. Within a few months I was talking about the letter with my school's History Club (official motto: History—Wow!) and seeing if any of the students knew, or could guess, what Spalding meant when he wrote certain phrases, especially "hop up and bite without salt." The students, as always, were great, and they enjoyed Spalding's jokes and his more impolite moments. The letter's mysteries proved as intriguing to all of us as its more historically significant points.

There are still passages and people in Spalding's letter that I have not been able to figure out. Other places deceived me at first—such as Spalding's mention of a newspaper editor he only identified as "Big." My first guess at who "Big" might be was the editor of the *Vermont Gazette*, a man named E. Marvin Smalley. His last name seemed likely to prompt Spalding, a jokester, to call him "Big." It now seems much more likely that one of Spalding's college friends, Lucius Bigelow, who became an editor, was the person behind the nickname. Reading Spalding's letter became a kind of game, one that got easier to play (and more rewarding) with practice.

My fascination with Stephen Spalding's letter, then, comes from many sources. It was initially mysterious and funny; it seemed in places clear and amusing, in others dark or clouded. Spalding's letter is just one of many thousands of extant Civil War letters, and at least some readers who have seen it suggest that it is not entirely unique. I am not sure how unique it is, or even how great it is; perhaps I've gotten too close to Spalding when I imagine him becoming another Mark Twain had he only lived longer.[15] But even if he is not special—and certainly his only truly distinguishing characteristic is his distinctive voice—his letter gives us a lot to think about, explore, and, yes, discover. The richest discovery has been how much is hidden below the surface of the letter—how much is in plain sight, but only if you know more than is on the page. (In fact, I suspect that if his meanings had always been obvious, his letter would have been destroyed rather than donated to the Vermont Historical Society.) Spalding has taught me that often a good historian needs to slow down and really pick over a document. If anyone were to ask me why I have chosen this letter to read so deeply rather than one of the thousands of others that survive, I would say that the pleasures of each new discovery about Spalding and his world fueled my desire to learn more.

The idea of spending lots of time on one source stands in marked contrast to the practice of rushing through items in order to sample broadly in the archival abundance of Civil War letters and diaries, mining sources for useful quotations or points of view that will back up a project's working hypothesis. That approach usually works fine, since all authors need evidence to support their opinions, and the constraints of travel budgets, deadlines, and even tenure clocks leave researchers with only so much time to interrogate who a correspondent or diarist might have been.[16] But one also can come away from such studies, even excellent examples of this type, wondering who the people were behind the quotations.

What I am suggesting is that—at least in my case—rereading and rethinking Spalding's letter over the course of several years has allowed me to delve into how this junior-level officer thought about and experienced the war. Instead of reading his letter for troop movements or political opinions, a long look at everything he has written tells us that Spalding brought to the war all the complexity of a human being leading a privileged but uncertain life. My long examination tries to get at—to discover—the frame of mind of a very young junior officer caught in the middle of a giant, complicated, jury-rigged, and decidedly deadly war effort. Rather than focus on high politics, my goal is to study Spalding's inner life. His string of jokes, I think, reveals what he valued, particularly his need to maintain his friendship with James Peck, his reader far away in Vermont. His humor, I argue, helped him to cope with the threat of death, as well as the idea that he was now risking his life to advance the abolition of slavery, a cause about which he had grave doubts. Likewise, we can read his letter to better understand how Spalding understood his place in society. A wealthy white man, he reveled (sometimes literally) in the thoughtless exercise of his position. While born into a position of comfort, Spalding never ceased to strive; his life shows us his consistent effort to better his standing in the army and out of it. This book's subtitle, then, reflects three subjects that crop up repeatedly in Spalding's letter: his use of humor; his socially and militarily privileged status; and finally, his ambition to achieve success on the broader stage of life. These subjects are not the standard fare in Civil War studies, but they show us more about American society in the middle of the nineteenth century than we might expect. Our past culture comes across—at least in the young Spalding's eyes—as more hierarchical, self-serving, and even vicious than it does in our more nostalgic moments. That there are also many redeeming and humanizing qualities in Spalding (notably fear and his quest for friendship) reminds us not to judge him too harshly.

What Spalding can show us is the picture of a somewhat unsteady man in his young twenties going about a very serious business. I will not even begin to suggest that he is typical; the value of this biography is in understanding a complex human being. Historians who try to reconstruct a past person's psyche, however, are playing at a very hard game, especially when sources are few and far between. Readers of the following pages will encounter suppositions on my part; the fragmentary nature of the evidence about Spalding requires guesswork on the part of his biographer. Throughout the manuscript, and especially at the end of chapters, I have tried to be clear about what we know for sure as opposed to what are my interpretations of the evidence. But I would like to stick up for the interpretive readings that I (as well as other professional historians elsewhere) have made. They are based on decades of immersion in the middle decades of the 1800s, and I can read that culture almost as easily as I can understand my own. If the past is a foreign country, I have visited there often enough to understand—most of the time—the lingo and culture. Spalding does not always speak as slowly and clearly as we are supposed to do abroad, and I am sure that I have missed some things that he meant to imply, but often I am enough at home to know what he means and to laugh at his jokes. Ultimately, the reward for piecing together his meanings will be one of the first detailed examinations of how a bright, articulate Civil War soldier dealt with very personal issues: his possible early death; distance from his friends (and less so his family); how to spend leisure time; how to get ahead; and the fact that what he did in these years when he was very young seemed likely to have an oversized influence on the rest of his life.

Chapter 1 contains a complete transcript of the Spalding Letter. The remainder of the book represents my best effort to make sense of it and the rest of Spalding's life. Stephen Spalding wrote a fabulous letter, by turns comic and serious, bawdy and broody. It is the kind of letter that makes you long for more, even if you know that it is just about the only thing that he wrote that has survived. So we are left to pick apart what Spalding meant in this one case, aided by historical records generated by the people around him. That is the point of this book—to figure out who Stephen Spalding was, what he meant in his letter, and how those insights can help us to make sense of his society and the war for which he volunteered. In the meantime, we will think a bit about what historians do, what they cannot do, and why they do it at all. If anyone finds this book anywhere near as interesting or as well written as Stephen Spalding's letter, I'll be thrilled.

Lt. SPALDING'S LETTER

1

SPALDING'S LETTER

I will write you at least once a week and you please do the same.

—Stephen Spalding

When Stephen Spalding wrote home on July 8, 1862, he surely did not think that we would be looking over his shoulder 150 years later.[1] His letter is too filled with fun and farce to have an intended audience much beyond his college friend James Peck. It has none of the seriousness of the letters that soldiers sent to their parents or of the heartfelt missives that were sent to wives.[2] Spalding's irreverent jokes make his letter stand out. The theme song from *M*A*S*H** would make appropriate background music for a letter that ranges from broad slapstick to philosophical ramblings about war and humanity. While his humor has nineteenth-century elements to it, especially his use of comic exaggeration, Spalding sounds more like a product of our own era than of the supposedly more sentimental Civil War years.

That Spalding seems out of touch with his own culture says more about our misconceptions about the seriousness of Civil War America than about whether Spalding was some sort of misfit. The soldiers he served with relished a good joke and went out of their way to get a laugh. Some of Spalding's comrades in 1861 lived in a tent labeled "Phunny Fellows." This was a time when one of Spalding's comrades in the Eighth Vermont wrote, just before a long march to capture the new rebel capital of Louisiana, that "we start to-morrow for Opelousas to convene the Legislature of Louisiana. It is two hundred miles distant, and Gen. Banks has kindly given his consent to allow us to go on foot." Vermonters in another regiment relished a story about Pvt. Fayette

Potter, whose antics are more suggestive of P. G. Wodehouse than a somber war documentary. Potter, it turns outs, did a very good dog impression, and when he burst into a tent barking his head off, one of the other soldiers suggested that he "Go long hound and catch the coon." And he did. According to the story, Potter "at full bay ran down the company street and down the company lines, and from thence to the woods a short distance off; as luck would have it, he had no more than struck the woods than he ran across a coon, and running it down caught it, and started at a run again for camp." He made it back about twenty minutes later to the delight of all.[3] In the midst of the surging patriotism after the attack on Fort Sumter, *Vanity Fair* commended three of its contributors who had enlisted with what it clearly meant as high praise: they are "as good fellows and *bons compagnons* as ever cracked a jest. We can ill spare their merriment."[4] Civil War Americans valued their comedy, and Spalding shared this culture. Both he and Abraham Lincoln took time out to read the humorist Artemus Ward.

Indeed, Spalding seems to have been a practical joker in person as well as a humorist on the page. One of the few stories we still have about Stephen Spalding shows him—and other soldiers—looking for laughs. The story was told by a fellow officer, George Carpenter, who wrote a history of their regiment after the war. Let it be our introduction to Spalding, whom we join with another officer, Adjt. John Barstow, riding ahead of a patrol in rural Louisiana. As they approach some woods, Spalding leans over and suggests to Barstow that they play a prank on their own men, marching behind them. Being "full of good humor," Spalding describes the practical joke to Barstow. Spalding says, "Suppose on reaching that covert we imagine ourselves ambuscaded, draw our revolvers, fire at the enemy, and make our escape." Barstow is all for the idea: "The fun of the thing suited the adjutant, and he readily assented," Carpenter writes. He continues: "Accordingly, when they reached the place, Spalding shouted, 'The Rebels!' and both men whipped out their weapons and began to shoot at the imagined foe. But their horses did not seem to appreciate the humor of the joke, or else were in no mood to enjoy it; for at the first shot they wheeled so suddenly that their riders were unseated and thrown, while they galloped back to camp, leaving the disgruntled heroes to be taken prisoner, or to retreat, as best they could."[5] George Carpenter, the historian, observes that this was a rare instance when men got to laugh at their officers. Spalding's prank, its reception among the men, and its later retelling remind us that everyone wanted a laugh: the officers wanted to play a trick on their men; the privates on foot laughed at their suddenly horseless officers; and the historian and his readers remembered the officers' fall from grace with a chuckle some twenty years later. We might also note that, especially in the case of Adjutant Barstow, the regiment's commanders did not seem to care that the two officers had played such a ridiculous and even dangerous trick. Barstow won rapid promotion and served later as governor of Vermont. Perhaps his superior officers liked a good laugh, too.

With that anecdote as our introduction to Stephen Spalding, here is his one surviving letter, in its entirety. Since Spalding did not employ paragraph breaks, I have broken it into four parts and provided brief introductions to each section. Anyone who wants to read the letter unabridged and uninterrupted may simply skip my editorial intrusions.

Spalding begins his letter with an account of how he received the letter from James Peck to which he is now replying. The prominent intrusion of Jim, a former slave who now works for Spalding, serves later as the departure point for chapter 3. Much of the rest of this early part of the letter describes Spalding's "1st real fit of the blues" and what he thinks might have caused his depression. His experiences of late have not been pleasant, Spalding tells his friend, and patriotism is just not a cure for so much heat, boredom, and work. His tone here is humorous, and almost everything he writes in this section is a joke. But it is hard to deny the honesty of his statement, "to return to the sober truth, I was almighty glad to hear from you." These two men were clearly friends, for all of Spalding's jokes. Here's the beginning of Spalding's letter:

Algiers Louisiana
July 8th 1862

Dear James
Yesterday I was sitting in my room, thinking over the mutability of all things human, and making myself as miserable as the Army Regulations allow. I had just finished a mental discourse damning everybody and especially the Eighth Vermont, when the door was

opened and my boy Jim whom I captured at "Tibedeaux" and who
by the way is *painfully black.* I seized a stool—the only household
furniture that I now possess—and slung it at his head. He dropped
the document he had in his hand and fled. I had been expecting a
note from Col Thomas ordering me under arrest for disrespectful
language to superior officers, and I was very agreeably surprised on
recognizing the familiar hand of my friend "Jeemes." I immediately
came "to the rear open order" and broke the seal. "Liber XXI" was
the first thing that met my eyes, and I immediately proceeded to
the city and procured, a Greek & Latin Dictionary—a copy of the
Life & sayings of Mrs. Partington & her boy Ike—and all the old
letters that Artemus Ward ever wrote. Armed with these formidable documents, I succeeded in the incredible short space of 2 days
& nights, in reading the whole letter quotations and all, and in a
fair examination could have ragged 2d [second] as easily as I used
to in College Times. But to return to sober truth, I was almighty
glad to hear from you, for I was having the 1st real fit of the blues
since I enlisted. The life that we lead gives us an excellent opportunity to exercise our thinking faculties and we improve that opportunity to the best of our abilities. Were it not for the simple fact
that we are "Patriots" and fighting in a "Glorious Cause" our courage I fear would give way. You can know hardly nothing of the nature of the life that we poor cusses follow in this *temperate* climate.
First and foremost is the excessive heat. To be sure "your uncle [il-
legible word]" does not find it uncomfortably warm, but all men
are not constituted alike, and one man will die where another
under the same circumstances will live and grow fat. *I* do not find a
linnen coat uncomfortable in the middle of the day. One with a
very limited observation can see that the climate is seriously affecting the health of the troops in this Dep't. The men are lazy. Officers
D[itt]o. and it takes a good deal of talking and punishing to get
them to do anything. A don't care a damn for nothing kind of a
feeling seemes to exist immensely in every patriots's bosom. For
Eight long weary months we have been ready to offer up our lives
on the alters of liberty, or any where else where fun could be had,
but the 8th of July finds us in this quiet place just out side of the
din and bustle of the "Crescent City." Another thing which troubles

us not a little is a small fly called in the Northern States, "musquito." They are very thick and keep a man constantly employed in brushing them away from his face and ears. After dark any evening you can with a single wave of the hand strike to the earth millions. Through the kindness of the War Department, the Soldiers have all received an excellent "musquito bar," and the night is no longer made hideous by that vexatious hum, peculiar to the animal. There are many things concerning the Eighth Regiment of Vermont Volunteers, which I would like to inform you of. But knowing that a civil tongue has saved many a young man from the gallows, I refrain from saying any thing detrimental. In the dim distance, however methinks I see a day when I shall once more stand on the soil of old Vermont, a free man, when my tongue will no longer be fettered, when I can stand up provided I am sober and a tale unfold that will grate harsh upon the ears of some. Say nothing about this. For you know a still cat catches the mice. I have a good deal of laborious work to perform just now, for the reason that my Captain is Provost Marshall of Algiers, and the Second Lieutenant is detached on the Signal Corps leaving the Company in my hands. I have had to make out the muster Rolls—pay Rolls, quarterly returns for Clothing—ordinance returns, Camp & Equipage returns, and several other returns. The only return I have neglected thus far is my own return home. I find that the whole burden rests with ease upon my shoulders, and I do not forget my daily "snoozes" which number two as of old.

At this point Spalding launches into a long account of his trip into New Orleans on July Fourth for what later soldiers would call R & R. This story fills two of Spalding's seven pages, and it is a minor masterpiece of the subgenre we might call "young men's drinking stories." There is much going on below the surface in this section of the letter, and it will be explored in chapter 4.

For the lack of anything more interesting I will give you an account of the way I celebrated 4th of July in New Orleans. [First] Lieut [Daniel S.] Foster of St Albans & myself early in the morning called upon the Col to obtain leave to be absent during the day. The leave was—*refused* and we started across the Stream with the avowed purpose of making the "welkin ring" before our return. We drank gin, whiskey, brandy, rum, beer, gin coctails modesty prevents me from putting in the K., Eleven other different kinds of coctails, Cobblers of all kinds, julips d[itt]o, smashes d[itt]o, and night found us in the hospitable retreat of Miss Bianca Robbins, a lady of northern parentage, and friendly to the Union. After a close investigation into the theory of Spiritual rappings, we started for Miss Burdells where during the day we had received a kind invitation to attend a grand masquerade ball. The moderate sum of 10.00 each, admitted us into the magnificent saloons. The scene viewed with the naked eye was truly splendid. The quintessence of beauty in the City were collected together dressed in the various costumes of the last 19 centuries. The rooms were magnificiently decorated with mottos worked in the choicest roses. Wines pressed from the vines that grow "on the banks of the Beautiful River.["] decked the side boards, while the tables groaned under the wight of choice fruits, cakes, and every thing to suit the most fastidious. At a given signal the band struck up and and [*sic*] the dance commenced. Picking out a young lady who as I afterwards learned, was an Alabamian and from one of the 1st Families in the State, I launched forth into the dizzy (extremely dizzy) mazes of the dance. It had been so long since I had attempted to execute the particular figure, which was a french polka with a hideous name, that I did not succeed entirely to my own satisfaction or any body's else, as I was informed afterwards. My friends say that I crippled for life a French naval officer by hitting him in the shins, while executing a very difficult whirl. Another was wounded in the nose while I was throwing my head back into a graceful position, toes were broken, dresses torn until a mist came over my eyes caused by whirling round too much and I retired to refresh the inner man. A graceful apology, aided very much by the end of a "six shooter" sticking out of my pocket put everything right, and the order came, to go on with the dance. The 1st Strain of music had scarcely died away when 2 British Officers came in with "Secesh" badges onto their bosoms, the music hushed, the dancing ceased, and the crowd gradually gathered around Johnny Bull, forcing him slowly along towards the wicket. Soon kicks, cuffs, hair pulling &c were in order and I venture to say that when they reached the door, 40 boots assisted them in getting on to the side walk. They landed far out in the middle of the road, and with more quickness than grace "Skedaddled." Having accomplished our object we returned, finding everything quiet on the Potomac. In thinking it all over I do not remember of ever enjoying myself better in my life. the absence of 57.00 my earthly all only added to my feelings New Orleans is a great place for fun. I enclose you a slip of paper I cut out of the Daily Delta.[6] You will see from what I have written that our chances for fun are good.

Having summed up his thoughts about his day (and night) in New Orleans, Spalding now brings his letter back to news about his present and guesses about his future. He tells Peck the war news from his department, but there is only so much to pass along. Louisiana in the summer of 1862 looked like it was becoming a backwater after the exciting fall of New Orleans that spring, an event in which Spalding had played no part. His focus on the degree to which the white people of New Orleans embraced the return of United States authority is normal for Union soldiers stationed there. He is less optimistic about the authenticity of the Unionism he sees among the locals than many other soldiers at the time, but opinions on this matter varied widely. Perhaps the most interesting aspect of this section is his general frustration with his inactivity; as we will see in the next chapter, Spalding had enlisted very soon after the war started, and here he sits about a year and a half into the war without ever having been in combat.

Company D from Bradford is acting as Provost Guard in the City. We have 4 Companies at Des Almons on the Opelousas Railroad. It was about six miles from this place that 4 men were killed 6 wounded besides 2 Lieutenants, all of Company "H." There is a force of Texas Rangers near there, numbering about 800 men. The lay of the land will not permit any brilliant military manouvers as the Railroad Track is the only road that men can travel on. On both sides are marshy swamps filled with all kinds of animals. I have seen 13 aligators on the Track at one time, to say nothing about divers snakes &c. The Rebels have burned the bridges, torn up the track and built a breastwork across it. The Pickets on both sides are in sight of each other every day. Col Thomas has repeatedly urged General Butler to give us some artillery. He says that as soon as the Reinforcements which he expects arrive he is going to take the route to Texas and wipe out all the various geurilla parties between here & the Texas Capital. We shall probably spend the latter part of the Summer on the Texas Frontier or among the Rocky mountains. Butler must be reinforced or we shall get into trouble one of these days Most of the troops in this Department are at "Baton Rouge." The 13th Conn. 12th Maine & 8th Vt are all the troops in the immediate vicinity of the City. Algiers—the place where we are at present is a small town numbering I should judge 10,000 inhabitants. It is situated on the right bank of the River and directly opposite the City. Ferry Boats run every few minutes so we can go to the City any time we choose. All the large Dry Docks were situated on this side and were destroyed when the Federal Fleet came up the River. They cost more than a million dollars. The people here for the most are of the poorer class and extremely ignorant. Their hatred for the Union and the Yankees is pure and undefiled. I would as soon attempt to reason with a dog as with the most intelligent of them. In fact this place is to New Orleans what the French village is to Burlington Our regiment is quartered in the Depot, the officers using the private offices for their quarters.[7] We congratulate ourselves that we are not shut up in a fort as many other Regiments are. We have free range of the country & watermelons, oranges and all kinds of fruit suffer some at the hands of our soldiers. I board at a hotel and pay the moderate sum of 7.50 per week. I sleep in a tent and like it very much. There is a good deal of sickness among the soldiers. The night air is almost sure death. The dew falls so heavy that the water runs off the eaves quite freely in the morning. There is nothing that reminds one of home more forcibly, than the sight of a black hearse bearing the remains of half a dozen poor fellows to their long homes. We have no difficulty enlisting men. The sod is scarcely thrown over our soldiers before new recruits are strutting round with their equipments. The 9th Connecticut recruited over 400 men in a very short time. 30 Corporals have been detailed to drill the recruits that they are going to raise. They contemplate raising several Regiments in this State. It is amusing to notice the effect that some of the sen[s]ation articles in the Mobile papers produces in the City. Confederate Notes go up 50 per cent. A smile, a sort of heavenly smile appears upon their faces and they look contemptuously upon all the federal officers and soldiers. Next day the news is contradicted, and glorious accounts of Federal victories come in. Their chops fall and they look as if they had no friends in the world. There is a perfect rush for passports North. Every available spot on every Steamer that comes in is taken in less than 4 hours after she touches the dock.

Spalding closes with the reassurances that we might expect when a friend in dangerous circumstances finishes a letter to someone about whom he cares. He makes sure to tell James Peck that his health is good, and to prove it he makes jokes about his drinking and his naps. He also asks Peck for more letters, reassures him of his friendship, and summons their mutual friends and past experiences to strengthen the bond between them. Predictably, there are jokes here, but they mask, one suspects, a nostalgic sentiment about their past lives in Vermont that is related to Spalding's "blues" about being stuck in Louisiana.

I drink from 700 to 800 times a day to keep my spirits up and I do not think that it wears on one. The advice you give me is good, but it wont work in the Army. I am enjoying good health and weigh 165 pounds. I hope that my health will not fail me & I guess it won't for I take pretty good care of "Stephen." I am thinking what a glorious time we will have when I get back. We will make as usual our summer trip to Burlington and disgust the fair damsels worse than ever. A visit to Jacks, a ride in the Undine & a snooze at "Lewes" will be in order. I do not imagine that we shall get home before next summer at the least calculation. We are too far from home to go back now. I am sorry that I cannot make my letter more interesting, but give us some fighting & I will. As it is, take nothing from nothing & nothing remains. The barreness of my my [sic] letters however must not deter you from writing for I enjoy a letter you write hugely. I will write you at least once a week and you please do the same. I will drink one quart of High Wines at precisely 10 P.M. on the night of ye Celebration. Give my best respects to Big, Po, Jack, Lou, Peck & Bradish, and all my acquaintances in Montpelier. If you go to Burlington please tell the young ladies of my acquaintance to hop up and bite without salt. Dont for Gods Sake enlist unless you can get the position of Major General. Remember it. Write on receipt & believe me Yours Friend in the Owl Steve. You will hear from Felix soon.

The following sentences were written in the margins of pages five, six, and seven:

If the Vermont Eighth ever get into a fight—they will be annihilated before they will run. A boy in my company fell off of the dock just now & was drowned. I had a man in his place enlisted and drilling just as he was sinking the 3rd time.[8]

Tell Big I get his paper regular.[9] We hear from the North every 2 weeks.[10]

Who is the fellow that writes for the B. Times and signs his name "Vermont"? Is it Lucius?[11]

Stephen Spalding's letter ends there, and we can analyze many parts of it. But before we start to try to figure out what this letter means, we should look at who Spalding was before he headed off to war. Earlier Spaldings had distinguished themselves in a variety of ways. Perhaps their greatest claim to distinction came from their first ancestor to come to North America, Edward Spalding. According to a family genealogy published in 1897, Edward Spalding arrived in Virginia somewhere between 1619 and 1623. Already among the first generation of Englishmen in Virginia, Edward Spalding then earned more honor for the family by joining the early English settlers of Massachusetts Bay. The family genealogy claims that by 1634 Edward Spalding had established himself in Braintree, Massachusetts, though no one appears able to explain why he would have made the move north. By 1655 Edward became a founder of the town of Chelmsford, where he eventually served as one of the selectmen and acquired many acres of land. By the end of the nineteenth century, then, the Spaldings believed they could claim founding roles in the establishment of two of England's earliest and most important North American colonies.[12] While it cannot be proven that the Spaldings of Stephen's time were aware of this lineage, it seems likely that they thought of themselves as a distinguished family with a rich history in New England and elsewhere.

Stephen Spalding, our author, grew up in a wealthy family that worked to train him for a prestigious career. Stephen's father, Levi Spalding, had been born in Sharon, Vermont, in 1805. Levi went into business at age twenty-one with a brother, but that partnership lasted only three years. Levi had better luck with a business he cofounded with Stephen Foster, and the fact that he named one of his sons (our author) Stephen Foster Spalding attests to the prosperity and warmth of this alliance. In partnership with Stephen Foster and others, Levi Spalding owned and managed several businesses in Stanstead, Canada, and Derby Line, Vermont. Levi gained an especially prominent community role as "one of the early presidents of the Derby Line bank" during the Civil War era, and the family genealogist notes that Levi "at his death left a very large estate to his children."[13] Despite the generally prosperous and respectable nature of the family, the genealogist did not usually write this, and one is tempted to think that Levi had, indeed, amassed a good-sized fortune.

Levi Spalding sought to translate his business success into a career for his son, Stephen. Levi meant for Stephen to follow him into his white-collar world, and Stephen started at the University of Vermont in the fall of 1856. University educations marked a man as belonging to a privileged few; Stephen joined only *nineteen* other freshmen that year at UVM. When he left the school in 1860, he did so as part of a graduating class of sixteen seniors.[14] It is hard to know if Stephen Spalding did well at school, though he did manage to graduate, and to do so in four years. He also joined the Lambda Iota Society, which was known more familiarly as the "Owl Society." By 1859, he had become the group's corresponding secretary, and as such sent out the 1859 invitation to its annual celebration at the Lake House in Burlington. The invitation he sent to members bears just a hint more personality and humor than similar invitations preserved from the years right before the Civil War. Spalding closed his note with an unusually cheerful line: "Your attendance is most Owlishly solicited, Fraternally yours." His owlish language stayed with the young man, as we have seen, all the way into Louisiana and the second year of the war, when he closed his letter to James Peck, "Yours Friend in the Owl Steve."[15] Judging by his continued friendship with Peck, who had also joined Lambda Iota, and his fond regard for Owls, Stephen Spalding seems to have valued the social acceptance he had won as a young man in a fraternal order.

Stephen Spalding used his graduation from the University of Vermont as a preliminary step to reading law. Sources suggest that he studied law in a variety of places, including New York City and his hometown in Vermont. The family genealogist has him reading "law in the office of J. L. Edwards, Esq., at Derby, Vt." The regimental historian believed that Spalding was studying law in New York City when the war broke out, which makes sense in light of his rapid enlistment in the Seventh New York State Militia after the Confederate attack on Fort Sumter. The same person also writes that Spalding went home to Derby to read law after being mustered out of the Seventh New York and before he joined the Eighth Vermont.[16] Spalding's prewar life primed him for a career free from manual labor. It is not a surprise that he was such a particularly good writer.

A few words should also be said about James S. Peck, the man to whom Stephen wrote this letter. Peck also moved in illustrious circles before the war. He attended UVM with Stephen Spalding, and they knew one another intimately by the time they graduated in 1860. In their junior year, they lived next door to one another. They spent their senior year as roommates.[17] Later in the war, Peck ignored his friend's advice against enlisting "unless you can get the position of Major General." Instead, he joined the Thirteenth Vermont Volunteers and worked his way up from sergeant to 2nd lieutenant, and then finally to adjutant. Peck probably was with the Thirteenth Vermont Volunteer Infantry at Gettysburg on July 3, joining that regiment's devastating counterattack against the right flank of Pickett's Charge. When the Thirteenth disbanded later in 1863, Peck reenlisted with other volunteers from his old brigade (Stannard's) into the new Seventeenth Vermont Volunteer Infantry. He again served as adjutant and apparently acted as the unit's major, though he never received an official appointment to that rank. While campaigning outside Petersburg, Virginia, on October 1, 1864, he fell ill with what doctors called "typhoid pneumonia." According to the doctor's report that accompanied his request for an invalid pension after the war, he "was attacked by pneumonia, resulting from excessive labor, care, and exposure to a severe rain storm of 24 hours duration without shelter, while in command of his Regiment, after the action of Poplar Grove Church." Prostrated by his illness, he was taken to General Hospital at City Point, Virginia. Peck must have healed, at least in the short term, and he served with the Seventeenth Vermont until the summer of 1865, when he was discharged. He immediately began receiving an invalid pension because of his "disease of the chest," which rendered him "entirely incapacitated . . . from manual labor."[18]

James Peck may not have been able to perform manual labor, but it seems unlikely that he had ever planned to do so. Instead, he parlayed his social standing, education, and distinguished record of service in the Union army into an appointment with the Vermont government as adjutant general. Peck appears to have taken his work as state adjutant general seriously, but the fact that he was hired for what most Vermonters of his time would have seen as a very nice job shows how far up in Vermont society he—and by extension Stephen Spalding—moved before, during, and after the war. He died in 1884. Peck and Spalding were born into a certain amount of privilege, but they still expected to work hard and to strive. The war would force them to endure grave hardships and survive many skirmishes, battles, and disease. Still, their social position made the potential rewards for their bravery and service quite substantial; Spalding's friend Adjutant Barstow made it all the way to the governor's chair.

When Spalding sat down to reply to his friend, however, all that lay in the future. On July 8, 1862, Spalding and Peck were still young men, just two years after graduation. They had befriended each other no later than their junior year, when they lived in adjacent rooms and decided to room together for their final year. Spalding's manner of talking about this friendship seems both modern (and hence natural) but also curious. Viewed historically, Spalding's way of expressing his affection for Peck marks a transition that American men undertook in this period. Many men in the decades before and during the Civil War discussed their friendships in a more openly sentimental and emotional style that a historian has recently categorized as "romantic friendship."

As another historian has written of the period, "friendship was every-where during the period; every surface that men exposed to one an-other is coated with cottony, saccharine rhetoric."[19] That men wrote frankly of their love for one another, and often posed for photographs with their arms draped around each other, has sparked discussions about the pervasiveness and acceptability of homosexual relationships in nineteenth-century America. That women also expressed their love and longings for one another in the same decades broadens our con-ception of the range and depth of same-sex friendships during Spald-ing's lifetime.[20]

For young men and women living in America's many sex-segregated academies and colleges, forming and expressing close same-sex rela-tionships was second nature. As David Deitcher writes, "intimate bonds between men . . . flourished in all-male havens of middle-class privilege such as the university."[21] A recent study of the notes college classmates inscribed in one another's autograph books as graduation neared found that antebellum men were influenced by the "widespread growth of sentimental literary culture." Membership in fraternal orga-nizations and campus clubs further strengthened bonds between col-lege friends. Many of the writers also expressed "a passionate desire for sustained future friendship."[22] That description sounds very much like Spalding and Peck, or, to borrow from Spalding's letter, very much like "Steve" and "Jeemes."

The prevalence of declarations of love and the need for physical proximity (whether sexual or not) in such letters help us to read Spal-ding's letter. Spalding obviously wants Peck's friendship, but he does not use the language of "romantic friendship." Instead, he hides his longings behind jokes and misdirections. It is not, for example, Peck that Spalding wants, but his letters; at the close of his letter Spalding asks for letters "at least once a week," "for I enjoy a letter you write hugely." Still, the arrival of Peck's letter elicits nothing more affection-ate than that "I was very agreeably surprised on recognizing the famil-iar hand of my friend 'Jeemes.'" If we contrast Spalding's words—even his sign-off, "believe me Yours Friend in the Owl Steve," with the lan-guage of Massachusetts senator Charles Sumner and Henry Wads-worth Longfellow we see the magnitude of Spalding's withdrawal from the kind of open declarations of affection that marked many men's letters at the time. It is hard to imagine Spalding writing, as Sumner did when Longfellow left for a European trip: "And so you are gone. What solace or happiness is there for me? I shall go to Boston at mid summer but it will be desert enough for me." Or James Peck sending these words to Spalding, as Sumner did to Longfellow: "I miss you always."[23] But then, Sumner and Longfellow specialized in—even made careers out of—earnest conviction and sentiment, while Spalding was more at ease with sarcasm and jokes. We have found male friendship on the brink of a historic shift.

One suspects, however, that Spalding's unwillingness to express his friendship with Peck was more a matter of style than a change in human needs. For Stephen Spalding, military service would pull him away from his friends and family soon after the war began in Charleston harbor. He would still need emotional support, and he clearly relied on James Peck for at least some of that companionship. But the war, as we will see, provided incentives for action. Whether the fires of patriotism or those of ambition burned brighter is an intriguing question.

2

PROMOTION AND SELF-PROMOTION
Spalding and the Seventh New York State Militia

> Dont for Gods Sake enlist unless you can get the position of
> Major General. Remember it.
>
> —Stephen Spalding

When Stephen Spalding wrote his letter, he was serving as a first lieutenant in the Eighth Vermont. But he did not start the war in that unit. Rather, he first enlisted in the famous Seventh New York State Militia. How he got into that unit, and what he did with them, will give us clues about Spalding's character, as well as his later preparedness for a lieutenant's bars. His elevation to officer rank among the Vermonters, presumably on the basis of his time with the well-known New Yorkers, opens windows onto the way the North fielded regiments during the rapid military buildup in the summer and fall of 1861. We also catch a glimpse of the vast ambition that drove many young men, some of them to their doom.

When writing the history of the Eighth Vermont Volunteers in the 1880s, George Carpenter often paused in his narrative to provide brief biographies of the regiment's officers. He did so with Stephen F. Spalding, giving his readers some details about his life before he joined the Vermonters. Carpenter places Spalding in New York City, studying law, when the Confederates attacked Fort Sumter. According to Carpenter, the attack changed Spalding's life immediately: "In less than six hours after the assault on Fort Sumter, he was on his way to Washington as a volunteer in the Seventh New York Regiment, and served with them three months. When his term of enlistment expired he returned to New York, where he enlisted a number of men for another regiment, and was commissioned second lieutenant. But being called to Montpelier by the dangerous illness of his eldest brother, he resigned his commission, and returned to the study of law in Derby." Once back in Derby, he began to recruit for the Eighth Vermont, being driven by both "his strong patriotism [which] would not permit him to remain at home" and his recently acquired "taste for military service."[1]

George Carpenter's history, published in 1886, is both a blessing and a curse for historians. Unfortunately, Spalding was already dead by the time Carpenter and others began collecting information, and we have no idea how Carpenter went about drawing up Spalding's profile. Whatever his sources, Carpenter provides information that is not otherwise available. When we can check Carpenter's statements against other records, he is often right. However, he also makes several mistakes in his brief sketch. Weeding out the falsehoods makes his garden of the past less pleasant, though it also becomes more interesting. Sometimes Carpenter's apparent errors do not matter very much. No one, least of all Stephen Spalding, served at the front for as long as three months with the Seventh New York in 1861. As for Spalding's military service between leaving the Seventh and joining the Eighth Vermont, Carpenter places Spalding in the wrong city. The National Archives contain no record of anyone named Spalding (or Spaulding, as his name is often spelled) serving in a New York regiment as a second lieutenant in 1861; instead, he was already in Montpelier on June 21, 1861, serving as a "recruiting officer" for a "brigade of Light Infantry, to be composed of picked men, and intended for special service by Gen. Scott."[2] His miniature biography contains other facts that are more clearly falsehoods, as we will see, and then the question arises as to how the fictions arrived in Spalding's brief biography. Did they originate in the faulty recall of a kindhearted former officer, or did Spalding start spinning his own deceits even before he joined the Eighth Vermont?

We know that Stephen Spalding did, in fact, enlist in the Seventh New York State Militia (which is not to be confused with a later regiment, the Seventh New York Infantry) in 1861.[3] In doing so, Spalding joined an elite unit whose history predated the war. Known in the 1850s as an especially well-drilled militia unit, it was perhaps even more famous for the wealth of its members. No one could just walk in and become a part of the Seventh; even privates needed references to join, a practice that continued in the days after Fort Sumter. (Stephen Spalding's entry may have been paved by a distant relative, Zephaniah Swift Spalding. Zeph had gained admission to the Seventh a few years before as a private, perhaps because his father was a judge on the Ohio Supreme Court, and his mother was the daughter of the chief justice of Connecticut. Such was the status of these New Yorkers.)[4] The city's wealthy sons took pride in their membership in the regiment, which came to embody much of the city's spirit in the days after the war started. One member of the regiment saw the Seventh as a "guaranty of the unquestioning loyalty of the 'conservative' class in New York."[5] Not for them the standard enlistment period of three months; the Seventh pledged itself for exactly one month and took up the task of getting to Washington, D.C., ahead of other New York regiments. But they were not hasty. Even in the midst of crisis, the Seventh spent two days raising $6,735 to defray its costs before it left the city. The New York Stock Exchange Corporation chipped in a thousand dollars.[6]

They left the city with all eyes on them. They paraded down Broadway on April 19, a march that has entered the nation's annals through two well-known oil paintings, including the often reproduced classic by Thomas Nast.[7] More immediately, the illustrated news weeklies filled pages with stirring engravings of the patriotic send-off, which both dwarfed and epitomized the ceremonies soon to be held in other towns and cities across the North.[8] The fame of the Seventh grew from there, eventually resulting in a statue in Central Park. The regiment reached Philadelphia, where it learned that the only regiment ahead of it, the Sixth Massachusetts, had been attacked by a pro-secession mob in Baltimore. The New Yorkers decided to board ships and land at Annapolis, thereby avoiding Baltimore. With the media following their every move, the Seventh and a second Massachusetts regiment marched from Annapolis through a largely hostile territory to a railway station south of Baltimore. There they at last connected with a train nosing tentatively north from the capital. The march entered the pages of America's most prestigious magazine, the *Atlantic*, through the pen of one of the Seventh's recent recruits, Theodore Winthrop. Winthrop describes the brief campaign across Maryland as a mix of beautiful scenery with just enough suffering and danger to make the men feel like they were soldiers. After high afternoon temperatures and a thunderstorm, the soldiers, he wrote, "wrapped themselves in their blankets and took their wetting with more or less satisfaction. They were receiving samples of all the different miseries of a campaign." But, happily, not too many miseries; no one shot at them, and they suffered no casualties beyond a few blisters caused by bad shoes.[9]

The Seventh scored another coup by getting to Washington ahead of their fellow campaigners in the Eighth Massachusetts. As only the second northern regiment to arrive in the capital, and the first to appear in six days, the Seventh took on the guise of saviors. With many imagined and some real southern soldiers poised over the city on Arlington Heights, all manner of anxious Washingtonians greeted the smartly dressed Seventh as if they were heroes. An impromptu parade from the train station took them to the White House, where Abraham Lincoln and the U.S. secretaries of war and the Navy reviewed them from under the portico. The presence of such high-level politicians indicates how vulnerable the government had felt for the past week, and how welcome the Seventh was when it arrived. But the regiment's parade route also shows their own sense of entitlement as powerful citizens; they did not just march down the road at a distance from the White House. As Pvt. Robert Gould Shaw, the future colonel of the Fifty-Fourth Massachusetts, wrote in a letter, the Seventh "marched straight up to the White House and through the grounds, where 'Old Abe' and family stood at the doors and saw us go by." The march ended at the Capitol Building, then a fortified position held in readiness to receive an expected Confederate attack. The distinguished gentlemen from New York known as the Seventh then took up residence in the House Chambers.[10]

As the Union army grew with the addition of more regiments over the next week, the men of the Seventh moved out of the Capitol Building, which had been both their barracks and their playground. Theodore Winthrop wrote that "we joked, we shouted, we sang, we mounted the Speaker's desk and made speeches."[11] Their second home in the District was Camp Cameron, where they would spend most of the rest of their term of service.[12] The Library of Congress and recent illustrated histories of the war have many photographs of the Seventh at rest at this camp. Play did not stop simply because they had left the Capitol Building; one photograph, entitled *Gymnastic Field Sports of the*

Gallant Seventh. A Four Story Pile of Men, shows men forming a human pyramid four levels high.[13] Visiting dignitaries, including President Lincoln, cabinet secretaries, senators, and foreign ambassadors, stopped by to review their afternoon parades. New Yorkers sent the soldiers so many gifts that their storehouse overflowed with "the most appetizing array of barrels, boxes, cans, and bottles, shipped here that our Sybarites might not sigh for the flesh-pots of home." The regimental quartermaster finally resorted to begging for the care packages to stop. His appeal did not work, and a newspaper report on May 22 noted the arrival of at least eight hundred boxes at Camp Cameron. Among the items sent were a cask of brandy and several pieces of artillery, hopefully not to be used at the same time.[14]

Fate held one more pleasant adventure in store for the New Yorkers. Left to their dull training at Camp Cameron, the men began to grow exasperated that they would soon head home without conducting another campaign, without getting one more plume in their hats. They eventually decided to delay their departure for about two weeks in order to participate in the first Union movement into Virginia on the night of May 24. Positioned in the rear of the line of march, the Seventh followed others over the Long Bridge across the Potomac and onto Virginia soil. The May night brought a lovely moon, nice marching weather, and the thrill of advancing onto the "sacred soil" of Virginia. Happily, the evening again brought no combat for the New Yorkers. A night of digging entrenchments followed, enough to give the gentlemen a taste of soldiering, though not too much of one. Such was the elite status of the Seventh that an engineer actually "asked our Colonel if the Seventh were willing to shoulder a pick and spade and *dig* during the night." (They agreed unanimously to do so.)[15] They then returned to a hero's welcome at Camp Cameron and waited a few days before going back to New York. By June 3, they were home and living as civilians. For all this, they were paid a modest sum, though, as we will see, what they received in social compensation far excelled anything the paymaster gave them.[16]

It is tempting to think about what Stephen Spalding would have made of all this. Certainly, he would have enjoyed himself. How could he not have loved the adventure, the proximity to the pleasures of the city of Washington, and the admirers sending the regiment casks of brandy?

But Spalding was not there. He missed all of the famous parts of the Seventh's campaign. Despite Carpenter's assertion that Spalding joined the Seventh within hours of the attack on Fort Sumter, Spalding waited and waited before he enlisted. Dates matter here: the Seventh left New York on April 19 and received its warm welcome from Lincoln and the people of Washington on April 25. It barracked in the House of Representatives until May 2. Stephen Spalding, it turns out, mustered in on May 11, almost a full month after Carpenter's biography would have us believe. His late appearance means that he was a member of the Seventh for about three weeks—from May 11 to June 3. In that time, he would have gotten some feel for soldiering. We know that he lived at Camp Cameron and acted the part of a private in the new Union army. But, even then, he missed out on the biggest part of the Seventh's history during the weeks he was with it. When the regiment invaded Virginia during its thrilling nighttime adventure on May 24, Spalding stayed behind with his company while it stood guard on Camp Cameron. Throughout his regiment's three-day Virginia campaign, he remained behind, ready to greet the returning, blistered conquerors who had actually set foot on Virginia. Then he went home, where he was due about eleven dollars in pay.

The details of Spalding's surprisingly short and uneventful time in the famous Seventh become clear in the regiment's vast archival holdings, located at the New-York Historical Society. (The Society holds ninety linear feet of records about the regiment, including 97 boxes and 445 separate volumes of material dating to all periods of the unit's long history.) Spalding served in Company I, a part of the Seventh that was then in a state of flux. On February 14, 1861, the unit changed from an "Engineers and Artillery" company into a light artillery company. In the process, they acquired two "brass howitzers."[17] The unit's historians neglect to explain the rationale behind the change to artillery, though perhaps it was a matter of recruitment. Company I entered 1860 shorthanded, with only nineteen men. By January 1, 1861, it had managed to gain an additional thirty-one recruits, but this still fell short of the one hundred or so soldiers of a full company.[18] The company did not see a large enlistment rush in the first months of 1861, and it was still under strength when it marched down Broadway on April 19. Muster rolls show that Company I left for Washington with two officers, four sergeants, and twenty-three privates, a total strength of twenty-nine men. The company's most famous member, the *Atlantic* writer Theodore Winthrop, enlisted just after Fort Sumter and in time for the historic march.[19] But Spalding did not.

Stephen Spalding came later, part of a contingent of seventy-one privates who left New York on May 11 and joined the regiment at Camp Cameron on May 13.[20] The recruits enjoyed their own mini-march through New York to their waiting steamer, a replay of sorts of the much larger, more often illustrated parade down Broadway by their illustrious regimental comrades. The small detachment, Spalding included, marched from their armory to the pier "amid great enthusiasm," accompanied by two companies from other New York regiments stuck in the city. One has a hard time imagining "great enthusiasm" being mustered for the send-off of a few dozen men, and the historian writing that account in 1870 may have simply been burnishing the reputation of his own unit. Or perhaps Spalding did receive a hero's dispatch; if so, he may have wondered if he had earned it when he returned after his three weeks of service.[21]

When Spalding and the other new members of the Seventh reached the pier, they boarded the steamer *Matanzas*, where a lieutenant had rented a large cabin for them. The New York regiment had quarreled with the head of the state's militia, and the Seventh could not obtain government funds to pay for the men's transportation to Washington. Instead of waiting to resolve the dispute, the lieutenant had booked the cabin at twelve dollars per soldier and then returned to the armory where the recruits had gathered. There he "suggested to the men if they wanted to go speedily, comfortably, and be well cared for, if they would pay $5 per man I would see to paying the balance. The vote was taken, and every man voted yes."[22] Spalding and the other recruits then had their parade to the *Matanzas,* and an uneventful trip to the capital.

If Spalding was late for the most glamorous parts of the Seventh's history, he was not alone. He and the other recruits for Company I participated in a large flow of men into the Seventh as it waited for action in Washington. The Seventh numbered some 991 men when it left New

York City, but the ranks swelled quickly with men eager to take part in both the patriotic adventure of the war's early days, and the fame the unit had already gained. Altogether, the muster book shows that 309 men enlisted in the regiment after its departure from New York City. Some joined early on, among them the fourteen men gained by Company D and the twenty-four added to Company B before the end of April. The new manpower soon forced Colonel Lefferts to write to New York that, with the exception of about fifty new men needed by the artillery company (the group that would include Spalding), the regiment could take no more soldiers. But still newcomers straggled in during the first weeks of May. One remarkable soldier, Pvt. Ed L. Milkan, mustered in on May 25, making him a member of the Seventh for only eight days before being mustered out.[23] The changing strength of the regiment, which climbed up to 1,270 at one point, posed problems for the regiment as it adjusted to life at Camp Cameron.[24] On May 11, 1861, for example, Colonel Lefferts admitted that "I have now in Camp 100 men who have no arms, for which I ask muskets."[25] That was only one of the problems caused by the influx of new men.

Company I's old members, already at Camp Cameron, did not welcome Stephen Spalding and the other recruits with open arms. For the veterans of Company I, the new arrivals meant an unwelcome change in housing, and (as we will see later) a crisis regarding the unit's leadership. The influx of dozens of men drove the old members of Company I out of the comfort of the outbuildings of Dr. Stone's estate at Camp Cameron and into tents. A hint of the grumbling from the unit's old members makes it into the usually cheerful histories told by members of the Seventh. The book-length 1938 history of Company I includes murmurs of dissent about the new men. A sergeant complained in a letter on May 17 that "since my last have an arrival of 61 recruits—all for Co I and I have never had such trouble in my life. Our rooms not being large enough, we have moved to the tented field and have had constant business. Added to this the old men and the new have been at sword points."[26]

But even after Company I moved into tents, they still led a fairly comfortable life. Historians might wonder, in fact, whether their new quarters provided any practical experience for future army life. Put simply, the New Yorkers enjoyed a fine life at Camp Cameron in these warm spring days. The regiment enjoyed the services of a French cook and his "corps of assistance." At least one tent boasted carpeting.[27] Illustrations of Camp Cameron show its cleanliness, organization, and an almost luxurious feel. Engravings depict ordered rows of large, standardized tents. Photographs show men in front of their pleasant-looking tents, which are often decorated with names; Robert Gould Shaw and his tent-mates slept in "Virtue's Bower."[28] Another group lived in a tent with a sign reading "Florence Hotel . . . Phunny Fellows."[29]

The beauty of the Seventh's campsite on Meridian Hill inspired the most spectacular depiction of Camp Cameron. The distinguished Hudson River school painter Sanford Robinson Gifford served with the Seventh, and he used his time in the regiment as the basis for several paintings executed during the war. His painting *Preaching to the Troops, or Sunday Morning at Camp Cameron near Washington, May 1861* was probably finished in 1861. The painting captures the beauty of the camp, with its open green field for the service, a row of trees in the middle distance, and a scenic vista stretching to the Washington Monument, the city of Washington, and the Potomac River. In the far distance are the buildings of Arlington, Virginia, Gifford's reminder of the unit's participation in the invasion of Secessia. In the foreground, all is as it should be in a peaceful world. Two columns flank the minister, giving a classical taste to the setting and hinting that the democracies of Greece and Rome still serve as the pillars of the people's government in Washington. The band in the lower left corner carries more instruments than there are guns in the entire painting, and there are women seated in the right foreground. A handful of visitors have come to the camp, including at least three members of a Zouave regiment—probably the Fire Zouaves, a New York City regiment made up of working-class men who, thanks to the war, pulled together with the friends of the Stock Exchange in the Seventh. The scene is the United States at its best, Gifford seems to say. There is class harmony, beautiful women, music, brilliant nature, and a sound, classically based government.

Gifford's painting depicts how pleasant Camp Cameron could be, but it also tells us something about the men enrolled in the Seventh. The painting shows men lounging on the ground and in folding chairs listening to the sermon. While the men in the painting seem to be paying attention to the minister, they are hardly a rapt congregation; the most intent listeners are the officers on each flank of the minister. But even they stand and sit a good distance from the preacher, valuing shade over proximity. Not even the dog in the lower right corner seems unduly excited.[30] This is no low church revival meeting where emotion will rule the day. Rather, these men are confident auditors, listening with their heads more than their hearts, as would befit a group of respectable, successful men unlikely to lose their heads about anything. And, above everything, the whole scene radiates beauty, from the cloudless sky to the bright-green grass, majestically dark trees, and the aspiring city covered with atmospheric haze. With more food than they could eat, good weather, and a magnificent camp, Spalding and his comrades had much to enjoy. They also probably did not learn too many practical lessons about soldiering.[31]

At least Stephen Spalding and his fellow recruits for Company I did not have to worry about the shortage of rifles that plagued the regiment in May. Company I would train as an artillery company, and they had weaponry readily at hand.[32] The regiment had at least four howitzers when it marched through Maryland, some of them aggressively mounted on railroad flatcars pulled by men in the forefront of the unit's advance.[33] They also received more cannon as they waited in Camp Cameron, sent by the regiment's wealthy patrons in New York City. Rutherford Stuyvesant personally purchased two howitzers, ammunition, and equipment and forwarded them to Washington on May 3. J. J. Astor Jr. bought an additional two rifled cannon and eight hundred rounds of ammunition with the help of the Union Defense Committee and had them sent to the Seventh.[34] For Spalding, the Seventh would be a fine training ground for the use of different cannon, and he would have had the ammunition with which to train at live firing.

But Spalding's appearance in an artillery company raises questions about his future service in the Eighth Vermont. The Vermonter would soon have command of a company of infantry, and we can wonder at just how prepared he was to take on the task of training others to serve as infantrymen. Reading the Seventh's records shows us just how unprepared he was even after leaving the regiment in early June. The most detailed information about the Seventh's stay at Camp Cameron comes from the unit's "Guard Book," a day-by-day account of who had passes out of camp, when they left and returned, and whether they overstayed their leave. Officers also recorded in the "Guard Book" who served as pickets for the day and on which "reliefs." Spalding makes few appearances in the "Guard Book," a likely indication that he was too untrained to fulfill most duties. He makes his first appearance on May 13, when he received a pass to leave camp. He left at 12:45 and returned a hairsplitting three minutes before his leave ended at 2:45. A two-hour leave did not allow Spalding to get into too much trouble, because Camp Cameron was about two miles from Willard's Hotel. Robert Gould Shaw, in fact, noted to his mother that "the short leave of absence they give us now makes it hardly worth while to go to town unless to get a bath which we do as often as possible, that is, about once a week."[35] There would be no early rehearsals for Spalding's later Fourth of July debauchery in New Orleans.

Five days after his first leave, Spalding enjoyed a longer time away from camp; he spent four and a half hours away and came back a half hour early. Four days later, he had another long leave but came back seventy-five minutes before he had to. None of this makes Spalding's conduct in any way extraordinary. Spalding may have been on his best behavior, being very new to the regiment and perhaps even a bit awe-struck by his cosmopolitan and experienced comrades. Or he may just have been very green and needed to figure out what was going on. The most telling fact in the "Guard Book" is that his officers did not entrust Spalding with keeping guard—or any other specific duty—until May 26. At that point, eight of the regiment's ten companies left for Virginia, and his commanders had very little choice but to put him to work. That day he served on the third relief, meaning that he stood guard from 10:30 p.m. until 12:30 a.m., and again from 4:30 to 6:30 a.m. He stood guard again on May 29, after the rest of the regiment had come back from Virginia with aching muscles and sore feet. This pretty much brought his useful service to the Seventh to a close.

The historian of Company I knew that officers were uneasy about the new men and their lack of training. He wrote that after Spalding's arrival at Camp Cameron, "it is to be hoped that in three days they were able to make a presentable appearance, for . . . the whole regiment was reviewed by President Lincoln."[36] Even the painter Sanford Gifford voiced caution about the new men after being promoted to "Corporal of the recruit squad." In the wake of the recruits' first parade at the company level, he wrote a public letter expressing that "we went with fear and trembling." Perhaps their lack of preparedness caused Spalding and the rest of Company I to miss the invasion. Certainly, the officers who planned the campaign into Virginia kept Stephen Spalding and his fellow late arrivals behind in the capital. Still, Spalding may have been disappointed about being left behind. One eyewitness to the reading of the orders for the advance on the fateful night claimed that "many" of the men in Companies I and K "almost shed tears of disappointment at their forced stay in camp."[37] Speculation about the degree of Spalding's inexperience—or more pointedly, his incompetence in military matters—would not be so important had Spalding not been able to parlay his time in the Seventh into an officer's rank in the Eighth Vermont a few months later. He was not ready to be a first lieutenant of infantry; he had served less than a month; trained in artillery, not infantry; and had barely been deemed worthy of doing guard duty as a private. His promotion makes clear just how jury-rigged the whole Union war effort was in the fall of 1861.

No matter how green he was in other matters, Spalding would at least have learned the importance of rank during his brief stay with the New Yorkers. While in the ranks, he saw how far his comrades would go to secure promotions and how many of them were able to leave the Seventh to become officers in new regiments. He had been in the regiment not more than three days when he witnessed a blistering fight for promotion at very close quarters. It happened this way. Probably sometime in late April, Sergeant Tyng received orders from Colonel Lefferts to recruit and train men in New York City to fill up Company I. Tyng seems to have done his job well, but he also hatched a plot among the new recruits, who included Spalding.[38] It appears that Tyng had both ambition and a hand for the kind of palace intrigue that occasionally surfaced in the early years of American democracy. Knowing that the new recruits would outnumber the older members of Company I, Tyng apparently convinced them to elect him to the vacant captaincy when they reached Camp Cameron. What promises he made to the new soldiers he had under his thumb during drill remains unknown. We do know that Tyng's plot was unmasked upon their arrival, and "high authority" in the regiment squashed his try for officer rank.[39] Within days of entering the military, Spalding had seen that rank mattered enough to plot for it, and he had seen higher rank used to crush the attempt.

Sergeant Tyng, in the end, returned to his old company at his old rank. Spalding, of course, remained in Company I. There he witnessed elections as the company reorganized to suit its new size. Spalding's initiation into this process again came quickly for the new soldier. On May 17, less than a week after seeing Camp Cameron for the first time, Spalding saw six of his fellow new arrivals promoted to corporal or sergeant.[40] Spalding remained a private; whether he stood for election is unknown. Either he knew he was unprepared for the jobs, or his fellow soldiers saw him as such.

Having an early initiation into the importance of rank may have prepared Spalding for what was to come: the Seventh teemed with men eager to translate their service into officer status in newer regiments. The regiment's reputation for sharp drill fostered the idea that a private from the Seventh could whip recruits into shape as an officer elsewhere. As William Swinton's 1870 regimental history recalls, "the talk of commissions was one of the leading subjects of conversation" at Camp Cameron. He quotes a letter from May 21, during Spalding's service in the regiment, that says that four privates and a sergeant had just received commissions in the same new regiment. The fact that Maj. Irwin McDowell, who swore them into Federal service, called the Seventh "a regiment of officers" underscored his belief that the regiment's privates had the expertise and social standing to command. McDowell's fame as the commander of the Union force at Bull Run helped spread his phrase to the world.[41] Two examples show what privates from the Seventh could expect if they jumped ship. Robert Gould Shaw left the Seventh at about the same time Spalding arrived to become a second lieutenant in the equally wealthy but just forming Second Massachusetts.[42] Also, Theodore Winthrop, the writer and very recent recruit to the Seventh, won a lieutenancy on Benjamin Butler's staff at Fort Monroe. (He would soon be killed at the Battle of Big Bethel.) Swinton's regimental history concludes with an annotated list of men who served in the Seventh before becoming officers in other units—and the list goes on for 105 pages. As Swinton phrased it, "the daily departure of comrades as officers of new regiments created a feverish anxiety in others to follow their example."[43]

Spalding seems to have caught the promotion fever, judging by his rapid appointment to officer rank and recruiter for a "Light Brigade" unit forming in Montpelier. That he had secured this new post by June 21, less than three weeks after his return to New York City with the rest of the Seventh, indicates that he acted quickly to gain officer rank. The question, however, is whether the fever caused him to misrepresent his service in the Seventh in order to win promotion. Was Carpenter's miniature biography of Spalding (which claims that he enlisted "in less than six hours after the assault on Fort Sumter") based on what Spalding said (with little fear of contradiction) when he returned to Vermont in 1861? It seems likely that he did tell this lie. A newspaper account from 1863 proves that, if nothing else, Spalding wrote to his father that he had volunteered immediately after Fort Sumter.[44]

Spalding had everything to gain by exaggerating his service in the Seventh. By saying that he had enlisted in the aftermath of Fort Sumter, he could claim patriotic credentials and say that he had participated in two of the most stirring events of 1861: the saving of the capital city and the big parade down Broadway. He also could boast of a full campaign's worth of tutelage in martial arts when he stood for election as an officer in Company B of the Eighth Vermont. Being a member of the Seventh was something to brag about, even if some people disliked their wealth and dandyism or had criticized the men's commitment to only one month of military life, especially before they extended their term to march into Virginia.[45] To be with them the whole way was to claim participation in something special.

But would he have feared being caught in his lie? Probably not. Records for the regiment were not available to the public, and no rosters seem to have been published at the time. And, of course, he had served in the regiment, so records would show that much at least. Few Vermonters would have been in a position to know his whereabouts in New York City during late April. Spalding would also have known about the regiment's activities during its first weeks without him. Camp Cameron would have been an easy place to pick up such details; Spalding would probably have been curious and asked what the men around him had been doing before May 11. It would have been far stranger for the "veterans" to have been silent about their efforts. So Spalding would know enough details to pass for a true veteran of the

Seventh's full campaign, and he probably had little reason to think that his Vermont comrades would find out the details of his service. If someone claimed to have seen him in New York City in April or early May, he could claim that he had been in the city doing recruiting duty, just as Sergeant Tyng had been. The "Guard Book" indicates that men also shuttled back and forth between the city and Camp Cameron on a fairly frequent basis in May, usually for medical reasons.

Of course, the faking of a substantial part of one's identity sounds more like a mid-twentieth-century Agatha Christie plot than a typical Civil War–era event. But Americans in Spalding's time worried about the existence of con men who fictionalized their past to get ahead. Historian Karen Halttunen has dubbed the decades from 1830 to 1870 "the era of the confidence man." This villain, she writes, emerged in writings about the newly anonymous cities, like Spalding's New York, where con artists preyed on virtuous, easily deceived people from the countryside. A con man was "a skilled actor" who played at being a friendly, honest man while masking his evil past.[46] In a world dominated by geographic mobility, respectable people imagined themselves surrounded by men who were not what they appeared to be.

People who lied about themselves figure prominently in the literature of the time. Both Herman Melville and Mark Twain consider the implications of a society in which individuals can make up their own history whenever they meet strangers. Twain, of course, usually joked about the resulting misunderstandings. In his memoirs about life in Civil War Nevada and California, Twain repeatedly meets men from the East who have reimagined their lives in order to get along better in the West. Indeed, one critic has said that Twain essentially did the same thing—reconstructing his days as a Confederate soldier in 1861 to such an extent that he became "the Lincoln of our literature."[47] If Twain could imagine retelling his past so wholeheartedly, then Spalding could add a few weeks to his service in the Seventh. Herman Melville's *The Confidence Man,* written in 1857, describes a steamboat cruise down the Mississippi during which everyone's identity is questioned and either verified or not, perhaps wrongly. Melville could not view these deceptions with Twain's comic disregard, but the whole novel's probing of the social ramifications of con men meeting con men highlights just how much Spalding's society ran on misrepresentations of one's experiences, talents, and background. Melville's novel suggests that if Spalding lied about when he joined the Seventh, he did so as part of a national epidemic of résumé padding.

Why did so many men want to be officers? Such striving may seem far removed from the patriotic motives that we impart to Civil War soldiers. But it would make sense for Spalding to have exaggerated; he would gain in pay, for one thing. Lieutenants received $105.50 a month, while privates were paid only thirteen dollars.[48] Spalding had probably already seen officers living more comfortable lives than enlisted men at Camp Cameron; his 1862 letter to James Peck laid out the privileges he enjoyed by gaining a commission: "Our regiment is quartered in the Depot, the officers using the private offices for their quarters."[49] He also would get the respect that came with an officer's commission, that fabled prize he had heard about ever since he had met Sergeant Tyng. Gaining a promotion—how to get one and who had received them—seems to have been the bread and butter of regimental talk at Camp Cameron. Lying would have served Spalding well.

Such a vivid display of ambition may seem out of character for Spalding's age, but that is only because we have rendered our past as more disinterested than it was. Even in the earliest decades of Spalding's century, Americans worried about the amount of self-interest they saw around them. As Jane Kamensky writes in her biography of a banker in early national Boston: "Americans reached, strived, *climbed*." (Stephen Spalding's father, Levi, was also a bank president, and he may have taught his son something about self-interest.) Another recent historian of Jacksonian Massachusetts has described the era's young men as "restless, striving, self-assertive spirits. They pursued ambitions beyond their parents' imagining." As a Michigan officer said about the army that marched on Bull Run in 1861, "we were all young then, and the imagination was more active, the ambitions were greater."[50]

Men had always wanted to get ahead, but rarely was such ambition so divorced from a sense of the communal good as it was in the antebellum decades. For proof, we need only look at the number of people who tore away from their families and towns to pursue California gold on the other side of the continent. It is hard to know for sure if Stephen Spalding was in the vanguard of aggressive individualism, but he certainly was not among its many critics. He was as modern in his pursuit of individual self-interest as he was in his comic style and his ways of expressing friendship.

More to the point, we have proof that Spalding carefully created images of himself to satisfy audiences. Spalding's letter shows us that he made up versions of himself. This is not the same as fraud; one usually only accentuates elements of one's character or background at the expense of others. In his letter, Spalding presents himself to his friend in exaggerated ways that surely were not true. Most obviously, he did not have seven hundred to eight hundred alcoholic drinks a day, and he probably did not have *all* of the different kinds of drinks at Bianca Robbins's establishment that he enumerates. The story of his drunken dance suggests a stock depiction of an inebriated dancer rather than a literal reality. One doubts if he really trotted off to New Orleans to get Greek and Latin dictionaries in order to read his friend's letter. All of these falsehoods are there for comic effect, certainly, and not to deceive his friend. But they suggest an ability and a willingness to invent stories about himself in order to gain a point. Having enlisted immediately after Fort Sumter made for a better story in so many different ways. It ennobled his enlistment with patriotic sentiment. It gave him license to retell the stories of the Seventh from a first-person perspective. It sounded better than what he could have said, truthfully: I joined for three weeks and did nothing much of any use. How could he have resisted telling this fiction about himself?

But perhaps it did not do him well in the long run. Did he fail to impress his commanding officers when he knew less about infantry drill than he should have, given his recent experience? Is that why he was never promoted? Did his lack of knowledge mean that he never gained the respect of his men as he fumbled through the initial weeks of drill outside Brattleboro? By the summer of 1862 he had discipline problems in his company, and an initial lack of respect for his knowledge may have sown the seeds of that problem. But here, as in so many other things about Spalding, we are left with more questions than answers. Nevertheless, we do know these things: Stephen Spalding did not seize the first opportunity to enlist in the war to save the Union. We can now look back at Spalding's letter, where he writes that "were it not for the simple fact that we are 'Patriots' and fighting in a 'Glorious Cause' our courage I fear would give way," and see that he is making fun of the country's overuse of those words at the start of the war. We know that ambition is a larger part of his character than veracity. We know that he received only three weeks of training as a private before he received an officer's commission. We know that he received more training in artillery than he did in infantry tactics, rendering him even less suited to officer rank than we might think. We know that during his time with the Seventh he never left camp, never marched in a campaign. We know, in other words, that the Union war effort was so haphazard, even in the fall of 1861, that someone with close to no qualifications ended up with a lieutenant's bars on his shoulders. This was going to be a war of amateurs.

3

RACIAL HIERARCHY
Spalding and Jim

The door was opened [by] my boy Jim whom I captured at
"Tibedeaux" and who by the way is *painfully black.*

—Stephen Spalding

Like most good letter writers, Stephen Spalding included characters
and scenes scattered over his seven pages. The dancing incident stands
out, with its escalating action and flying British officers, but other parts
of the letter feature small stories. The opening scene of Spalding receiving a letter from James Peck is one of these vignettes. It includes
two players, Spalding and his servant, Jim. For better or for worse, the
interaction between the two men starts the letter and sets its comic
tone.

Of course, Spalding's joke about hurling a chair at Jim will now
strike readers as more offensive than funny. But there are things to be
learned from it all the same. Spalding's racial views might best be described as white supremacist. The fact that many people shared that
perspective in the 1860s makes it only a bit more excusable. Since some
people publicly argued for racial equality, we have to conclude that
Spalding chose to be the way he was. This is one of the things that
makes Spalding historically important. He wrote and acted from the
perspective of someone at the top of a social pyramid, and no evidence
suggests that he questioned his place there. He would have been called
"conservative" in his time because of his sense that some people were
made, by nature and God, better than others; "liberal" reformers preferred more egalitarian models of society. The next two chapters analyze the tensions between Spalding's stratified view of society and the
movements toward equality going on around him. In particular, this

chapter explores Spalding's ideas about racial hierarchy and how they influenced his actions. The next chapter will explore his ideas about masculine supremacy. Spalding's sense that he lived at the top of a series of social stratifications fueled his humor and affected how he interacted with people. His elitism, usually an empowering set of beliefs, was being challenged as American society and politics moved toward greater inclusiveness. In the remaining chapters we will see Spalding's privileged status come under assault from both the poorer men whom he commanded and perhaps from his fellow officers. But in the next two chapters, we will see Spalding enjoying the social status his race and sex gave to him.

When it comes to racial matters, what was funny to James Peck and Stephen Spalding may not be so amusing to modern readers. The Vermonter's description of his servant as *"painfully black"* smacks of a long-standing racist tradition of equating blackness with a host of sins and evils; Spalding is pained by the blackness of his servant's skin.[1] Describing Jim in this way immediately places him on the wrong side of the color line. So, too, does Spalding's unapologetic seizing of a stool, the better to "sl[i]ng it at his head." This violence, presented as a laughing matter, brings to mind the punishments of the Slave South, as well as northern acts of racial aggression before and during the war. It seems to fall into an established pattern. Historian David Cecere's study of New England soldiers and their racial attitudes finds that in the first two years of the war, New England whites wrote of blacks as "subhuman, simple-minded, amusing pets, often the butt of jokes." While Cecere also says that New England volunteers displayed "inconsistent and often contradictory racial reactions to blacks," it seems that Spalding's joke about abusing Jim is consistent with a broad swath of Civil War letters.[2]

But it is possible to read the scene in other ways. The freedom of employers to abuse their servants (and of valets to torment their bosses) is a big part of the history of Western theatrical comedy. Spalding's vignette begins with a stage direction: "I was sitting in my room thinking." His mock-serious comment that he had been pondering "over the mutability of all things human" heightens the sense of comic exaggeration. (It also invites readers to take him at his word. If he really were pondering over how much "all things human" change, he might well be considering just how much race relations—"all things human"—were changing around him.) The theatricality of the scene continues with the stage direction of "the door was opened and my boy Jim" entered. That the stool is thrown is much more important than whether or not a blow is struck, and indeed Spalding leaves off any effect of the toss. To hurl furniture at a servant who has acted correctly is surely an exaggeration, this one told to highlight our main character's state of gloom and frustration as the story opens in one of the war's backwaters. Similarly, we could read "*painfully*" as an ambivalent adjective; in modern usage at least, people can be "painfully white" or "painfully thin" in a culture that still all too often values whiteness and a slim physique.

So we as modern readers are left to wonder why Spalding starts his letter this way. To answer that question, we need to explore the fuller contexts of the world in which Jim, Spalding, Peck, and the Eighth Vermont lived. We can examine the unit's partisan politics, the policies they were ordered to enforce, how the veterans of the Eighth remembered their service, and how Spalding's friends wrote about racial issues. By exploring Spalding's world more fully, we will be able to see what prompted Spalding to write this odd beginning to his letter.

We can draw a first clue about Spalding's racial politics from his curious phrasing about Jim's origins. Spalding introduces him as "my boy Jim whom I captured at 'Tibedeaux.'" This phrase suggests that Spalding does not think too highly of his servant. Americans have a depressing history of addressing black men as "boys," regardless of their age. By doing so, whites deny black men their rights as citizens, as well as their abilities in other fields, ranging from sex to mature reasoning. That Jim may have actually been a boy needs to be considered, but the phrase "my boy Jim" is too standard a phrasing of control and superiority to ignore. The words "whom I captured" is more surprising and more intriguing.

It is hard to know what Stephen Spalding meant when he wrote that he had "captured" Jim at Thibodaux. The first confusion comes from trying to imagine how Spalding might have gotten to Thibodaux. Over the course of the summer, the Eighth Vermont may have sent patrols to Thibodaux, which lay to the west of Algiers. For example, three companies skirmished at nearby Raceland in late June. The problem, however, is that Spalding's Company B was not part of that campaign, and there would have been no reason for Spalding to have accompanied them. So how could Spalding have "captured" Jim? Either Spalding somehow made it to Thibodaux in a campaign that has gone unrecorded—this is by no means unlikely, since one suspects that the Raceland skirmish made it into Carpenter's regimental history only because it resulted in the Vermonters' first combat and casualties—or Spalding was exaggerating his military conquests.

While it is possible that Spalding made it to Thibodaux in time to capture Jim, it seems equally likely that Jim escaped from a plantation near the town. He could have done this by running away and making his way across enemy lines to the Eighth Vermont's pickets. Or he may have taken advantage of having the Union army come through the town, which we know happened at least once when the Twenty-First Indiana passed through Thibodaux in early May.[3] One way or another, enslaved men and women were getting to Union lines in considerable numbers that spring and summer. Capt. John De Forest of the Twelfth Connecticut describes the scene in a June 15 letter, written about three weeks before Spalding wrote to Peck. De Forest notes that there were forty "Negro laundresses" working in the Thirteenth Connecticut, while his own regiment employed sixty blacks as nurses and hospital laborers, company cooks, and as "servants to officers." Another 150 black women and men had established a camp nearby.[4] In other words, Jim could have joined a "contraband camp" and then looked for work among the Union regiments. Or Jim may have meet Spalding along the picket line, and the Union officer seized the chance to employ him. These scenarios give Jim most of the credit for his escape and employment by Spalding. If this is indeed what happened, then Spalding has failed to acknowledge Jim's role in planning and making his escape.

We cannot know definitively how Jim came to be with the Union army by early July 1862. But we do know how Spalding writes about it. He writes of Jim, "whom I captured at 'Tibedeaux.'" The verb "captured" is a curious word choice. In what way could Spalding have "captured" Jim? What, after all, does one capture in war? Usually enemy soldiers are "captured," but it is almost certain that Jim was not serving in the Confederate army. There has been an ongoing debate in popular culture about the extent to which the Confederate government allowed or encouraged black men to enlist in their army, but the weight of evidence shows an absence of "black Confederates" in the ranks.[5] This is particularly true in Louisiana in 1861 and 1862, where even *free* black men willing to serve in Confederate ranks were never issued arms, despite the severe manpower shortages Confederate commanders experienced after troops were sent north to fight at Shiloh.[6] Even if he had been with a Confederate soldier as a servant, how could he have been captured without the kind of skirmish that would have made Carpenter's history?

It is more likely that Spalding "captured" Jim in the sense that he had seized enemy property. This means that Spalding saw Jim as a slave, not a person. Jim was a thing to be captured, much as Sherman would capture Atlanta or a Union ship might capture a blockade-runner. If this is the case, then we could argue that Spalding's conception of slaves was pretty consistent with the federal government's policies in the summer of 1862. Starting in May 1861, the Lincoln administration had unofficially adopted Maj. Gen. Benjamin F. Butler's classification of fugitive slaves as "contraband of war." The term "contraband" quickly fell into widespread usage in the North; the idea was that the U.S. government could legally confiscate any property used by the Confederates for the purpose of making war against it. For the Lincoln administration, this was a convenient legal concept that allowed it to simultaneously keep and employ most southern slaves who made it to their lines while also denying that the war was aimed at abolishing slavery—an idea opposed by some northerners and most Border State whites siding with the Union.[7] In this sense, Spalding could mean that he had captured rebel property and was holding it (not him) for his own use. Custom would have demanded that Jim was paid a wage, but Jim was hardly in a position to demand a high salary.

It seems likely, then, that Jim had escaped to Union lines, where he found that he was in a kind of gray area in terms of his status. He would be treated as a free, wage laborer, but he would not be legally free. He was no longer enslaved in daily practice—he could leave Spalding's employ for another job—but he had to hope that the United States both won the war and changed its policies regarding slavery. He could no longer be sold or severely beaten, but he was employed by a man with great power as a Union officer and who joked, if nothing else, about throwing furniture at him. Spalding denied Jim the credit for his escape from slavery, called him a "boy," and, as a final act of disrespect, stated that Jim reacted with cowardice to Spalding tossing a stool at him: "He dropped the document he had in his hand and fled." As an author of a piece of theatrical comedy, Spalding has now concluded his opening scene. Peck's letter has arrived, and Spalding is alone to read it. According to Spalding's exaggerated account, reading it took him two days, his course blocked by Latin and Greek passages and literary allusions high and low. Jim, we might suppose, was illiterate, and his hasty exit is necessary for the reading to commence. Neither Jim nor anyone of his race will appear in the rest of Spalding's letter.

The absence of any mention of slavery—or, indeed, of any African American other than Jim—in the letter is remarkable. Forty-nine percent of Louisianans were enslaved before the war.[8] Other Union soldiers stationed in southern Louisiana make frequent mention of African Americans. To make sense of Spalding's omission of blacks from his letter, we had best go back a year and see how and why the Eighth Vermont came into being, and what its origins mean about Spalding and the other officers with whom he served.

What we find is that the Eighth Vermont came into being under very specific political circumstances. In October 1861, with the United States licking its wounds after the First Battle of Bull Run, the Lincoln administration asked Benjamin Butler to go on a recruiting tour of the New England states. Butler had two qualifications for this job. First, he had created a fine record for himself. He had rushed troops to Washington in the first week of the war, wrested control of Baltimore from a hostile mob, and created the useful category of "Contraband of War" for fugitive slaves. Second, Butler had been an outspoken Democrat before the war, and Lincoln, a Republican, needed his help to demonstrate that the war was not a single-party effort. If Butler could raise a division of troops among New England Democrats, he could have their command. This was, in essence, the infantry force that he eventually used to secure New Orleans and create the Department of the Gulf, his command until December 1862.

Butler approached his recruiting drive among New England Democrats as a top-down enterprise. According to his autobiography, he first secured the appointment of prominent Democratic politicians to command his new regiments. New England's Republican governors had previously tended to give command of regiments to either their own party loyalists or to Regular Army officers willing to take up Volunteer commands. Most of them, however, gladly appointed Butler's Democrats as colonels as long as recruits were mustered for the cause. That Lincoln had given Butler a letter requesting that they do so no doubt helped.

Butler visited Montpelier in October 1861 and asked Vermont's governor to commission a Democratic member of the state legislature, Stephen Thomas, to command the Eighth Vermont. Thomas had been a delegate to the 1860 Democratic nominating convention in Charleston, South Carolina, where he probably met Benjamin Butler, then a delegate from Massachusetts. Indeed, Thomas had been to every national Democratic convention since 1848.[9] George Carpenter's history of the Eighth Vermont states that Thomas then selected his regimental staff and recruiting officers, including company captains. Lieutenants, like Spalding, were elected by their commands. It is hard to know for sure how important partisan allegiance was to Butler and Thomas as they considered this lowest level of the officer corps.[10]

Does this mean that Spalding—or his father—was a Democratic activist? Butler's confrontation with Republican governor John Andrew of Massachusetts suggests that the Spaldings may have been Democrats. During that contentious meeting, Butler apparently said: "I preferred to have them, if I could get them, a regiment of Democrats, every officer to be a Democrat, and especially the colonel. . . . I told him that I had the permission of the President to have the recruiting of a New England division of Democrats, and I wanted them of the most pronounced and well-known type; . . . and that I desired to recommend the officers to him for his appointment."[11] Butler's words suggest that he saw his entire officer corps as fair game for Democratic patronage. With so many of the colonels in Butler's force experienced politicians who attended national conventions, it is hard to imagine them passing up the chance to nominate their fellow partisans to the ranks of prominent and well-paid officers. In a world in which heroism in war was often a step to political success, Democrats (like Republicans) would have liked to have as many of their people in the officer corps as possible.

We can also see Spalding acting as a young Democrat in the one big professional decision he had made by the time General Butler traveled to Montpelier to organize his Vermont regiment. Soon after his graduation from the University of Vermont, Spalding made his way back to Derby Line. There, sources agree, he read law with John L. Edwards. In the age before law schools, young men studied with established lawyers to learn their trade, much as apprentices worked for skilled artisans in most trades. Spalding's choice to work with John L. Edwards very probably reflected his political allegiances, since attorneys usually regarded the men who worked for them as protégés. In this case, Spalding was taken on by Edwards, who would be the Democratic candidate for governor of Vermont in 1868. (He remained enough of a Democratic partisan to receive votes as a congressional candidate in a subsequent election.) The two men must have been reasonably well matched eight years earlier in order to work well together, and it is unlikely that Edwards came to his Democratic allegiance soon before 1868. Clearly, he did not take the nomination out of expedience; like all Democratic gubernatorial candidates in this time, he was clobbered in the election, winning only 26 percent of the vote.

Other evidence that Spalding adhered to Democratic politics is circumstantial but intriguing. When C. C. Spalding, a cousin of Stephen Spalding, opened a newspaper in Newport, Vermont, a neighboring town to Derby Line, in 1863, he was greeted with intense suspicion about his politics. The opening of his newspaper office sparked concerns in the largely Republican town. "We were somewhat surprised to find," he wrote in his first issue, "directly after we had opened our office, that a report had been very industriously circulated to the effect that the Newport paper was to be a violent anti-administration, secesh sheet. This thing, however, did not astonish or offend us."[12] The rumor could, of course, have started because the Spaldings in the nearby town were known to be Democrats, a fact that would have made the rumor predictable and unlikely to "astonish" C. C. Spalding. Even when C. C. Spalding's paper took a pro-war stance, it did so as a "Union Party" paper and did not endorse the Republican Party. By 1865, a strictly Republican paper, the *Newport Express,* opened for business, presumably to compete against the Democratically inclined Spalding one.

Being able to link Stephen Spalding to the Democratic Party makes it easier for us to understand his comments about his servant, Jim. Northern Democrats were conservatives on matters of race and slavery during the Civil War era. Illinois senator Stephen Douglas's famous statement during the Lincoln–Douglas debates that he did not care if slavery were voted up or down represents the heart of the northern Democratic position. But northern Democrats broadened this position by adding a fierce opposition to black equality in the North. Democrats opposed the integration of public schools and racial intermarriage, labeling the United States a "white man's country." As Stephen Douglas declared: "We do not believe in the equality of the Negro socially and politically. Our people are white people; our state is a white state, and we mean to preserve the race pure without any mixture with the negro."[13] As such, the party stood as much for white supremacy as it did for indifference to the expansion of slavery.[14] Benjamin Butler, the man responsible for raising the division in which Spalding would serve, had employed these kinds of racist positions to curry favor with voters and with the Democratic politicians in Washington who controlled patronage appointments in his district. Most recently, Butler had fought so persistently against the inclusion of black men in the Massachusetts state militia that he was stripped of his rank by an antebellum Republican governor.[15] There is no reason to believe that any of the Democratic politicians in his command differed from Butler on racial issues. In other words, the United States Army that went into Louisiana in 1862 was top-heavy with officers who did not see emancipation—let alone racial equality—as a priority in the Union's war effort.

Spalding's exact racial positions cannot be determined beyond what he says about Jim and one story told about him after his death that we will explore in a moment. But other Vermont Democrats made themselves heard. Democratic newspapers often discussed the merits of abolition and the likely outcomes of legalizing racial equality. The Democratic newspapers rarely admitted that they liked slavery, but their ambivalence about bondage was overpowered by a stronger dislike of black people. The *Burlington Weekly Sentinel,* for example, claimed that they had "no love for the negro-slave system," only to then begin attaching conditions to its end. Slavery may not be good, they thought, but abolition would be worse. "Abolition," they wrote, "and not Slavery is the cause of all our present national troubles."[16] They also tried scaring Vermont voters with the idea that freed blacks would find their way to the Green Mountain State unless the United States "let both the Southern Negroes and their masters quite alone." In keeping with this idea, the paper opposed what became the Second Confiscation Act as it made its way through Congress.[17] In concrete ways, the state's Democrats opposed abolition, even as they proclaimed their theoretical dislike of slavery.

We can also get a sense of the Eighth Vermont's racial politics from letters written home during the war by members of the regiment. Some were just plain hostile to abolitionists. Pvt. William Haskins blamed his harsh life as a soldier on abolitionist ministers whose ideas arose from "envy . . . because they cannot hold slaves." Other soldiers displayed the same rhetorical juggling act as the *Burlington Weekly Sentinel,* balancing a hatred for slavery in theory with acceptance of it in practice. A month before Spalding wrote about Jim, Pvt. Benjamin F. Morse of Company E expressed doubts about what he saw unfolding around him. "The plantations look well but the negro is a lasy creature at the best" he wrote, before continuing his negative assessment: "if ever I come home I shall not be an abolition[ist] not that I think slavery is right but it is a bad institution to meddle with let them that have got it bear the curse of it." Morse clearly did not think of blacks as his equals, and he would not disturb slavery, though he contradictorily indicates that he knows it is not "right."[18] Adjt. John L. Barstow, one of Spalding's friends and the regiment's adjutant, also expressed a theoretical dislike of slavery: "I hope its day is gone, so far as getting labor for nothing is concerned." However, when Barstow wrote to his wife, he included blacks in a list of sights he had seen, placing them in suggestive company: "Every rod of travel showed us something new. pelicans, turtles, Swan's geese, ducks, Alligators Water Snakes, Negroes—were seen by turns and some times together."[19] The list places African Americans far down on the evolutionary ladder, away from humans and consorting with beasts. It is neither a happy nor a surprising association.

Two books written by veterans of the Eighth Vermont in the 1880s and 1890s tell long stories about the Vermonters' encounters with African Americans. George Carpenter's regimental history gives us an inside look at the racial beliefs of Spalding's fellow Vermonters, even from the distance of its 1886 publication date. The book argues that the black people they had met decades ago in the towns and sugar fields of Louisiana were not their equals. Still, they did not want to seem too sympathetic to slavery, and striking that balance required some fancy rhetorical footwork. George Carpenter confronts the issue as soon as the Eighth Vermont arrives in Algiers and the men meet black refugees from slavery in considerable numbers. Carpenter asks what were the men to do about these large groups of fugitives? His answer is revealingly vague, but couched in humanitarian terms: "The sentiment of the regiment was not unanimous. Part, recognizing human slavery as an unmitigated evil, felt that it would be wrong under any circumstances to remand the fugitives back into servitude; others contended that a body of troops, in the discharge of their proper duties, could not lawfully interfere with private property, or undertake to decide on the justice of the alleged owner's claim. But very naturally the sympathies of the soldiers prompted them to render every reasonable aid to any colored brother whom they found groping his way to freedom."[20]

To back up this statement, Carpenter turns to the story of a fugitive slave who had made his way to the Eighth Vermont. We need not assume this man was Jim; in fact, hundreds of men escaped to Union lines around New Orleans in the summer of 1862. For months the Eighth Vermont held the front lines of the western approaches of the city, the route along which slaves seeking freedom from the coastal sugar parishes would have come. Whoever this anonymous man was, "he complained of cruel treatment, and showed the recent marks of a chain around his ankles, the sight of which stirred the indignation of the men. He seemed willing to work." The man's owner soon appeared, however, and began beating him with "a heavy leathern strap." The fugitive then started to run through the camp, closely pursued by the owner, who never stopped whipping him. "This spectacle," Carpenter notes, "was more than the Yankee boys could witness unmoved, so they too joined in the race, and every time the master struck his slave they would give him a kick." The would-be owner gave up his quest and returned home alone.[21]

This was not an unusual sequence of events. Other Union soldiers, perhaps to their own surprise, came to side with the bloodied fugitives in their midst. For example, when an enslaved woman named Mattie Jackson tried to gain the protection of the Union army in St. Louis in

1861, she was turned away. But she received a warmer welcome a few weeks later after her owner struck her across the head "with a stick of wood," causing blood to run "over my clothing, which gave me a frightful appearance." Refusing to change into clean clothes, Jackson returned to the Union garrison and won entry and temporary protection.[22] But the frequency of this kind of confrontation does not mean that every fugitive slave won refuge in Union lines or that welcoming Union units did so unanimously. Such was the case in the Eighth Vermont.

The excitement caused by the abused slave's appearance in the Eighth Vermont's camp did not end with the rout of the person's owner. As Carpenter notes, the regiment's lieutenant colonel, Edward M. Brown, made a stink about his men's actions. Brown had the regiment formed into line and "addressed some severe language to the men." He told the soldiers that they had come "into the service to obey orders, and not to interfere with personal property, whether in slaves or anything else." Carpenter explains that Brown's address fell flat with the soldiers, who instead of seeing the error of their ways became all the more sure that they were "not to return the fugitive slaves."[23] Brown soon left the regiment to become Benjamin Butler's handpicked editor of the *New Orleans True Delta*, the official newspaper of the city's new Unionist government, but perhaps by then he had outstayed his welcome with the Vermont men.

Even with Brown's departure, Spalding's regiment did not become a hotbed of abolitionism or racial egalitarianism. It was happy to employ three or four "colored cooks," Carpenter writes, and obviously Jim became Spalding's valet at about this point.[24] But at least one soldier believed the regiment returned some fugitive slaves to their owners as late as June 1862.[25] Also, the regimental history includes tales of black criminality, even as it explicitly omits all stories that reflected badly on white men in the unit. Readers hear a black cook named Stamps confess to plundering plantations, though we do not hear how Colonel Thomas eventually ruled in his case. In another passage, a group of slaves kill their overseer and place his corpse in a mule cart. The Vermonters encounter the slaves and their grizzly cargo on a road. The enslaved people "declared that the overseer had been a hard master, and very 'outrageous,' what ever that might signify, on which account they were confident that their murderous act was entirely justifiable." One can almost see the sneer on Carpenter's face as he writes "what ever that might signify." The Vermonters "reprimanded the murderers severely" and placed several of their leaders under arrest and sent them to New Orleans.[26]

Perhaps most ominously for anyone hoping the Vermonters would become a force for racial equality, Carpenter follows this story of murderous blacks with a story of a white secessionist woman who turns into an angel of mercy while nursing an ill Vermont soldier. The moral was clear to Carpenter: "there were honest secessionists, who loved their enemies and tried to do them good."[27] While many other white Union veterans would defend abolition and welcome blacks into the Union's postwar veterans group, the Eighth Vermont remembered the war differently. That Carpenter (and the other men who collected material for his history) chose to combine stories of good Confederate women and bad black men suggests that these Democrats of the 1860s saw white racial unity as a way to foster national reconciliation in the 1880s.[28]

Blacks make favorable cameos in Carpenter's history, but even then there is an odd brevity or incompleteness to the tales. We meet "'Old Joe,' a colored man whom all will recollect," as he single-handedly captures two Confederate soldiers hiding in a cane field. But the incident passes in a few sentences, without any details. The most curiously incomplete story unfolds over four pages in April 1863. In this tale, a black man, Ole Dick, has passed through rebel lines to warn the Eighth Vermont that the enemy will attack in force very soon. He has, in fact, overheard a rebel gunboat captain discussing the plans in his master's house. This would seem a proper occasion to commend the man who had put himself in grave danger to warn the Vermonters, but Carpenter stops short of doing that. Instead, he relates the event as a very long monologue by Ole Dick, whose warning is lost in a maze of ramblings in a barely comprehensible dialect. Thus, a randomly chosen sentence of Ole Dick's supposed speech reads: "But do lake wuz so big, and I wuz so fur from shore, dat I cudn' see ez I wuz gittin' ahead any."[29] Nearly any Vermont reader would have trouble with page after page of this dialect, and ultimately most would probably wonder about the equality of the speaker.

Rather than acknowledging Ole Dick's service, Carpenter introduces the whole story as just something funny that had happened to the regiment. The black man does not give valuable military intelligence; instead, he "gave the boys what some one very properly styled a Sunday evening entertainment." At the end of Ole Dick's tale, the Vermonters do not ready themselves for an attack; instead Ole Dick is overcome by the sight of "soft bread and coffee," which he ends up talking about "in his comical style" with great enthusiasm.[30] For Carpenter, the Eighth Vermont's experiences in Louisiana did not inspire treatment of blacks as equals, or even as people to take seriously. With a few exceptions, he instead tosses figurative stools at them and moves on.

Moses McFarland's much shorter published recollections—totaling about seventeen pages—also include tales about slaves who have gained their freedom. The picture, which could be painted as one of liberation and victory, is instead presented as a comedy. While McFarland says he personally refused a planter's request to return two fugitive slaves, he fails to make any case for racial equality. He boasts that he has had "ample opportunity to study the nature, character and disposition of the colored race," but the study has produced a less than favorable picture. Blacks were there "in great numbers," he says, and that is perhaps McFarland's dominant impression of them. The Eighth Vermont's camps around Algiers had blacks "filling all the warehouses and every nook and corner, clamoring for food and clothing."[31] The Vermonter also acknowledges the plundering conducted by slaves escaping their plantations:

> All along our route, . . . the whole colored population evidently thought the year of jubilee had come and with it the right of possession to anything and everything the plantation afforded, which would in any way serve their present purpose and add to the grotesqueness of our rapidly increasing caravan. Vehicles of all kinds from the mule cart to the plantation barouche were made to do unwonted service behind almost as many kinds of four-footed beasts. These carts, wagons and chaises were loaded with every conceivable and inconceivable thing that the most imaginative African could think of as being either useful or ornamental on the "jubilee" road. Our caravan, living panorama, "greatest show on earth," continued to grow all night long.

At least to this Vermonter, the caravan was a show worthy of P. T. Barnum—high praise indeed—with its mismatched vehicles, various beasts, and odd assortment of goods. McFarland would have it as a show, but he also called it "a spectacle not without its lessons and one never to be forgot."[32] But what was the lesson? He does not say. McFarland's lesson seems to be that blacks will rob whites of all they can carry if given the chance.

The Eighth Vermont's tepid response to the opportunity to gain promotion by transferring into the United States Colored Troops (USCT) also suggests the depths of the unit's racism. The USCT regiments were composed of black men in the ranks, but they were assigned white officers. White enlisted men, noncommissioned officers, and officers received promotions in the course of transferring from their original regiments into the USCT. With higher rank came substantially higher salaries, the chance to command more men, and perhaps a more leisurely life with less drilling in the hot sun. Sugar plantations and New Orleans proved to be fertile recruiting grounds for black regiments, and there were only so many white units in the Department of the Gulf from which to draw the officer corps for the new regiments. The catch, as many whites would have seen it, was that you had to serve out the war in the company of black men. As one member of the Eighth Vermont explained in a letter home, his captain had turned down the rank of colonel because "he does not like niggers and will not accept it."[33]

The men in the Eighth Vermont responded to this chance for promotion with a noteworthy apathy. In all, only fourteen men transferred to the USCT, half of these from Company A.[34] Company A's captain, Hiram Perkins, probably urged men he trusted to come with him after he became a major in the USCT. But Company A also had a unique history that accounted for its willingness to transfer into black regiments. Originally slated to go into the Sixth Vermont, Company A ended up in the Democratic Eighth Vermont when its first regiment was oversubscribed. In other words, Company A was not part of Benjamin Butler's Democratic force, and as a result it more accurately reflected the generally Republican, antislavery population of the Green Mountain State.[35] In contrast to Company A's enthusiasm for promotion into the USCT, only one man joined the black regiments from Spalding's company. The exception was Pvt. Edward Mooney, who jumped at the chance to become a lieutenant. Spalding, notably, did not take promotion on these terms.

The small community known as the Eighth Vermont, then, appears to have believed in racial inequality. As Democratic politicians, readers of Democratic newspapers, and historians who constructed specific meanings about what their war in Louisiana was about, the men who surrounded Spalding on July 8, 1862, were not inclined to see Jim—or Ole Dick, or Old Joe, or Stamps—as their equals. This did not mean they would necessarily side with a nasty, whip-brandishing slaveholder out to reclaim a black man who "seemed willing to work," but it did mean that the Vermonters were probably alarmed by the changes in racial policy that surrounded them. At both the national level, and in terms of the world they saw unfolding around them in Louisiana, the conservative Green Mountain men could see signs that their army was weakening slavery.

With the Emancipation Proclamation still two months in the future when Spalding wrote of Jim, it is tempting to think he would have been at ease with the national government's racial policies. But much had already changed, even if we tend to see Lincoln's proclamation as the starting point of the war for liberation. The government's unofficial adoption of Butler's "Contraband" policy had hurt slavery by giving thousands of people experience with freedom. In August 1861, Congress had passed the First Confiscation Act, which essentially recognized the "Contraband" policy as law. By March 1862, a new federal law barred Union officers from returning slaves to owners, even loyal ones. Congress quickly followed this with laws to abolish slavery in Washington, D.C., and to make sure that it never spread into any Federal territories. When he wrote his letter, Spalding could not have known that Congress would soon enact the Second Confiscation Act, which freed slaves of rebel masters who lived in Confederate-held areas. But the handwriting was on the wall. The Republican Party was tending toward the abolition of slavery, and none of the earlier changes would have escaped Spalding's notice, since he received the Democratic *Burlington Times* at mail call.

The more immediate situation around Spalding in Louisiana offered both consolations for white supremacists and many causes for anxiety. Historian C. Peter Ripley argues that the federal policies in the state lacked emancipatory vigor. He points out that the Confiscation Acts applied only to Confederate-held regions, which left slaves inside Union lines legally enslaved. Slaves, Ripley observes, might justifiably wonder if the United States was more concerned with having a viable plantation labor force than with freedom, let alone equality. For much of the early summer, Butler also excluded fugitive slaves from his lines if the army could not employ them. In addition, Union officials enacted labor contracts that held workers to the land for periods as long as a year at a time.[36]

But black Louisianans did not seem impressed by the policies that kept them either enslaved or, if they were refugees from rebel areas, earmarked them for plantation-style labor. "The theory worked poorly in practice," Ripley writes; "blacks, to judge by their actions, apparently no longer considered themselves slaves. They understood what the war was going to do to the labor system and took full advantage of the situation."[37] The daily sight of African Americans acting like free people, with power in numbers if in no other way—no doubt alarmed Spalding and his fellow conservatives. By this point, Spalding probably doubted that any law passed in faraway Washington could ever rebuild slavery. The scene McFarland described of blacks plundering plantation houses would speak more loudly than any fine print in the First Confiscation Act.

If Spalding was upset about the course of the war being charted in Washington, at some level his own actions must have worried him. He had seized the opportunity to secure Jim as a servant, and while he had thus gained an easier life, he had also contributed his mite toward breaking the back of slavery in the Pelican State. It seems likely that Spalding, whose letter exhibits considerable intelligence, saw the contradiction between his intellectual commitment to white supremacy and the emancipatory effect of his own actions. He also would have experienced the disjunction between his belief in racial inequality and the intellect, ability, and humanity Jim presented to him every day. A great many northern soldiers who felt these tensions resolved them by changing their minds; they may not have reversed their racial ideas, David Cecere tells us, but their thinking became more complex and enlightened.[38] But that would not be Spalding's path. Instead, he resolved the intellectual conflict caused by the daily sight of Jim and thousands of other blacks asserting their abilities, cultures, and freedom by striking out against them.

A careful look at Spalding's opening vignette reveals that his humor is more about domination and intimidation than it is about literal racism. He recognized that Jim was *"painfully black,"* as racist a comment as one can find, but his humor was not based on the imagined characteristics of a supposedly inferior people. Put simply, he was different from many other Civil War veterans who deployed humor when writing about other races. His humor did not stem, as Mark Twain's sometimes did, from the alleged brutality of Hawaiians in *Roughing It* or the laziness and fraud of Arabs in *The Innocents Abroad*. Spalding chose not to include long descriptions of African Americans behaving badly. His humor was not the same as Sam Watkins's racist jabs at smelly or shiftless blacks in *Co. Aytch*.[39] While there is a slapstick element to his chasing Jim away with a flung stool, we might also add that this is not the racial humor of prewar minstrelsy. Jim may run away, but unlike the black-faced whites in minstrel shows Jim does not develop into even the shell of a character. He is not a Zip Coon or a happy slave; he neither sings nor speaks. It is hard, therefore, to interpret Spalding's anecdote as one would a minstrel act or plantation novel.[40] Rather, Jim appears only long enough to show that Spalding is still very much in control of the man he has helped to liberate. He is a target, and only a target.

Spalding's involvement in a second story concerning former slaves in Algiers helps elucidate his pattern of silencing African Americans around him, of robbing them of their newly enlarged circles of freedom and power. George Carpenter's regimental history tells a story about Spalding that occurred shortly after the unit arrived in Algiers. The chronology and setting establish that the story dates from around the time Spalding wrote his letter. Carpenter prefaces his brief story by saying that it is "illustrative of the versatile humor of Lieut. Spalding." As officer of the guard, Spalding asked Adjutant Barstow and Carpenter to make his rounds with him. His fellow officers agreed, and they and Spalding set out into the night. They did not like what they found. "At that time there were several thousand contrabands in and around the camp," Carpenter writes, "many of whom were quartered in large warehouses near the river, where they held nightly religious meetings,

and kept up the noisy fervor of their grotesque prayers and weird singing until a late hour." After midnight, Spalding and the other officers
found one of these meetings, then "at its greatest height."[41] Unwilling
to allow the proceedings to continue, Spalding interrupted them. Carpenter approves of what followed: "Striking a dramatic attitude, Lieut.
Spalding uttered in a stentorian voice, 'Were I ten thousand times a
prince, I would not trespass on the ashes of the dead.' The words of
Shakespeare abruptly broke the flow of a negro melody like a thunder-
clap, while startled worshippers on all sides cried out, 'Dar be no dead
heah, Massa!' 'If you do n't stop this noise,' pursued the lieutenant,
'there will be a great many of you dead.' It is needless to add that quiet
reigned in that warehouse for the rest of the night."[42]

George Carpenter saw this as a joke, publishing it under the running head "Fun-Loving Officers." It now seems bizarre to regard this
virulently racist act as a joke. However, it is essentially the same joke
that Spalding uses to open his letter to Peck. Stripped to their essen-
tials, both incidents involve an encounter between Spalding and newly
freed African Americans. In both cases, Spalding dislikes the blacks
around him. Likewise, he threatens them with violence. In both stories,
Spalding forces the blacks into submission, either through flight or silence. Both times, he drives them off the public stage and out of the
historical narrative. In the letter to Peck, Jim never reappears after
Spalding runs him off, and the letter contains no further reference to
blacks. Although George Carpenter does not keep blacks out of his regimental history entirely after his report of Spalding's encounter with
them, they will never be heard singing again. A prominent part of the
black communal existence is banished from the record. Or so it seems.

As historians, we might note the use of humor in both of these passages. In both cases, presenting Spalding's actions (either actual or
imagined) as laughable affairs masks the power politics behind them.
And, as in his letter to Peck, Spalding uses not only physical force—a
stool or his status as a gun-carrying officer of the day—but also his superior education to carry his point. Surely one of the reasons Carpenter
thought this was a funny story was the apparent juxtaposition between
the university-trained, Shakespeare-quoting white man and the blacks
who lacked any formal schooling at all. Shakespeare beats any "negro

melody" for these Vermonters. It looks like Spalding has all of the power.

And yet, we can poke holes in this image. Best of all, either Carpenter or Spalding did not actually know his Shakespeare. Put simply, the line attributed to Spalding ("Were I ten thousand times a prince, I would not trespass on the ashes of the dead.") is not from the Bard of Avon. In this sense, we might now say that the joke is on Spalding and Carpenter. Basing their status on their superior education, they turn out to have built on a weak foundation. But there are other reasons to doubt that the men of the Eighth Vermont had complete control over the situation in Algiers that summer.

Despite his very real power at the warehouse that night, Spalding would have seen his version of the war for the Union slipping away whenever he was waited on by Jim or heard blacks singing. The white man's country of the Democratic Party was evaporating in the hot Louisiana summer, and Spalding saw clearly the need to fight for it. We might here remember that humor is more often the weapon of the powerless than of the powerful. This is especially true of the kind of modern sarcasm and cynicism to which we have already compared Spalding's; what is a catch-22 but a statement of one's helplessness in the face of an all-powerful bureaucracy?

As Sigmund Freud tells us, jokes are usually about power. Although Freud was writing later in the nineteenth century, Spalding lived the same bourgeois life as many of Freud's patients. He had attended university, grown up in urban centers, including his postgraduate year in New York City. For Freud, jokes can be divided into two types: innocent and "tendentious." Tendentious jokes are the ones that apply to Spalding; they can concern either smut or, and this is what matters for us, a "*hostile* purpose." Modern civilization's repression of violence as an acceptable form of behavior has forced us to act against our foes through language: "by making our enemies small, inferior, despicable or comic, we achieve in a roundabout way the enjoyment of overcoming him—to which the third person, who has made no efforts, bears witness by his laughter." Spalding's case bears this out. He cannot use blatant force against Jim or the religious congregation, nor can he touch the Republican Party or President Lincoln militarily. Freud suggests that many tendentious jokes "are especially favored in order to make aggressive-ness or criticism possible against persons in exalted positions who claim to exercise authority. The joke then represents a rebellion against that authority." Most helpfully, he also points out that since people in power "are protected by . . . external circumstances from direct dispar-agement," many jokes aimed at them appear to be told about "inferior and powerless people."[43] Thus will people make fun of marriage bro-kers when the really shameful conduct and ideas belong to the people who engage their services. To make jokes about how ignorant freed-men are of Shakespeare or how easily they can be intimidated, is ulti-mately to strike back at the former slaves' patrons, the Republican Party.

So there is every reason to believe that Spalding meant to demean Jim in every way he could when he wrote to Jim Peck. And probably Peck thought it was funny that Spalding could throw a stool at his *"painfully black"* servant. Abuse was warranted, if only to keep blacks in check—to keep them from taking any liberty or liberties out of the chaos the war had created in Louisiana. The Republicans in Washing-ton were endangering slavery, and Democrats were warning one an-other that racial equality would be forced upon them. It was time to strike back, and Democrats like Spalding knew that shouting down a black congregation was the kind of action that needed to be done. Bar-stow and Carpenter knew it was the kind of action that needed to be condoned, both in person at the time and in print twenty years later.

It is important to note that we know Spalding considered himself unable to attack the leaders of his regiment. He writes to Peck: "There are many things concerning the Eighth Regiment of Vermont Volun-teers, which I would like to inform you of. But knowing that a civil tongue has saved many a young man from the gallows, I refrain from saying any thing detrimental. In the dim distance, however methinks I see a day when I shall once more stand on the soil of old Vermont, a free man, when my tongue will no longer be fettered, when I can stand up provided I am sober and a tale unfold that will grate harsh upon the ears of some. Say nothing about this. For you know a still cat catches the mice." Judging by his perceived need for self-censorship, Spalding seems to have decided humor was the safest way to express his com-plaints about the war, and even then his jokes needed to be directed at the Republicans' powerless allies.[44] George Carpenter, also unable to attack the martyred Lincoln or emancipation directly in the 1880s, took the same approach. We might, therefore, conclude that Spalding was not as powerful as he seemed to be when we started. In fact, his joke is a sign of just how weak he felt in the face of all of the changes unfolding around him. Ultimately, that Spalding found a safe outlet in humor could be good news for egalitarians; humor is often a way for the powerless to vent their frustrations without actually taking action.

So there is every reason to believe that when he wrote to Peck, Spalding meant to demonstrate his control over Jim. But his need to crack jokes at Jim's expense—his need to include Jim in his letter at all—suggests that with Republicans threatening slavery, it was not completely safe to be violently racist in Butler's Department of the Gulf in 1862. Presenting his racism as a joke enabled Spalding to exert his racial authority in a way safe from retribution. That he felt obligated to take refuge in humor tells us that blacks were not without their power. In part, this is because Jim may have been a formidable person. Given the number of refugees from slavery crossing into Union territory at the time, Spalding must have had a large number of men to draw from, and Jim somehow rose to the top of the applicant pool.

While he has left no record of his thoughts, Jim almost certainly regarded working for Spalding, with all of his youth and faults, as better than what he had escaped from in Thibodaux. We might compare Jim with John Washington, a slave who made his way into a Union camp in Virginia in 1862. Washington's life as an urban slave could have been much worse, and he had even found opportunities to earn money and assume responsibilities. But freedom was sweeter, even if the first work he found with the Union army was the same as Jim's job. As Washington writes of the night he crossed into Union lines: "A Most Memorable night that was to me[.] the Soilders assured me that I was now a free man. . . . They told me I could Soon get a Situation Waiting on Some of the officers. I had already been offered one or two." After he started working, Washington celebrated his job and his wages: "I felt for the first time in my life that I could now claim Every cent that I should Work for as My own. I began now to feel that Life had a new joy awaiting me. I Might now go and come when I please."[45] Taking Washington as a stand-in for the silenced Jim, we might well think Jim worked hard to keep his income and his foot in the door of freedom. Jim's drive and talents certainly may have caused Spalding to doubt how long his racially ordered world could last.

There is another reason why Spalding may have believed that his racial privilege was being eroded even as he sat down to answer Peck's letter. Emancipationists dotted the ranks of even a regiment as conservative as the Eighth Vermont. Spalding could not have helped but see their efforts to afford African Americans the social space and resources they needed to force open the doors of opportunity. Pvt. Justus Gale, whose Company A provided the disproportionate number of officers for the USCT, was one such voice. He subscribed to Vermont's leading antislavery paper and asked relatives to forward the *New York Tribune* to him. He wrote to his father in mid-June about the physical abuse of a twelve-year-old boy by his owner and condemned one of "our" officers for failing to punish a "slave driver" who had shot one of his workforce.[46] Writing in Algiers late in the summer of 1862, Gale relayed reports that black troops were being recruited in Louisiana. He thoroughly approved: "I wish they would arm all the slaves there is in the south and set them on & spat their hands and holler ateboy," he wrote. "They are ready to go at the rebels like a mess of blood hounds." Gale's lovely reversal of the traditional bloodhound image reflects his belief that blacks were his equals, and maybe even a bit more than that, if only in terms of their motivations for combat. Another soldier in Company A included the phrase "that the millions of oppressed should become free people" in his list of war aims. Unlike many northerners who accepted the notion that African Americans were inherently lazy, this soldier looked around and saw that they "work eighteen hours a day" on sugar plantations.[47]

A soldier in the Eighth Vermont went further by arranging to have his favorable evaluations of African Americans published in the *Brattleboro Phoenix*. His first comments about Louisiana's blacks came very soon after the regiment arrived in Algiers. Writing as "W," he pointed out that there were many blacks who had "been deserted by their owners," a telling refusal on his part to grant blacks agency. If he was slow to recognize that slaves might elect to leave their masters, he still acknowledged that they were "without exception, quiet, orderly, and much more 'sinned against than sinning.'"[48] He still thought they were "sluggish" and "easily influenced," but these negative stereotypes would fade as he grew to know more blacks. Two months later, he thought African Americans were "very industrious, need no driving whatever, are very orderly, and contribute vastly to the health and cleanliness of the Camp." By the end of August he looked forward to the day recruiters visited the contraband camps around Algiers.[49]

The unit as a whole may also have moved toward emancipation as the war progressed. The Eighth Vermont sporadically maintained a camp newspaper, the *Soldier's News-Letter*, edited by Pvt. A. W. Eastman of Company K. A surviving issue from May 1863 shows how far the editor (and presumably his subscription base) had come since their enlistment in 1861. One editorial announced that the question of what to do with escaped slaves "is losing its knottiness, as the nation loses its naughtiness and as it is more clearly seen what they can do and are doing for us." In a rhetorical question, the editor asks whether the country should "neglect" these people "rather than treat them as we should other unfortunate fellow citizens in the same circumstances." It is hard to understand now just how radical a phrase Eastman used when he described the former slaves as "fellow citizens" in this passage, but the editor had taken a very advanced position. Perhaps even more dramatically, Eastman then endorses the idea of a "Home Colonization Society," through which whites could assist blacks "in establishing schools, churches, press &c." The Society should also give former slaves land for a colony in the United States to enable a "full and fair trial of the Free labor system, on a plan which recognizes the Manhood of the black, and his right to the proceeds of his own labor, in his native land, and also to more than an 'equal right with a rebel' to enjoy under the protection of the American flag the rights of an American citizen." The same issue praised two regiments of black troops serving in the same part of Louisiana as the Eighth Vermont's editor.[50]

The most dedicated abolitionist in the Eighth Vermont, however, was Pvt. Rufus Kinsley. While Spalding and Carpenter tried to silence a black congregation in 1862 and again in 1886 when their history was written, Kinsley took the opposite approach. He records black church services in his diary, and when historian David C. Rankin shepherded the diary into publication in 2004, Kinsley's entries moved the black congregants back onto the public stage. They are silenced no more. Regarding other racial matters, Kingsley's diary leaves readers with no doubt about the violence, moral indifference, and emotional cruelties of slavery in Louisiana. He spent time in the contraband camps with escaped slaves and heard stories that made their way into his diary. One day he heard of a married man who had purchased a woman by whom he fathered three girls. Years later he had sex with these young women, his daughters, and proceeded to sell two of his grandchildren. Just one day after writing this letter, Kinsley told of caring for an escaped slave so beaten that "there is little hope that he will live."[51]

Seen from Jim's perspective, Kinsley's actions would have spoken louder than his diary entries. Late in June, a few weeks before Spalding wrote his letter, Kinsley cryptically noted in his diary that he "hid a negro from his master." By September 1862, Colonel Thomas delegated him and two other men (including Kinsley's brother William) to administer the contraband camp near the regiment. Kinsley took charge of drawing rations for the four thousand to six thousand people in the camp, and oversaw the cooking and distribution of food "to each family."[52] He did more than meet the minimum job requirements. On September 21, he won assurances from Colonel Thomas that a school would be added in the camp. The same day he records his first attendance at a black church. Unlike Spalding, he came to appreciate both the sermons and the congregants. He wrote no editorial comment about the first service he attended, but the next week he was enthusiastic. "At church again with the Contrabands," he wrote. "Most of them know more Scripture than half the Yankees, notwithstanding they can not read a word. But, they *never forget any thing*." By the next summer, he was wholly won over, calling the "singing beyond all description: inciting first to tears, then to shouts: original, and full of power, whether of pathos, of warning, or of exultation."[53] It is not too much of a reach to speculate that Spalding would have seen Kinsley's efforts and noticed African Americans' progress toward establishing their own communities along the Mississippi. This must have challenged Spalding's belief in racial hierarchies and his sense of what the war and his military service meant. How would Jim have seen Kinsley's actions? The first child born in the contraband camp was named "Freedom Kinsley."[54]

Lieutenant Spalding's joke to his friend mattered little in the course of the war, but it still bears study as an expression of racial conservativism in a time of upheaval. Spalding's literary abuse of Jim shows one way that northerners could resist the social changes of the war years. It reminds us of the conservative North, and just how vibrant its racist culture could be. Historians have chronicled the power of northern racism during the Civil War era, including often successful campaigns to stop black suffrage drives, limit black legal rights, and segregate public spaces. There is too much evidence of racial conservativism to be ignored.

But historians can also make too much of their power. Even in a conservative regiment such as the Eighth Vermont Volunteers, different constituencies had the opportunity to act on behalf of their vision of the future. Even in the Eighth, whites rallied to help "contrabands." The North, for all of its faults, was far more egalitarian than the Confederacy, which lacked not only men like Rufus Kinsley but even people like Justus Gale. Nor was Jim powerless when he became part of the regimental world. That Spalding felt obligated to toss a literary stool at him shows that the young Vermont officer felt the need to put him (back) into his place. He had to show himself and Peck that Jim's presence did not mean Spalding had changed his mind on abolition. Humor allowed him to prove to his friend that Jim enjoyed no power in his new status, all without incurring the wrath of antislavery officers and politicians.

But it was still only that: a joke. A comment made between two whites who already knew their political positions. We should remember that jokes are one of the primary recourses of the powerless, of the soldier caught in a war he believes is slipping away from the ideals for which he originally enlisted. Things were changing all around Spalding, and he tried to stop them as best he could. But he would lose this fight for all the rest of his short life, and he would have to make his peace with his government's decisions and even his own emancipatory acts: hiring of a fugitive slave and making war against the Confederacy. Perhaps humor was the only way to face the fact that the Eighth Vermont—and even Spalding himself—now acted as agents of change.

4

MASCULINITY
Spalding's Fourth of July

> If you go to Burlington please tell the young ladies of my acquaintance to hop up and bite without salt.
>
> —Stephen Spalding

When Stephen Spalding sat back and told his tale about how he had spent the Fourth of July 1862, he rattled off close to two big pages of text. The story dominates the letter, filling up the reader's imagination with action and characters, none the least of whom is Spalding himself. According to Spalding, by the time the sun came up on July 5, he had gone AWOL, spent an astonishing fifty-seven dollars, drunk just about every kind of booze imaginable, and attempted to dance. His inebriated dancing resulted in torn dresses and physical harm to his neighbors on the dance floor. He had gotten into a brawl, helping to throw two British naval officers out of a party and into the middle of the street. He had found his way into at least one brothel. Finally, he managed to stagger back to camp. In all of this, he had been joined by another young Union lieutenant, Daniel Foster. Despite the city's reputation as a hotbed of Confederate sympathies, Spalding and Foster never seemed to be in any danger. In fact, Spalding never seemed in any doubt about his place, either culturally or personally. He seemed at home in New Orleans, even though he was a long way from his native Vermont.

Spalding clearly wanted James Peck to know that he had had a good time on the Fourth, and he told his tale with verve and humor. But there is no reason to think he exaggerated very much. For historians, the letter serves as a reminder that Union soldiers and officers interacted with southern civilians in a variety of ways. As we will see, both

Spalding and his men visited New Orleans for what modern American soldiers would refer to as R & R. Cities serve as commercial centers, and the Vermonters came to rely on the Crescent City for food, drink, and amusements of many kinds. By July, Spalding and his men could easily find their way to the pleasures of the city, having spent May patrolling its streets. Fighting crime more than the rebel army, they had learned about the city's least reputable neighborhoods. That experience may well have helped Spalding carouse as successfully as he did when it came time to celebrate his nation's birthday in July.

But familiarity with the city's streets, bars, and brothels would have helped Spalding navigate New Orleans only so well. What mattered more was Spalding's deeper understanding of shared urban cultures, particularly in regard to how gender worked. Spalding felt at home in New Orleans because he could enact the same masculine roles that he had performed as an undergraduate in Burlington, Vermont, and as a young law student in New York City in 1860 and 1861. No one could ever argue that New Orleans perfectly resembled any northern city, but its large immigrant populations, the predominance of wage labor, and the mixture of wealth and poverty must have struck many northern soldiers as familiar.[1] New Orleans, in other words, provided Spalding and other Union soldiers with commercialized rest and relaxation, particularly leisure moments that allowed them to continue to occupy gender roles with which they had grown familiar while living in the North. The urban South offered a northern soldier like Stephen Spalding the relief and natural ease that comes to a person living amid an alien landscape and people when he finally discovers himself on familiar cultural ground. Southern cities offered many Union soldiers familiar commercial experiences and gender ideologies.[2] For Stephen Spalding and many northern soldiers, New Orleans and other southern cities could be home away from home.

The soldiers' familiarity with urban southern gender ideologies may have been especially true for northern men affiliated with the conservative Democratic Party, as was the case with Spalding's regiment. Of course, Democratic leanings were not universal even in the Eighth, and this led to cultural divisions in the Union army. Historian Lorien Foote has found that Union army split on how to define masculinity, with the largest questions arising from whether or not alcohol, sex, and profanity had any place in the life of a soldier. As a rule, Republican men tried to shun drinking, illicit sex, and swearing, while other men engaged in those practices.[3] This division over masculinity was muted in the Eighth Vermont, since the officers and men generally veered in conservative, Democratic directions. Like other Democrats, the men in the Eighth Vermont embraced conservative positions on masculinity, including their love of alcohol and their willingness to enjoy masculine privileges regarding sex.[4] Unlike Republicans, Democratic men seized what physical pleasures they could without expressing guilt or ambivalence. Coming from an urban culture that fostered alcohol consumption and commercialized sex, Spalding and other northern Democrats found in New Orleans many places that catered to their interests. Spalding and many of his fellow soldiers knew how to act in New Orleans without even thinking about it.

Lieutenant Spalding had his own way of articulating the cultural comfort that came with familiar masculine pleasures: "New Orleans is a great place for fun."[5] Even though the city now has a pro-Confederate reputation that celebrates some white women's opposition to the Union military, the city's voters in 1860 had given more votes to both of the Unionist presidential candidates, John Bell and Stephen Douglas, than to the radical John Breckinridge. When secession came on the ballot in January, secession won the city by only two percentage points.[6] The people's willingness to cooperate with the Union government after May 1862 merely continued that moderate trend. Most of the city's people, even in its white population, grew accustomed to the Union army by early July at the latest, and many had welcomed it earlier than that. By the time Spalding visited on July Fourth, the Union blockade had been lifted, the United States had restored a stable currency, and it had fed and employed many residents.

By June at the latest, northern soldiers safely explored the city. Spalding and Lieutenant Foster were not the only members of the Eighth Vermont to get into New Orleans on the Fourth. William Smith and Jonathan Allen crossed through New Orleans on their way to the shore of Lake Pontchartrain but complained that "there was no celebration, here and I think it was the dullest Fourth I ever spent." Spalding and Foster may have been the only ones to enjoy themselves the whole day. Justus Gale left the only other account of Independence Day in the

Eighth Vermont, and he spent it in a railroad car in Algiers, suffering from "dierea," writing letters, and watching it rain "very pleasantly." He told his brother that he knew this made for a dull letter, but life had its compensations: "I guess I had the best musketoe bar last night."[7] While Gale had a slow day, Union troops were often seen in the city's stores, theaters, and bars.[8] New Orleans spent most of the war welcoming soldiers in blue.

Spalding probably had more fun than his fellow Vermonters on the Fourth because he could afford to find his pleasures in the city. As officers, he and Foster had more money at their command. The fifty-seven dollars Spalding spent equaled about four months' pay for a private, but only about two weeks' pay for a lieutenant. This was one of the privileges that Spalding enjoyed, but only one of them. His family's status, his rank, his paycheck, his new servant, and his race placed him near the top of the social hierarchy. But his trip into New Orleans illustrates a further aspect of his social privilege; he was a man in a culture that granted men many liberties. Masculinity counted for a lot in the United States during Spalding's life.[9] That was never more apparent than when Spalding and Foster hopped the ferry in Algiers and landed in the Crescent City.

The men in the Eighth Vermont revered the public drinking of alcohol as one of the emblems of manhood. Spalding and Foster, both about twenty-two or twenty-three years old, relished their alcoholic freedom, but they were not alone.[10] Their regimental culture was awash in hard liquor. The regiment's fondness for drink emerged even before they had left Vermont. While still in training camp, Col. Stephen Thomas marched a company of men (who presumably joined him reluctantly) into nearby Brattleboro to demand that merchants stop selling liquor to his soldiers.[11] Throughout their time in Louisiana, the soldiers (like Spalding and Foster) found many opportunities to skirt Thomas's policing. Many Civil War soldiers took to drink, and one recent study has found men assigned to the "loneliness and boredom" of garrison duty to be especially susceptible to temptation.[12] Such was the case with the Vermonters stuck in Algiers. The Eighth Vermont's embrace of alcohol as a potent sign of their masculinity can be seen in the reaction of Pvt. Justus Gale to seeing New Orleans women drinking liquor. "Liquor is just as common here as water is in Vt," he wrote; "you

can hardly go by a door in this City without seeing the glass and bottle
siting on the bar. there is about as many women here that get drunk as
there is men in the north that get drunk."[13] Gale's disapproval of inebriated women reminds modern readers of the extent to which public
drinking remained a male preserve in the 1860s. Conservative men
drank proudly, and jealously guarded their right to do so. The signifi-
cance of alcohol emerges when they reminisced and joked about the
war after it ended.

Which is not to say that Republican troops avoided alcohol like perfect teetotalers. Future doctor and Company A private Charles Cooper
happily took up considerable space in his short memoir with a comic
story about alcohol abuse. Cooper's story starts with Sgt. Oscar Good-
ridge of his company. Detached with two anonymous privates, Good-
ridge returns to the main force in an unsteady state. Cooper jokingly
describes the three men as "very happy," though he judiciously (and
sarcastically) denies that they had been drinking too much: "not that
they were all drunk by any means for they were a very temperate Regt.
but a few barrells of La. rum had been discovered, the heads knocked
in and water pails had been filled."[14] The same night, others in Company A, probably after sampling the "barrells" of liberated rum,
"thought they must do a little foraging." Soon "every man" in the company was feasting on "chickens, geese, pigs & sheep" and enjoying "a
general hilarious time."[15] If anyone suffered court-martial or lost standing with his comrades because of this drunken feast, Cooper neglects
to mention it. Instead, by story's end public inebriation results in a
good time and bonds together "every man" in Cooper's company. Cooper features the masculine bonding provided by rum even in
Republican-leaning Company A. Masculine attachment to drink provided (at least in retrospect) a source of bipartisan consensus.

In 1896, Moses McFarland, a former captain in the Eighth, wrote
Some Experiences of the Eighth Vermont West of the Mississippi. His
memoirs take up fewer than twenty pages but include four drinking
stories, two of which go on at length. His tales of rural binges sound
like college memories, fondly remembered for their camaraderie and
humor. McFarland's first drinking tale follows him and a scouting
party as they enjoy "a friendly introduction" to a newly discovered barrel of whiskey. Shortly after drinking his fill, McFarland mounts a trou-

blesome mule (is there another kind?) that he has confiscated. Warned by some blacks about the mule's idiosyncrasies, McFarland jokes that he was "not far enough from the whiskey barrel to be easily frightened by rebels or kicking mules." Predictably, he soon lands "flat on my back in the road."[16] Another of McFarland's scouting parties ends with the captain paying for an open bar at a saloon for his twenty exhausted men. The barkeeper comes to regret charging McFarland only three dollars for his twenty soldiers, whom he claims drank an astonishing eight gallons of whiskey. McFarland advises him, jokingly, that before he agrees to host thirsty soldiers again, "he would do well to inquire if the men belonged to the Eighth Vermont."[17] Comic encounters with drunk pickets and looters also appear, rounding out a picture of men at liberty and feeling their oats (and other distilled grains).

Drinking takes on an overtly gendered aspect when McFarland tells more serious tales of hard liquor. If the funny stories of the Eighth Vermont sound like fraternity escapades remembered fondly in old age (with hangovers and stomach upset forgotten), the introduction of women into the stories means that events take on the serious tone of the parlor. McFarland tells two stories in which he receives liquor from planters' wives, and the rules of polite society dictate both of the proceedings. In one instance, he enjoys the hospitality of a Confederate officer's wife, though he adds approvingly that she "was not a fanatic." He tells her, seriously, that he is sick and has been advised to drink brandy but cannot find any. She gives him an entire bottle and refuses all of his efforts to pay her. He respects her for her hospitality, but he really admires her for her femininity. She occupies her circumscribed female role as host, does credit to her husband, and stays clear of politics. To make her femininity the focus of the story, he concludes by contrasting "such women and the women of New Orleans," who had disgraced their sex by spitting on Union soldiers and called down upon themselves Butler's Woman Order, "denouncing them as women of the town plying their vocation."[18] He praises her loyalty to her Confederate husband, which is presented as personal and right. Her loyalty is familial, not a political loyalty to the Confederacy. McFarland recognizes and values her obedience to traditional gender roles.

In a second story, women, whiskey, and good manners bridge the divide separating Confederates from Moses McFarland and his men.

Nina Silber has found that many northern men longed for an emotive reattachment of the North and South in the 1890s, when McFarland wrote his memoir. They imagined decorous southern ladies as the agents through which the reunion could occur.[19] McFarland tells just such a story when he recounts how he and his men approached the plantation of Captain Ranseau, who commanded a nearby Confederate cavalry company. With the handful of Confederates fleeing before his troops, McFarland finds himself negotiating with Mrs. Ranseau, the only white resident left on the plantation. All goes well, the wheels of society greased by whiskey and etiquette, at least as McFarland chose to remember the scene. He remembers having "suggested" that his "men would appreciate a little good whiskey." When Mrs. Ranseau "very promptly and courteously set out what proved to be a very excellent article," McFarland's "men paid their hearty respects" to both her and the alcohol.[20] The Union troops then searched the Ranseau house, but they allowed Mrs. Ranseau to "show us over the house,"[21] a gesture that eliminated the threat of unlicensed plunder. So far this is pretty normal, but McFarland's adventure takes an odd turn, enabled by the woman's properly gendered hospitality and the plying of alcohol.

Getting ready to leave, McFarland, in the role of gracious guest, "requested [Mrs. Ranseau] to give my compliments to Captain Ranseau on his return and say to him that on such a day I desired to meet him at Boote [Boutte] Station, and that on the honor of a gentleman no advantage should be taken of him." Everything here is as it should be in a society united by manners, not divided by war: Mrs. Ranseau hosts McFarland and extends her generosity to his men. They get a tour of the house from her. McFarland states that he hopes to meet her husband and pledges his "honor" as a "gentleman" to treat him well if they do. Better still, Captain Ranseau accepts McFarland's invitation, and the two men later meet to have "a friendly chat."[22] A fly gets in the ointment during the chat when Ranseau asks McFarland to retrieve two of his "valuable negroes" and McFarland refuses, but the fact that slavery was the only cause of disagreement between McFarland and the Ranseau household merely accentuates that all should be right between them in the 1890s with slavery ended (and white supremacist rule restored in Louisiana). With slavery off the table, women should be able to go back to serving alcohol to men, who will then get along splendidly.

Seen in the context of McFarland's joyous binges, Spalding's drunken carouse through the city on Independence Day should not come as a surprise. Neither should the flurry of jokes about alcohol that dot Spalding's letter, including references to drinking so much upon his future return to Vermont that he would not be able to stand up, even to denounce his officers, and the fact that he drank "700 to 800 times a day to keep my spirits up." But even so, Spalding's alcoholic consumption daunts the reader, and one imagines, or perhaps hopes, that he has exaggerated for comic effect when he states that he and Foster "drank gin, whiskey, brandy, rum, beer, gin coctails modesty prevents me from putting in the K., Eleven other different kinds of coctails, Cobblers of all kinds, julips d[itt]o, smashes d[itt]o."[23] Spalding shows no remorse about indulging in all of this, even when his resulting lack of coordination leads to mishaps on the dance floor. Presented as comedy, the havoc caused by his drunken dizziness damages neighboring shins, noses, toes, and dresses. All comes right, he tells Peck, with the help of his just-visible pistol and the need to keep the business of the party moving along. For Spalding, as for other men, drinking nearly topped the list of what made being a man such a happy and privileged status in these years.[24]

But men held another social right. Spalding hinted at a second prerogative held by men when he jokingly inserted "modesty prevents me from putting in the K" after he had written "coctail" (instead of "cocktail"). Readers might be tempted to read this as a throwaway joke at which Peck could snort before moving on to the rest of his friend's staggering bar tab. But there is more to Spalding's "coctail" joke than meets the eye. It serves to flag an alert reader's attention that Spalding did more than drink at "the hospitable retreat of Miss Bianca Robbins." By claiming that "modesty" prevents him from writing out the word "cock," Spalding lets Peck know that the same modesty will inhibit him from going into even more provocative sexual details. Spalding continues, including more telltale jokes along the same lines as his "cock" joke. Peck would not have had to stretch too far to figure out what we know from the historical record; Miss Bianca Robbins ran a prosperous brothel. Her death in a steamship accident in 1866 earned her a brief notoriety, and lists of people killed in the accident sometimes identified her by her profession. The *Monroe (LA) Ouachita Telegraph* described her as "a woman who kept a fashionable Bagnio in New Orleans." She left an estate of 100,000 dollars.[25] Her death triggered an unseemly court case over control of her estate and the valuable jewels that went with it.[26]

Knowing that Bianca Robbins kept a brothel suddenly makes Spalding's fifty-seven-dollar expense account for the day more understandable. It also clarifies his jokes. Robbins may have been "a lady of northern parentage," but one now doubts whether Spalding's description of her as "friendly to the Union" concerned the North and the South as much as it did men and women. Spalding's line about his "close investigation into the theory of Spiritual rappings" prior to his departure for a party at Miss Burdell's now also requires a reinterpretation. Spiritualism, or spirit rapping, flourished in the mid-nineteenth century, and many people accepted the idea that the dead could communicate with the living through mediums and by producing noises in answer to stated questions. Spalding and Peck, however, probably had nothing to do with the people who believed this claim. Spiritualists shared a social and political circle with a host of other liberal reformers, including abolitionists, feminists, temperance advocates, vegetarians, and pacifists, all of whom Democrats held in contempt.[27] Spalding's line about closely investigating spirit rapping meant to mock the Spiritualists, but more than that it served as a euphemism for sex. In this case, the knocking on the furniture that spiritualists would have heard as messages from the dead was actually coming from a prostitute and her client loudly fornicating. Spalding, in other words, told Peck he had left the "k" out of "cocktail" to let him know that modesty forced him to put the true account of his afternoon's affairs into a thinly veiled, humorous code that Peck could easily decipher.

After leaving Miss Robbins's brothel, Spalding went to Miss Burdell's for a "grand masquerade ball." Burdell cannot be firmly identified as a brothel-keeper from historical records, but the evidence points in that direction. Spalding's description of her event sounds like the masquerade balls staged by brothels with increasing frequency as the century progressed.[28] The costumes, alcohol, food, and dancing suggest that her event took place in a brothel, but the ten-dollar cover charge guarantees that this was no ordinary private party. The presence of so many military officers of different nationalities (American, British, and French officers are mentioned) means that Miss Burdell invited men who were in the city temporarily, not her personal friends. That Spalding had "during the day" (perhaps at Miss Robbins's business?) "received a kind invitation to attend" that evening's festivities indicates that men were invited on short notice. One might even speculate that Miss "Burdell" was close enough to being Miss "Bordello" to have been a code or joke between Spalding and Peck. If Miss Burdell did manage a brothel, then we can see how readily Spalding navigated the city's commercialized sex industry.

New Orleans has long held a reputation for relaxed moral codes of conduct, and the city earned this distinction in the middle decades of the nineteenth century. Both before and after the war, the city did little to police prostitution. Historian Judith Kelleher Schafer has concluded that "evidence abounds in the New Orleans newspapers and court records that prostitution in the city flourished virtually unchecked throughout the antebellum period."[29] The sex trade, in full swing as the war started, received no checks on its growth from the Butler administration once Union troops arrived. Despite the fact that the Union administration of the city receives high marks in terms for its fair enforcement of laws in 1862, prostitution nevertheless continued unabated. One historian, who has found little evidence that the Union army actively curtailed the sex trade anywhere during the war, notes that Benjamin Butler did "little to control the brothels" in New Orleans.[30] Historian Catherine Clinton has found a steady increase in prostitution during the war, citing evidence from Nashville, Richmond, and other places to make the case for a "boom in prostitution from 1861 to 1865."[31] So Spalding would have had abundant opportunities to go into a brothel if he so desired. But would he have wanted to? Was brothel-going likely to have been part of his past in Burlington and New York City?

Several factors point toward the likelihood that Spalding would have been familiar, and comfortable, with brothel culture by 1862. Spalding's youth, his relative wealth, and his likely identification with the Democratic Party pointed him to the brothel life. Starting in the

1830s and 1840s, Democratic politicians in New York City allowed prostitution to flourish. The party's newspapers, especially William Gordon Bennett's *New York Herald,* covered the sex trade with more fascination than disapproval. Starting with their exploitative and profitable coverage of the murder of a well-known prostitute, Helen Jewett, in 1836, the *Herald* and other "penny papers" ran up large circulations with sensationalist coverage of brothels and crime. The murder in 1841 of Mary Rogers, a woman famous for her involvement in sexualized advertising and illicit sexual relationships, only fueled an already raging fire.[32]

New Yorkers coined the term "sporting culture" to capture the young men's fascination with sports and sex that was so evident on many city's streets. Young men in sporting culture favored outward expressions of masculinity, especially sports ranging from horse racing to boxing. But they did more than try one another's athletic prowess. Historian Amy Srebnick finds them involved in both politics and prostitution. Politically, she sees the young men as a merger of "older working-men's politics with the newer club house politics of Tammany Hall," which puts them firmly in the Democratic Party camp by the 1840s. She also locates "their advocacy of prostitution and brothel culture" as an important part of the construction of American masculinity.[33] Brothel culture involved paying for sex but also included participation in a world of men who attended brothels together, drank there, discussed individual prostitutes, and generally used brothels as social gathering places. Visiting a brothel need not embarrass a man in this culture; rather, the trip gained a young man admission into a group of like-minded men. Brothel-going could be a social as well as a sexual enterprise, as much something to be proud of as hidden—as long as the audience was other young men.

The surest proof that sporting life could be boasted of comes from the pages of the city's so-called "flash press." With titles like *The Libertine, The Whip,* and the *Weekly Rake,* these illustrated newspapers covered the brothel scene, using only the thinnest veneer of moral disapprobation in their attempts to skirt the city's censorship laws. Circulations soared, giving publishers ample reason to try to squeeze out issues despite legal difficulties.[34] Similar papers sprang up in Philadelphia, Baltimore, and Boston, while copies of the New York City papers found their way into the rural North via the mail.[35] In other words, people in New York and other northern cities during the mid-nineteenth century lived in a culture where sex could be discussed, and bought, relatively openly; we should not imagine a strict Victorian taboo on sexual topics during the antebellum decades.

The men of the sporting culture did not occupy the field alone, however. They were part of what Helen Lefkowitz Horowitz calls a "lively, multivalent conversation about sex in their time."[36] Moral reformers, both men and women, did what they could to curb prostitution, to help women leave the trade, and to embarrass men who visited brothels. The largest antiprostitution group, the Female Moral Reform Society, started in New York City in 1836 and quickly spread to cities and towns throughout the North. The Female Moral Reform Society's newspaper published the names of brothel clients in the hope of embarrassing men into cutting off their trade, but at least with the single men in sporting culture that may not have been much of a deterrent.[37] By the 1850s, political parties in the North took sides on sexual issues, with Democrats supporting male sexual privileges and Republicans calling for greater self-restraint and a crackdown on illicit sex. All of this debate meant that when Spalding set foot in Gotham in 1860, he knew about prostitution and its ready availability. Visiting brothels would reinforce his identity as a conservative on matters of male sexual privilege. All he would lose by brothel-going was his money (and maybe his health).

We see sporting men's literally shameless attitude in Spalding's letter, which lets Peck know exactly what he had done on Independence Day. He did not have to reveal that information at all, obviously, and the fact that he did tells us about the freedom with which he and Peck could brag about their exploits with, and exploitation of, prostitutes. It is perhaps useful to remember that Peck labeled his letter "Liber XXI," or Book 21, implying strongly that he had already written Spalding twenty other letters.[38] If this correspondence had started only when the Eighth Vermont entered service in the very late fall of 1861, then Peck had been averaging at least one letter every two weeks. These two men seem to have known one another very well, even well enough to joke about sexual matters.

Spalding and Peck may have, in fact, visited brothels together during their Burlington years, though this is undoubtedly only a guess. The main hint in this direction comes from the close of Spalding's letter, when he urges Peck to remember him to a host of other men that they both must have known. In the midst of this male world, Spalding writes, "If you go to Burlington please tell the young ladies of my acquaintance to hop up and bite without salt." The meaning of Spalding's phrase, "hop up and bite without salt," has unfortunately been lost over time. Two slang dictionaries published at the time do not include the phrase in any form.[39] The tone, however, does not appear genteel. Ladies of the period did not, as a rule, hop up and bite anything, even less so without the encouragement of salt. If, then, Spalding and Peck knew women to whom they could give orders, as Spalding's sentence does, then what kinds of young ladies were they?

While admittedly conjectural, speculation that Peck and Spalding shared a common history with prostitution would explain Spalding's willingness to discuss the subject. It would also justify his apparent assurance that Peck would both get the jokes and see the adventure in the same positive light in which Spalding saw it. A shared knowledge of brothel culture would also make the jokes funnier; philosopher Ted Cohen tells us that the "deep satisfaction in successful joke transactions is the sense held mutually by teller and hearer that they are joined in feeling."[40] In other words, Peck would bring his knowledge and assumptions to Spalding's joke. He would be able to envision the masquerade ball, hear the not-so-spiritual rapping, and make the same assumptions about women who worked as prostitutes as his friend in Louisiana. If true, the common bond of brothel-going between the two men would have cemented their friendship and served as a basis for their shared sense of themselves as men.

Stephen Spalding, in other words, wanted to share his brothel experience with his former roommate, now absent. His outing, arguably, improved with the sharing, creating a bond between the two men of far greater permanence than that between Spalding and Bianca Robbins's employee. Nor was Spalding alone in writing such letters, even among the ranks of the Eighth Vermont. Pvt. William T. Church also wrote a comic letter to a friend, Ed, about his sexual exploitation of women in Louisiana. Only one letter of what must have been an exchange of at least three letters between William and Ed survives. In the first two, both now missing, William Church must have told Ed about the woman he had hired to do his laundry and how much he paid her. Ed, replying, seems to have asked him what services, exactly, he received for that pay, implying perhaps that the laundress also worked as a prostitute. Church's reply, which is extant, comically pretends to be shocked at the implications of Ed's letter. He then launches into a lengthy rant, ridiculing Female Moral Reform Societies for their antiprostitution efforts. Throughout his sarcastic digression he mocks those who oppose the sexual exploitation of female employees: "Now Ed I have one very serious charge against you and that is being to inquisitive. when I consider the import of that question you proposed to me my mind becomes seriously affected: *What* inquire of me if my wash womman did anything more than to wash and mend for me: What why it beats all I ever heard in my mortal career. Now you know that I have allways ben a contributer to the Ladies Moral Reform Society in Boston & New York and various other virtuous Societys. why Ed I have in my posession a large Silver *Medal* given to me by [small tear in the paper] [a com?]mitee of the different societies and inscribed on it a token of disrespect for protecting those that their steps lead to *Hell*. if you wish for any more proofs of my virtuous abilities I refer you to Ben Graves, Hiram Coloney Now I hope that will be all that is nessary to convince you."[41] Perhaps the most important word in Church's letter is "disrespect." He has been given a medal as "a token of disrespect for protecting those that their steps lead to *Hell*." Of course, the Female Moral Reform Societies committee would have honored his "respect" for prostitutes, not his disrespect of them. But for Church, as for Spalding, disrespecting prostitutes was all just part of the joke.

Another member of Spalding's regiment joked about male sexual privileges, daring to do so with his own wife. In October 1862, Deming Fairbanks wrote to Mary Spencer Fairbanks, his wife, about all of the "pretty darned nice looking gals" in Gretna, a town close to New Orleans. Would Mary have seen the humor of his next thought, which was to tell her that these local beauties were "all after me as fast as blood hounds"? Perhaps it was a private joke, and she saw it as part and parcel of a friendly letter in which he also expressed his desire to send her "great nice oranges."[42] Or perhaps Deming Fairbanks let his wife know that the sexual license afforded to, and enjoyed by, the other men in the

Eighth Vermont could carry over to him as well. Whether or not his wife was in on the joke, the letter suggests that men could joke about illicit sex whether they were married or not. Living when and where they did, the Vermonters knew that their rights as men included sexual freedom as well as the right to hard liquor.

What of the women involved? Then, as now, the degree to which an individual prostitute is victimized by masculine privilege varies. Historical studies of prostitution demonstrate a wide variety of backgrounds and experiences among women in the trade. Studies of antebellum New York City's commercialized sex industry emphasize the diversity of sex workers; women could work temporarily or make careers of it. They could be streetwalkers or work in brothels. Some—really only a rare few—became famous and could chose for whom they would work. But historian Timothy Gilfoyle and others suggest that for most women, prostitution was neither lucrative nor truly voluntary. The work was usually taken only as a last resort to destitution. As Gilfoyle concludes, "the major factor inducing young women to sell their bodies was the low wages for [other] female labor." Women faced with low pay and bouts of joblessness had few options when confronted with homelessness and starvation. Gilfoyle adds that "when work was slow or money slack, milliners, servants, and peddlers alike resorted to prostitution." Girls in their teens often worked in the industry.[43] Historian Christine Stansell sees the same dynamic frequently causing women to undertake sex work on a short-term basis. Drawing on William Sanger's survey of New York prostitutes done on the eve of the Civil War, Stansell finds that many women who sold their bodies lacked a male income in their household at a time when "women on their own earned such low wages that in order to survive, they often supplemented waged employment with casual prostitution." While she also finds other causes for turning to prostitution, Stansell's picture of prostitution is only marginally more empowering than Gilfoyle's.[44] Sexualized commerce, in other words, included a range of women, motivations, and situations. But most interpretations of antebellum and Civil War prostitution start with the exclusion of women from highly paid careers and the sweatshop wages paid for most women's work. For Stephen Spalding in New York and New Orleans, many of the women he would have found in brothels had very few options but to sleep with him.

Not all men lived and thought as Stephen Spalding, Daniel Foster, and William Church did. The most outspoken abolitionist in the Eighth Vermont, Rufus Kinsley, also serves as the regiment's unofficial spokesman for the evangelical, sentimental vision of women. Though he was vastly outnumbered in the Eighth by those who lived by traditional rules of masculinity, Kinsley would have found more company in most other northern units. Recuperating from a long illness, Kinsley wrote to a friend that when he was sick "I lay and thought of my mother, and my Aunt Elvira, and a number of other mothers in Fletcher, and of some who are not mothers yet, but who hope to be by and by; and how ardently I wished I might fall into their hands, during sickness, at least, if not longer." Perhaps wondering if he had implied too much sexual desire, Kinsley added, "There is no care like mother-care; no love like mother-love, eh Charley?"[45] One suspects that many of his fellow soldiers in the Democratic Eighth Vermont would have sought other kinds of love first.

Which brings us back to the fact that Stephen Spalding, like most white men in this period, experienced power and privileges that few women ever had the thrill of feeling. Some Republican-leaning men might refuse to abuse those powers, but Spalding and his fellow conservatives drank their way through Louisiana, perhaps enjoying that right even more frequently than they had in their hometowns. Spalding never seems to have doubted his right to enter a brothel and pay for sex. Finding a brothel and navigating its rules and culture seemed easy for him, at least as he describes it, despite his being far from home. He gives no evidence of having considered how the women involved in the transaction may have felt. His social power was to be exercised and, perhaps equally importantly, bragged about later in the interest of building a gender-based friendship with Jim Peck. Being a man involved not just honor or restraint, as some gender historians have hypothesized. Masculinity revolved around the practice of gaining sexual access to as many desirable women as one could pay for or cajole. The sex act itself, and the later sharing of one's conquests and adventures, proved a significant part of masculinity among the conservative Vermonters. New Orleans had provided the Eighth Vermont with alcohol, and Stephen Spalding and others with commercial sex. As such, it needs to be reconsidered as a place of recreation, in which people welcomed U.S. money and opportunities for exchange. That exchange happened seamlessly and quickly, and speaks to a culture of masculinity shared by men in both northern and southern cities. For Spalding, taking advantage of his power over women was as natural—and perhaps even less in question—than enjoying his racial privileges relative to Jim.

Stephen Foster Spalding. Courtesy of the
Vermont Historical Society.

James S. Peck, who received Spalding's letter.
Courtesy of the Vermont Historical Society.

Lt. Stephen F. Spalding, from George N. Carpenter, *History of the Eighth Regiment Vermont Volunteers*. Courtesy of the Vermont Historical Society.

Men of the 7th New York State Militia at Camp Cameron in 1861. The man holding the tent pole strongly resembles Spalding's image in the photograph held by the Vermont Historical Society. Library of Congress.

Spalding could have trained on these artillery pieces, shown here at the
7th New York State Militia's Camp Cameron. Library of Congress.

"Camp of the seventh reg. N. Y. near Washington on 14th St." Spalding lived in a
neat and well-equipped camp throughout his first military service.
Library of Congress.

Part of the 7th New York State Militia's Camp Cameron. Note this tent's ample furniture and equipment. Library of Congress.

The painter Sanford Gifford at Camp Cameron, with other soldiers and an African American man, seated. Spalding would have seen many examples of white and black relationships before employing Jim in Louisiana. Library of Congress.

"Algiers from Bywater," by photographer Jay Dearborn Edwards, between 1858 and 1861. Spalding wrote his letter while living in this densely populated town across the river from New Orleans. Courtesy of the Historic New Orleans Collection, acc. no. 1982. 32. 16.

"Canal Street and Algiers Ferry Building" by photographer Jay Dearborn Edwards, between 1858 and 1861. Ferries offered Spalding and other Vermonters stationed in Algiers in 1862 access to the joys of life as a Union soldier in New Orleans. Courtesy of the Historic New Orleans Collection, acc. no. 1982. 167. 9.

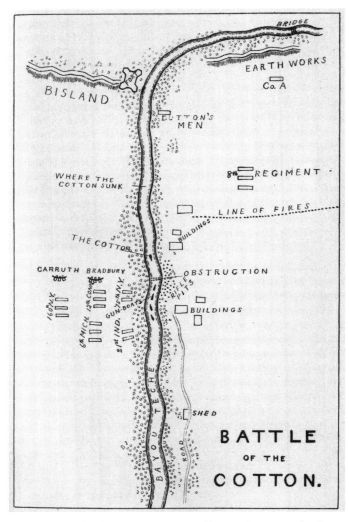

Map of the Battle of the Cotton, 1863. Spalding's 8th Vermont fought up the right side of this map, capturing the rifle pits marked, and ending the fight where it is shown. Note "Dutton's men" and "Co. A" are shown in advance of the rest of the regiment, where Spalding remained. From George N. Carpenter, *History of the Eighth Regiment Vermont Volunteers*. Courtesy of the Vermont Historical Society.

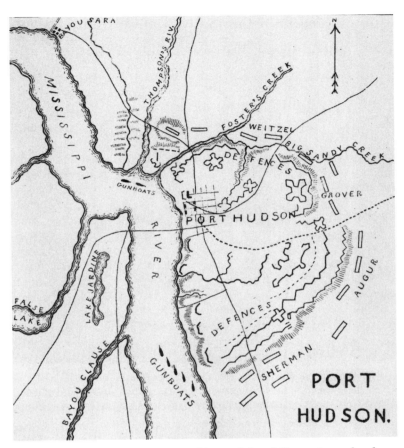

Map of the siege of Port Hudson. Spalding and the 8th Vermont served under General Weitzel, whose position is shown along the town's northern side. From George N. Carpenter, *History of the Eighth Regiment Vermont Volunteers*. Courtesy of the Vermont Historical Society.

"Approach to Reb. works on right flank at Port Hudson." Photograph by McPherson and Oliver. Spalding would have charged across land such as this during the two Union assaults on Port Hudson in 1863. Library of Congress.

5

RANK AND INSUBORDINATION
Spalding and the Awkward Court-Martial

The men are lazy. Officers D[itt]o. and it takes a good deal of
talking and punishing to get them to do anything.

—Stephen Spalding

Three days after Stephen Spalding wrote his letter to James Peck, his
colonel appointed him to be one of the three judges for a regimental
court-martial. The court assembled thirteen days later, on July 25,
1862, to try eleven men for their crimes. Lieutenant Spalding may have
been uncomfortable throughout the day. Among the judges, he was the
junior party; his fellow judges included Major Dillingham and Capt.
Henry Dutton of Company H, one of the regiment's rising stars. Adding to Spalding's awkward position was the fact that four of the eleven
men on the docket came from his company. Spalding may have found
himself caught between two powerful constituencies. If he were ever to
receive a promotion, he would have to impress the other judges, something perhaps done best with a stern approach to discipline. But in
order to curry favor with his own command, whose ire he could ill afford to arouse, he would need to find ways to moderate the army's extremely harsh concept of justice. Could he find a way to placate both
groups?

In at least one important way, Spalding brought his discomfort on
himself. Many of the defendants were charged with having gotten
drunk and misbehaved—exactly what he had just boasted to James
Peck of having done. How could he sit in judgment of men who had
only done as he had done? His hypocritical position seems to have
plagued him even before he sat down in the improvised courtroom.
Historian Lorien Foote points out that officers could summarily punish

soldiers whom they felt were guilty; as the ranking officer of Company B, Spalding chose not to take this path. Instead he decided to have these men judged by a larger panel.[1] Perhaps that indicates that he lacked the credibility to hand down harsh punishments on his own. Bringing the soldiers before the court would allow him to share responsibility for the sentences with two other judges. Whatever Spalding thought, his soldiers obviously wanted to get into the city and drink just as much as he did. In that sense, most of the Eighth Vermont—including the soldier-historian Moses McFarland, his men, Lieutenant Foster, Stephen Spalding and the guilty privates—shared a (perhaps blurred) vision of masculinity enhanced by alcohol. But the privates in this courtroom would be punished for their debaucheries, and the unequal and adversarial nature of the officer/enlisted man relationship came to the fore. Spalding could throw stools and intimidate blacks. He could hire largely powerless women to have sex with him. But the men in Company B had the collective power to make his life miserable if they decided to do so. Spalding occupied a high place in the regiment's hierarchy, but just how dominant he could be as an officer was up for negotiation on July 25.

One of the more intriguing, but unanswerable, questions posed by Spalding's presence as a judge is why Colonel Thomas appointed him. Why would a colonel with many lieutenants at his disposal pick Spalding as a judge, especially if Thomas knew anything about Spalding's adventures only a week before he appointed him?[2] Perhaps it was just Spalding's turn. Or maybe Thomas hoped to benefit from Spalding's antebellum legal training. Perhaps he wanted the court to have Spalding's close knowledge of the four men from his company who were on trial. Another possibility makes the colonel a bit more Machiavellian. Perhaps Thomas had heard about Spalding's escapades on July Fourth, and he chose Spalding to force his young officer to reflect on his conduct. Sitting on this court would require Spalding, if he was at all of a reflective turn of mind, to consider how his behavior was perceived by his fellow officers and by the men in the ranks. Guessing at the colonel's possible motivations allows historians a good deal of leeway for maneuver. But they remain guesses. What we do know is that the events of July 25 tell us how power operated in Spalding's society and how it influenced the inner workings of the Union army.

Being appointed judge at a court-martial in your own regiment was a serious matter with broad implications for your standing among both your fellow officers and the men under your command. Capt. John De Forest, who served on a court-martial in Louisiana at the same time, strongly disliked the job. Drilling in the hot Louisiana sun, he wrote, was "mere sport" compared to being president of a court, especially when his fellow judges had no more experience than he had with law. His conviction rate can be used for comparison with what Spalding and his fellow judges handed down. De Forest reported that his court found forty-five of fifty accused men guilty, and that all of the convicted men lost pay and that half of them—twenty-four—ended up wearing a ball and chain.[3] The worst aspect of court duty, however, was his powerlessness as a judge. "I can't avoid condemning and punishing, for everybody is guilty, and nearly everybody pleads guilty," he wrote. He seems to have wanted to avoid issuing the harsh punishments called for by the army's regulations, and yet he considered himself subject to the same law: "I must chastise according to the articles of war, or I may catch it myself." Every man who came before him, he noted, had been drunk when he committed his offense.[4]

In Spalding's courtroom, the first case was that of Pvt. William Murphy of Company E. It set the tone for the day's events. Officers accused Murphy of absenting himself from the regiment for three weeks. Even upon his return, Murphy proved to be a recalcitrant soldier. When ordered during drill to "fall into line," he answered: "I never will do duty in the company again. I will die first." Historians have written about the difficulties Civil War officers experienced in convincing volunteer soldiers to conform to army discipline, and Murphy's conduct exemplifies the problem. Did Murphy have reasons for abandoning his unit and, later, disobeying his officers, or was he just uncooperative by nature? Regardless of who was to blame, the court meted out a harsh punishment. Spalding and his fellow officers docked Murphy one month's pay and forced him to "wear a ball and chain on his right leg for 20 days." The chain was four feet long, and the ball was to weigh a brutal sixty-five pounds. To add shame to the physical and fiscal pain of the sentence, the court added that Murphy was "to have one half of his head shaved."[5] Clearly, the judges felt empowered to levy stiff punishments.

Pvt. William Murphy presented Spalding and his fellow judges with a severe challenge to army discipline; desertion and refusing orders struck at the heart of the military order. Some might even regard the sentence handed down against Murphy as light considering the extent of his rebellion. Perhaps Murphy was lucky to have rebelled so early in the war. Lorien Foote argues that "there was a widespread perception during and after 1863 . . . that a class of undesirable men had infiltrated the ranks of the army and that these men had to be handled with strict discipline, harsh punishments, and coercion." Looking at Regimental Books and courts-martial records, she sees a willingness among officers "to use violence and corporal punishment against subordinates who refused to obey orders, and the increased use of coercion at all levels to force men to stay in the army and fight."[6] By staging his rebellion early in the war, Murphy may have escaped a harsher fate; Foote includes cases of Union officers spontaneously shooting men who disobeyed orders. That violence was perhaps the ultimate sign of the gulf that she finds between officers and men, a gap that was exacerbated by the reality that differences in army rank usually mirrored the hierarchies of class and ethnicity of northern society. Men in the ranks, Foote writes, quickly sensed when officers, the so-called "shoulder-strap gentry," failed to recognize the manhood and equality of the men beneath them. When we ask ourselves what Lieutenant Spalding thought during the court-martial, we need to consider just how big a gap Spalding saw between himself and his men, and how little his men might have thought of him.[7] Did all power lie with the judges on this day?

The next two cases show the range of crimes with which the court had to deal. One was sad, and almost cute: Pvt. Peter Allard had been found trying to steal melons from a nearby farm—indeed, he allegedly "was found therein partially hid among the weeds and grass." Allard ended the day five dollars poorer. The other case demonstrates that Spalding shared his fondness for drink with another man in the Eighth Vermont. At some point, Pvt. A. J. Stickney had found himself stuck in the regiment's guard house, accused of drunkenness. He did not go quietly, however. Officers charged him with "disorderly conduct" on account of his "continual swearing and cursing, and by his refusing to keep quiet." Stickney's accusers, perhaps employing some understatement, said of his lengthy, profane, and drink-fueled outbursts that they "kept the camp in an uproar the principal part of the night, contrary to military order." Stickney pleaded guilty—no doubt the prosecution could have called witnesses—and forfeited one month's pay. One can imagine that so far Lieutenant Spalding felt that the day was going along fine; none of the accused had done what he had done, even if he and Stickney shared a fondness for stiff drinks and many of them. Spalding at least had not stolen melons, disobeyed orders, deserted, or entertained the regiment with profanity for hours at a time.

It is tempting to think that the next case alarmed Stephen Spalding. It is also possible, however, that he felt no sense of shame at all if there was a wide gulf between him and his men. The defendant, Pvt. Thomas Ferrin of Company E, was accused of doing only what Spalding had done. He even did it on the same day; there seems to have been something of an illegal exodus from the regiment's camp in Algiers on the nation's birthday. Nor could absenteeism have been only a recent phenomenon, as the colonel had issued an order on June 19 limiting the number of passes that would be given out to "Enlisted men." In addition, any passes that were granted needed multiple signatures and would be given only to clean, smartly uniformed soldiers who petitioned very early in the day.[8] Ferrin did not go through this cumbersome process. Instead, like Spalding and Lieutenant Foster, he decided to spend the day away from the camp without telling anyone of his intentions. His officers charged him with "running the Guard and getting drunk" on July Fourth. Predictably, his commanders found that "on his return [Ferrin] was very much intoxicated." Ferrin, unlike Spalding, found himself hauled before the court. He pleaded guilty.

The court agreed that Ferrin was guilty, and Spalding had to sign off on a stiff sentence. Ferrin's punishment resembled that handed down to William Murphy, the man who had deserted and then refused to drill, saying he would rather die. Ferrin, too, lost a month's pay and had to wear a ball and chain attached to his right foot. Again the chain was four feet long, and the ball a hefty sixty-five-pound shot. The only differences were that Murphy, the deserter, had his head shaved and would wear his for twenty days, while Ferrin retained his hair and was to be encumbered for only ten. But that was still a week and a half of complete misery. The equation of deserting for three weeks and pub-

licly refusing a direct order to drill with going AWOL for a day and returning drunk meant that Spalding's own offenses were being ranked
right up with very serious offences against army protocols.

The severity of the court's sentence against Ferrin (for offenses identical to Spalding's) comes out in comparison with the judgments
handed down against other guilty men that day. The other men brought
before the court received lesser sentences, highlighting the seriousness
of Ferrin's drunken Independence Day. Pvt. G. G. Smith, for example,
was accused of "leaving his post while on duty and going to sleep in his
quarters."⁹ Smith, however, received leniency from the court after
pleading guilty. He was only eighteen years old, and the court recognized his "extreme youth . . . and his former good behavior."¹⁰ The mix
of a serious crime (if something of a funny offense, given teenagers'
love of sleep and the obvious nature of the crime) and leniency was a
six-dollar fine. Six dollars was half a month's pay, a serious amount, but
not a ball and chain. Spalding was seeing conduct identical to his own
judged with severity compared to the crimes of G. G. Smith.

After this start to the proceedings, the court turned its attention to
four members of Spalding's own company. While there is no way to
know how Spalding, the junior officer on the court, influenced the proceedings, the way the court behaved on three of the four cases enables
us to speculate about how his peculiar position may have weighed on
him. The first three cases, we can note, all had to do with excessive
drinking—a phenomenon that Spalding was both familiar with and
found amusing enough to relate to his friend. Pvt. John O'Mere was
found guilty of "getting drunk on duty," in particular "while standing
guard as sentry." The next private, Andrew McIver, left his post as
guard for "hours," returning "drunk and wholly unfit for the duty of a
Guard." In the third case, Pvt. Francis Hagan left camp and got drunk.
These men were found guilty, and their crimes mostly mirrored those
of Thomas Ferrin, who had gone absent without leave on July Fourth
and returned drunk to camp. But Spalding's men were not destined for
the ball and chain, as Ferrin was. Rather, the court docked O'Mere one
month's pay. McIver, who abandoned his post to go drinking, lost a
month's pay and had to do ten days of police duty in the company's
quarters. Hagan, whose crimes seem identical to McIver's, got off even
more lightly. He was sentenced to lose a month's pay and to do five days

of police duty in the company. The court in his case went on record saying that it had been "lenient on account of the previous good conduct of the prisoner."[11] This information presumably came from Spalding. So we can ask the question: did the young lieutenant look for ways to get his men off lightly? Certainly they received lighter sentences than Ferrin did—none would wear a ball and chain for ten days. Did Spalding work to reduce their sentences out of kindness, or did he know that his conduct on the Fourth made *any* sentence he handed down seem hypocritical and very likely to be resented? Had he not succeeded in saving his men from the worst sentences, he almost certainly would have lost popularity and perhaps even control over his men.

Historian Steven J. Ramold's study of Civil War army discipline gives us reason to think that Spalding may have tried to get his men less severe sentences than those meted out to men in other companies. Ramold finds evidence of the same gap between officers and men that Lorien Foote has written about. Soldiers in the ranks often found their officers to be "instruments of the army discipline that diminished their personal liberties, and therefore became the target of general scorn and displeasure." As commander of Company B, Spalding knew he would need the cooperation of his men in the coming months. Officers known to be too fond of regulations soon acquired the contempt, or worse, of the men they had to lead.[12] The fact that officers could legally acquire alcohol from the Commissary Department, while soldiers and NCOs were banned from possessing it, accentuated the divide between officers and privates. Ramold further notes that drunken officers, a category that Spalding may or may not have fit into on a regular basis, often had the most difficulty maintaining discipline.[13] Finding himself caught between his men on the one hand and the army regulations that he must enforce on the other, Spalding may have tried to win over his men by making sure that they at least avoided the ball and chain. As Ramold concludes, the army's court system worked well, in part because it was often marked by "flexibility, leniency, and individuality."[14] But in this case it did not work fairly for Murphy or Ferrin.

The remainder of the court-martial passed relatively quickly. Only two more cases remained. One private refused to do guard duty and forfeited ten dollars as a result. The final case featured a more tempestuous charge. Pvt. Hosea Aldrich of Company K had also refused to perform guard duty but had done so in a more flagrant manner. His refusal was peppered with "abusive language" directed at his sergeant, whom he called "a damned fool," and probably other things that did not make it into the court record. He lost one month's pay and had to drill for an extra two hours a day for ten days while wearing a "well packed" knapsack.[15]

The hostility that Aldrich, Murphy and Stickney displayed toward their officers and NCOs suggests that privates in the Eighth Vermont could aggressively challenge their commanders. The fact that soldiers could question orders and survive requires us to look in a new way at Spalding's position on July 25. Aldrich, Murphy, and Stickney lashed out against their commanders with vigor and at great length. We tend to imagine harmonious relations among Civil War soldiers and their officers, especially in volunteer regiments that elected their own officers and NCOs. But how open were the elections? Capt. L. D. Clark of the Thirteenth Vermont wrote that officer elections were "really pretty much arranged by the leading citizens and selectmen of the several towns there regimented, before we commenced to vote, and the boys were given the great privilege of ratifying the selections made for us. Some resented this way."[16] Such elections would have re-created existing divisions and power structures in society, and units would be riven by class, ethnic, and religious gulfs between privates and those above them.

For his part, Spalding seems to have promoted certain kinds of men, giving free range to his ethnic prejudices. His blind spots should not surprise us, given that he grew up in a society that had fostered a successful nativist party that warned against the growing number of immigrants and Catholics in the country. Unsurprisingly, the three privates from Company B who stood in front of Spalding in the courtroom (whose ethnicity we can find on the muster rolls) came from social backgrounds at odds with Spalding's own past. John O'Mere had been born in Ireland about twenty-eight years before. Army life apparently failed to live up to his expectations, and he deserted in Alexandria, Louisiana, in May 1863. Andrew McIver had immigrated from Scotland, and, like O'Mere, had been a farmer before the war. Francis Hagan, who received leniency from the judges, was born in Canada East and was nineteen when he enlisted.[17] Did he get a softer sentence because he had exhibited good conduct, because he was young, or because he had not been born in Europe? An even more speculative question remains: did Spalding bring immigrants before the court, while handling native-born men with unofficial reprimands and warnings? Questions abound. Did Lieutenant Spalding feel any discomfort because he had to judge people for crimes he had also committed? Did a knowing colonel force him to sign off on hard sentences to let his young officer see how strongly the army condemned his conduct? Did Spalding, like Captain De Forest, regret his inability to issue weaker sentences than those required by the army's regulations? Did Spalding recognize his hypocritical position and reduce the punishments imposed on his own men in order to curry favor with them? Or did he experience no discomfort at all, believing (perhaps without even thinking about it) that what was funny for him to do posed a threat to the army if done by enlisted immigrants? Spalding's society empowered people like himself to do certain things while denying the same liberties to others. Spalding's family enjoyed considerable rank in his small town, and his future career as an attorney would give him a role in determining who had violated the law. Attorneys, more than anyone else, won elections and therefore wrote laws.[18] Wealth influenced who could stay in Derby, and who had to leave to find work or land. The Eighth Vermont Volunteers no doubt reflected hierarchical aspects of the society from which it was drawn.

It is reasonable to think that conflict was inevitable within the Union army. The men in the ranks may have felt a natural and continuing resentment against their officers, and the officers in turn may have been either oblivious to this sentiment or dismissive of it. In the midst of considerable uncertainty about how Stephen Spalding viewed his place in Derby and in Company B, we know some things for sure. There can be no doubt that July 25 was a day in which the wheels of power turned in the Eighth Vermont. Officers punished severely soldiers over whom they had always had more power, even back home in Vermont. We know that Spalding held up his conduct on July Fourth as a funny adventure to be rewarded with friendly laughs, while similar conduct by privates earned stiff punishments. We know that soldiers in Company B were not punished as heavily as soldiers in other companies. We cannot know for sure why that was, but I think the men in

Company B—the accused and their friends—had the power to make Spalding uncomfortable unless he worked for reduced sentences.

Spalding himself used an interesting turn of phrase when writing to Peck about how he commanded men he judged as "lazy." He wrote that "it takes a good deal of talking and punishing to get them to do anything." During the court-martial we see the "punishing" that Spalding wrote about. But what of the "talking"? Clearly Spalding and his men engaged in ongoing negotiations about how much work and obedience Spalding could expect. Unlike the African Americans Spalding met or the prostitutes he hired, white men knew that they had rights and balked when they were not recognized. Power in the Union army, as at civilian job sites, polling places, and churches, did not rest only with the elite in the nineteenth century. On this day when he exercised considerable power over other men, Spalding also felt the limits of his authority in ways that he would not when he dealt with African Americans or white women.

6

FACING DEATH
Spalding and the Unfunny Joke

Yesterday I was sitting in my room, thinking over the mutability of all things human, and making myself as miserable as the
Army Regulations allow.

—Stephen Spalding

Stephen Spalding sounds compellingly honest about himself when he
writes that "there is nothing that reminds one of home more forcibly,
than the sight of a black hearse bearing the remains of half a dozen
poor fellows to their long homes," his arresting term for graves.[1] Despite having been in and out of the army for over a year and a half, Spalding had just begun to confront the reality of a military death when he
sat down to write to James Peck. Serving in the Seventh New York
State Militia had been painless, and the Eighth Vermont had been fortunate as well. But the summer of 1862 began to take a toll. Facing
death made Spalding homesick, as he admitted, which contributed to
"the 1st real fit of the blues since I enlisted."[2] He turned to humor to
fight his homesickness and depression, but in the process made himself sound terribly callous, as we will see.

Certainly Spalding had reasons to feel down. The summer heat of
Louisiana affected most of the Vermont men. Hailing from the Canadian border, Spalding complained "first and foremost" about "the excessive heat." Drilling annoyed men in decent weather but was worse
in the heat. Spalding described the problem as obvious: "One with a
very limited observation can see that the climate is seriously affecting
the health of the troops in this Dep't. The men are lazy. Officers
D[itt]o." Lazy, wilting soldiers became Spalding's problem with the departure, in rapid succession, of two of his fellow company officers.

Capt. Charles B. Child left when he took over as provost marshal of Algiers on June 10, and Lt. F. D. Butterfield moved to the signal service on June 27, 1862.³ Left in sole command of Company B, Spalding now had to make men do things. His letter's next sentences show him having to coerce soldiers into doing their jobs. He wrote that the heat-induced indifference required him to do "a good deal of talking and punishing to get them to do anything. A don't care a damn for nothing kind of a feeling seemes [*sic*] to exist immensely in every patriots's bosom." This was partially a joke, like so much else in Spalding's letter. Patriots—real ones—would triumph over such adversity. But Spalding knew better than to expect patriotism from his soldiers, at least after eight months of service. The miserable Gulf Coast heat and humidity drained spirits and left soldiers not caring "a damn for nothing."

Other matters combined to make the situation worse. Mosquitoes plagued the Union soldiers. Humor again, masking frustration: mosquitoes, Spalding wrote, were "very thick and keep a man constantly employed in brushing them away from his face and ears. After dark any evening you can with a single wave of the hand strike to the earth millions." Mosquitoes tormented other Vermonters as well. Roger Hovey told his sister that "the mosquitoes and flies are pouring in upon me from every side and biting me dreadfully." Justus Gale called the area west of Algiers "musketoe valley" and wrote to his sister that she could not imagine how important mosquito bars were to the men of the Eighth Vermont. Another New England soldier joked that Louisiana mosquitoes were "not as large as robins." Having become a doctor after the war, Pvt. Charles Cooper of the Eighth Vermont wrote that the insects "explained the mystery [of] why so few [people] had lived here." Able to bite "through a thick woolen blanket and pair of pants," the large mosquitoes proved a formidable foe, and he diagnosed the regiment's problems as "a malarial fever." Kathryn S. Meier's recent study of soldiers in Virginia in 1862 links weather and insects to mental health issues such as loneliness, depression, and homesickness.⁴ Spalding, even with War Department mosquito bars, saw this firsthand.

Other problems plagued the Vermonters. Poor officers seem to have bothered some of the men, compounding the difficulties of weather and insects. Diarist Rufus Kinsley of the Eighth Vermont noted in early June 1862 that "the field officers are not above mediocrity."⁵ Pvt. Justus

Gale also complained: "Our officers kep us shut up tight and [we] are hardly alowed to go the out side of the guard, and if we do we are forbid to take any thing that would ad comfort to us or any body else." He concluded his complaint with a nod to postwar life: "there are some men in our regt. that wil get but few favors from us if we live to get out from under them."[6] Even though Spalding probably disagreed with Kinsley and Gale on most matters, the three men agreed on this point. The Eighth Vermont seemed to be undergoing a rough summer, and the commanding officers proved unable to hold the unit together.

Spalding, as usual, made a joke of it all. He had complaints about the unit, he wrote to James, but military law forbade him from expressing himself openly on the subject. Nevertheless, he did write:

> There are many things concerning the Eighth Regiment of Vermont
> Volunteers, which I would like to inform you of. But knowing that a
> civil tongue has saved many a young man from the gallows, I refrain
> from saying any thing detrimental. In the dim distance, however
> methinks I see a day when I shall once more stand on the soil of old
> Vermont, a free man, when my tongue will no longer be fettered,
> when I can stand up provided I am sober and a tale unfold that will
> grate harsh upon the ears of some. Say nothing about this. For you
> know a still cat catches the mice.

The heat, the mosquitoes, and the boredom tried the patience of many soldiers; a recent study of Union troops in coastal North Carolina doing "occupation duty" similar to that done by the Eighth Vermont finds men there complained of all of these problems.[7] Gale's and Kinsley's dissatisfaction must be taken seriously. Spalding's jokes about the officers—about going to the gallows and being too drunk to stand up and deliver his scathing critique of them—encourages his reader to disregard the seriousness of his unhappiness. But that is just his way of expressing himself. We know from other evidence that he and the rest of the Eighth Vermont suffered under inadequate leadership during this hot, trying summer.

The summer of 1862 was hard on the Vermonters. They complained openly at the time about boredom, loneliness, and homesickness. The regiment had missed all of the campaigning that resulted in the Confederates fleeing, deserting, and mutinying around New Orleans

during April and early May 1862. By mid-May they had arrived in New
Orleans but had done only garrison duty. Their month in New Orleans
had been uneventful, because most of the city's people had speedily ac-
quiesced to (or even celebrated) the Union presence. Since then, garrison duty in Algiers had been equally dull. The *Brattleboro Phoenix*'s
anonymous correspondent in the regiment did his patriotic best to tell
readers a happy story on July 15, but the truth soon won out:

> [O]ur wounded officers and men are doing remarkably well, our sick
> list is small, and the sanitary condition of the command is . . . high.
> We are passing through a trying ordeal, compared with which an ac-
> tive campaign were a relief. We are stationary, monotonously guard-
> ing an unattacked position, without excitement or the sight or sound
> of a foe. . . . We are learning, as the hot season slowly passes over us,
> that hardest of all lessons, to "labor and to wait." The danger is of be-
> coming dispirited and disheartened under the combined power of
> the sultry climate and the depressing circumstances.

Like Spalding, other correspondents complained that they had nothing to tell their friends and families back home. "You want me to write
all the news," Roger Hovey sighed. "Well," he wrote, "as far as *news* is
concerned, we do not get much, and as we are not *doing* any thing I
cannot write much news." An even more disgruntled Justus Gale told
his father that "I wish I could tel you of something that our regiment
had done but I cant think nor don't know of any thing they have done
yet worth spending the ink to write about."[8]

All of these problems bred loneliness and homesickness. Trapped in
unpleasant circumstances with the novelty of enlistment and military
life worn off, Benjamin Morse wrote to his wife about his homesickness. He used a clever turn of phrase to drive home his point in a funny
way, but his point was serious: "I aint home sick but for only one thing
& that is home that is where I want to *be*." Writing in July, about three
weeks after Spalding's letter, Morse wrote again of homesickness, saying that "no tounge can tell how I want to come & see you to you my
thought[s] are first in the morning & last at night . . . some times I see
you in imagination & for awhile talk in my mind as though we were
together these moments are the happiest moments of my life here."
Others shared Morse's sentiment; Dexter Fairbanks complained in

September that it "seems rather lonesome here" and would be far worse had it not been for the company of his cousin, Orange.[9]

Even the usually sunny postwar history of the Eighth Vermont agrees that the unit dragged its way through the summer of 1862. Essentially a celebration of the regiment, George Carpenter's history admits that "this book deals solely with the credible deeds of officers and privates, and, on the ground that nothing else deserved to be preserved in permanent form, consigns all else to oblivion."[10] Still, the book confesses that the regiment endured a rough spell that summer. Of these months, Carpenter writes, "it was no uncommon thing . . . for members of the regiment to have severe attacks of home-sickness."[11] But Carpenter follows this serious remark with a comic story, telling of a soldier who worried that his homesickness will "prove fatal if he remained in that climate." The soldier acts on his fears and resolves to earn a discharge. He "feigned to be a fool" by taking a baitless fishing rod down to the Mississippi River every day, only to return intentionally empty-handed. He receives his discharge papers once his officers decide that only the "under-witted" would pursue such a course of daily futility, only to have him happily proclaim that "these [discharge papers] are what I was fishing for."[12] Interestingly, Spalding follows his statement of homesickness and death—the "long homes"—with a joke, just as Carpenter does in his history.

Through it all, we can see that death proved to be far more unsettling than poor officers, heat, or mosquitoes during the summer of 1862. Deaths had been relatively infrequent in the first months of Spalding's service in the Eighth Vermont, just as they had been when he was in the Seventh New York State Militia. From March 1 to the end of May, only eight men had died, and Spalding might have looked on some of these deaths as not especially threatening examples of mortality. Two of the earliest deaths had fallen on some of the unit's oldest men, John Boyce, forty-eight, and Richard Boyce, forty-four. Four men had fallen mortally ill on Ship Island, a place that had not endeared itself to the Vermonters, perhaps because of its salty water. Once they left Ship Island, health returned. Only two men had died in May.

June changed all that, and Spalding had this recent spate of deaths on his mind when he took up his pen on July 8. As Spalding mentions in his letter, four men from Company H had been killed during a skirmish at "Des Almons" [Bayou des Allemands] on June 22. Known later as the Battle of Raceland, the Confederates had killed two thirty-one-year-old corporals and two eighteen-year-old privates.[13] Spalding's Company B played no role at Raceland, but he would have talked with the survivors in the days afterward. The usually cheerful Jonathan Allen, who had been at Raceland, reported that his Company H "is a sorry looking and sad hearted Co. the Capt. is quite down hearted. the men wish for another chance and swear they will have revenge." Allen's letter names all of the people killed and elaborates on the nature and extent of the wounded men's injuries.[14] Civil War combat was deeply traumatic, and soldiers—especially those new to battle—often had to work hard to recover their emotional and psychological equilibrium in its aftermath.[15] Allen's detailed letter proves, in its own way, the novelty of combat casualties and the degree to which he needed to write about the carnage in order to process the company's losses. Allen and his comrades were not veterans in any sense of the word, and they and Spalding had to find their own ways through grief and a heightened sense of mortality. Allen processed what he had seen in part by writing a detailed list of what had happened to each man hurt in the skirmish. Even though he missed Raceland, Spalding would react in his own, very different, way.

To make matters worse, life in camp proved to be even more lethal than the skirmish at Raceland. Nine men died from disease in the regiment during June, with the later part of the month proving worse than the start. Three men passed away on June 23 and two more on June 27. Except for the wondrously named Victory Rotary, who died on June 2 at age thirty-one after being shot by a Union guard, all of the deceased were young men—not more than twenty-six. In fact, factoring out Victory Rotary, the average age of death was a hair under twenty-two, less than Spalding's age. The unfortunate men who fell ill, died of disease, or drowned had worked jobs before the war that suggest hearty constitutions: wheelwright; teamster; farmer; laborer.[16] Illnesses continued even as Spalding wrote; Joseph Horn, age twenty-one, died the day after Spalding wrote his letter. Like the other men who had sickened and died after Rotary's death, Horn wasted away in Algiers in close proximity to the living members of the regiment.

The sharp increase in the number of deaths and funerals in late

June means that Spalding composed his letter at a potentially sensitive time for the young man. There is no reason to believe that he was particularly close to any of these young men, but that does not mean that he was unaffected. Spalding's relatively brief life had included long stints away from his family at the University of Vermont and again to start his legal training in New York City. Any deaths he may have encountered in those years would have been handled by other people's families. Women would probably have presided, at least informally, over the mourning rituals. But the Eighth Vermont was an all-male world. How would the dead have been mourned? Who would have mourned them? One senses an emotionally constrained atmosphere in most Union military units; tears flowed freely on occasions, but only at certain times and during certain kinds of ceremonies. Confronting death without the help of women or relatives proved to be a difficult experience for many Union soldiers.[17] In this regard, Spalding was probably not an exception. He may not have known quite what to do, or even what to think. And so, he made jokes.

Historians have made promising forays into the uses of humor during the Civil War. Much of what they have written has focused on published stories, material that one historian calls humor "written by and for those at home." These stories deal with deaths, though with severe limitations. Alice Fahs describes Civil War humorists as setting themselves up against the sentimental conventions of mainstream patriotic rhetoric, including its glorified depictions of heroic death. Bravely facing death might make for a fine parlor story, humorists seem to be saying, but try finding volunteers for it in the ranks and you will be a long time looking.[18] Spalding's letter gives us something else; instead of a home-front professional writer, we hear from a soldier who is confronting "the sight of a black hearse bearing the remains of half a dozen poor fellows to their long homes."

Spalding gives James Peck what historian Robert Bonner calls a dose of "dark humor." Bonner describes the comic elements in Civil War letters as "the beginning of a comic sensibility that has remained part of the response of the 'grunt' to modern war for the next century and a half."[19] While Bonner does not mention death as one of the topics soldiers write about—the soldiers he studies complain of poor food, shelter, sanitation, and officers—Spalding's comic mood and complaints about similar topics seem to fit Bonner's description. In addition, Jon Grinspan's study of Civil War humor indicates that by writing about death, Spalding may have been part of a trend among northern soldiers. Originally, Grinspan writes, many northerners "winced at the thought of joking about casualty lists. But veteran Union troops . . . embraced hard war humor, and their comedy slowly trickled into the northern homefront."[20] In these ways, Spalding seems to be on the forefront of a new way of using humor to deal with war's horrors and the sense of powerlessness that soldiers can experience in its midst.

Spalding scrawled the joke that demands our attention across the top of page five, but it is not merely an afterthought. Spalding's most honest, intriguing joke is: "A boy in my company fell off of the dock just now & was drowned. I had a man in his place enlisted and drilling just as he was sinking the 3rd time." In fact, Spalding likes this joke—or needs this joke—so much that he makes it twice. Earlier in his letter he remarks that "the sod is scarcely thrown over our soldiers before new recruits are strutting round with their equipments[.]" This is a joke, in both its iterations, because it is clearly an exaggeration—dead soldiers are not replaced quite so quickly as this. New soldiers do not literally show up so quickly that they can watch the man they are replacing drown. But comic exaggeration does not mean that we should not take this joke seriously.

Spalding's joke—made twice—reflects his urgent need to process two matters that fill up other parts of his letter. First, he had to come to terms with death. Second, the Union army was trying to absorb hundreds of new recruits that it was enlisting from New Orleans's white population. New recruits enlisted rapidly in New Orleans in the summer of 1862, and Spalding's joke revolves around how quickly the city's men volunteered to serve in "northern" regiments. Despite the city's present reputation as a hotbed of Confederate feeling, the Union army successfully enlisted the city's white men into its ranks. The first volunteer joined up the day after the Union army disembarked on the city's levees. Less than two weeks later, the United States government opened up a recruiting station to handle the influx of volunteers. By September, Maj. Gen. Benjamin Butler reported that "more than 1,200" Louisiana whites had enlisted into his regiments, including the Eighth Vermont. By late October, Butler had begun raising separate white Louisiana regiments for the Union cause, with one fully manned and a second and third well under way. These recruits were the first wave of more than five thousand white Louisianans who served in the Union army during the war.[21]

Spalding's interest in white Unionism in New Orleans and Algiers pops up throughout his letter. To Spalding and others, the authenticity of white Unionist sentiment had important implications for the war effort. If the Confederacy did not enjoy the full support of its white population, the war would be shorter and easier to defend ideologically. Most Americans believed that white men had the right to self-government, and if all southern whites endorsed the Confederacy, then the Union war effort lacked validity, as even northern newspapers admitted.[22] Hence, Spalding paid attention to the loyalties of the people around him. He observed that the people in Algiers "for the most [part] are of the poorer class and extremely ignorant. Their hatred for the Union and the Yankees is pure and undefiled. I would as soon attempt to reason with a dog as with the most intelligent of them."[23] That would be bad news for the Union if it were universally true. On the other hand, if southern whites had been dragooned into secession by a few slaveholders looking to protect their human property, and if nonslaveholding whites had come to regret their hasty support of southern independence, then the war would be one of liberation. Perhaps even more important for Spalding, who was beginning to look for a rapid return home, tepid support for the Confederacy would make the war easier to win. The successful mutiny among the six-hundred-man Confederate garrison of Fort Jackson south of New Orleans in April, together with the widespread desertion from the Confederate army and Louisiana's militia in April and May, spread hope that the Confederacy was on the brink of collapse.[24]

The influx of Louisiana whites into the United States military also mattered to Spalding because it impacted his life directly. Spalding notes the rapid rate of enlistment, telling his friend, "We have no difficulty enlisting men." This good news, however, is tempered by the necessity of making further detachments from Spalding's Company B and the rest of the regiment to train the new volunteers. He writes that "30 Corporals have been detailed to drill the recruits that they are going to raise[,]" because "they contemplate raising several Regiments in this State." We might be tempted to regard this as more of Spalding's comic exaggeration, which was a common enough form of humor that one Civil War veteran wrote of "that essentially American cynic humor which often finds amusement in wild exaggeration."[25] But at least in this instance Spalding wrote only the truth. On the same day Spalding wrote his letter, regimental headquarters issued Special Order No. 36, ordering five of the regiment's corporals to assist a major from the Thirteenth Connecticut at the "U.S. Barracks below the City of New Orleans." Among the five were two from Spalding's Company, M. W. Farr and H. P. Haney.[26] The detailing of these two men would have further degraded the command structure of Company B, thereby making Spalding's job of getting his men to obey orders that much harder. As such, the arrival of Louisianans into the Union army was a mixed blessing for Spalding.

The Louisiana recruits constituted news during the dull summer months. Spalding repeated what must have been a piece of camp gossip when he told his Vermont friend that "the 9th Connecticut recruited over 400 men in a very short time." This was an exaggeration, though only by so much, and one can see how the rumor got started.[27] In reality, the Ninth Connecticut took in 124 recruits in New Orleans before Spalding composed his letter, a high number considering the city's pro-Confederate image, but not quite Spalding's "400 men."[28] His high estimate might be blamed on ethnic prejudices. Most of the recruits who came into the Union army at New Orleans were immigrants, as historian G. Howard Hunter has demonstrated.[29] From its inception, the Ninth Connecticut enjoyed a mixed reputation as a distinctly Irish regiment, with reports of their escapades on the train from New Haven to Camp Chase in Lowell, Massachusetts, causing trepidation in the hearts of the mill city. Later attempts to bust out of Camp Chase and into Lowell's downtown further tarnished, or perhaps embellished, the regiment's reputation. Spalding may simply have assumed that Irishmen from New Orleans would flock to the Ninth Connecticut.[30] Even though they might help end the war more quickly, Spalding might not have welcomed the foreign-born volunteers who required the services of two of his corporals. His reluctance to give them a warm reception may help us to understand the callousness of his joke about their arrival in the Eighth Vermont.

We know, then, that the second half of Spalding's joke ("I had a man in his place enlisted and drilling just as he was sinking the 3rd time.") is basically true. New recruits were piling into the Eighth Vermont. The first half of his joke, unfortunately, is also true: a man in his company had just drowned in the Mississippi River. Ten days before Spalding wrote his letter, Andrew McKenzie of Company B had died. We cannot learn much about Andrew McKenzie; he enlisted at eighteen, having lived in Wickham, Canada, before he volunteered.[31] He joined up on December 18, 1861, and was mustered in at Camp Holbrook in Brattleboro, Vermont, two months later. His enlisting officer neglected to record McKenzie's height and hair color, even though he should have done so.[32] The "Casualty Sheet" filled out on his death, reproduced here, is spare to the point of neglect. In the form's "Remarks" section, the company clerk could think only to write "No Effects," a sad commentary about this Canadian teenager's life and death.[33]

And yet the regimental history, published long after McKenzie's death in the Mississippi, includes a tantalizing story about his enlistment. George Carpenter tells readers that "all his comrades will recollect Andrew McKenzie, who was drowned at Algiers, and how he became a member of Company B. After the company was full he wished to enlist in it, and it was agreed that if he would go South with them, the boys would share their rations with him until a vacancy occurred. He went, and at New York one man deserted the ranks, and McKenzie took his place."[34] We can question the truth of this story quite easily, noting that McKenzie's service records say that he was mustered in on February 18, in Vermont, and that the regiment did not reach New York City until March.[35] But the truth of the story is not what is most interesting. More fascinating is Carpenter's assertion that "all" of the men of the Eighth Vermont will remember McKenzie, which seems hard to believe in light of the brief record of his death and the inaccuracy of Carpenter's own story about him. Nevertheless, someone *must* have remembered him enough to include him in the regimental history beyond simply listing him in the roll call printed in the back of the volume. And if he was young, memorable, and perhaps so eager to serve that an apocryphal story sprang up around his enlistment, it makes Spalding's cavalier joke about his drowning seem even more callous. Or perhaps, even more likely, it is an attempt by Spalding to guard himself against the emotions that the death of such a young man may have stirred.

It would seem obvious that Spalding should not have made a joke about the boy's drowning. And yet he did, despite his education and his usually more keen intelligence. Why did he do so? The answer may lie in the fact that the moment we make a joke about something it becomes less scary. The subject becomes something that we have mastery over, as evidenced by the very fact that we can laugh at it. Indeed, I have done this myself in recent years. For me, and I suspect for Spalding as well, making such jokes can be comforting, not because they are inappropriate but because they conquer death for a moment, even if they are not our best material.

Living at quite a distance from McKenzie's drowning, historians have the luxury of analyzing Spalding's reaction to the young man's death. Spalding's joke partially denies the reality that a man he knew rather closely had just died. To say that "I had a man *in his place*" is to come very close to suggesting the interchangeability of the men in his command. His second version of the joke makes much the same point. "We have no difficulty enlisting men," he writes. "The sod is scarcely thrown over our soldiers before new recruits are strutting round with their equipments." The joke strongly implies that the first man's death simply does not matter. The replacement of one body for another leaves the company unchanged.

To say this of Spalding's jokes—made at his young age—is not necessarily to judge him harshly, or even to judge him at all. Clearly, Spalding was having a hard time, as he even admitted to Peck. His very first sentence to Peck alerts us that Spalding is thinking about death and is saddened by it: "Yesterday I was sitting in my room," he writes, "thinking over the mutability of all things human, and making myself as miserable as the Army Regulations allow." His opening is a joke, but it introduces the "mutability" of the human body and his "miserable" emotional state. Spalding comes up to the brink of admitting fear and adult worries about death but pulls back from exposing himself that much to his friend. Newly exposed to death on a frightening scale in the past weeks, Spalding flirted with openly talking about his fears to his friend. He chose, however, to circle around the topic, perhaps even thinking that Peck, a civilian still, would not really understand his fears. Joking with him no doubt seemed a safer course. But Spalding's letter, with its awkward jokes and fanciful language, nevertheless gets us to the undeniable place that its author was worried about dying, dying too young, dying too far away from his family and friends.[36]

Spalding was also probably thinking that most of the deaths around him were too commonplace. They lacked heroism; they were not memorable. Men died of disease even at home, even in peacetime. Drowning was both horrible and common in the Eighth Vermont that summer. Joseph Croteau, a twenty-year-old Quebec farmer, drowned on June 18.[37] Edmond Saul drowned on the same day as Edward McKenzie, perhaps the victim of the same accident, though even this is uncertain. Saul was forty-four when he died, a common laborer who had been born in Cork, Ireland.[38] Nothing about any of these deaths was heroic. People never imagined that the men they cheered off to war would die of disease or in the muddy Mississippi miles from Confederate troops.

The drowning death of Edmond Saul offers us a chance to see another way that a Union soldier could react to the deaths around him. Saul, the forty-four-year-old Irishman, served in the same company as Rufus Kinsley, whose diary entries have complemented Spalding's elsewhere in this book. Certainly more religious than Spalding, Kinsley also believed in racial equality and abolition. He was also older, about thirty-one years old. For these reasons, Kinsley wrote a more generous note about the drowning death of Edmond Saul than Spalding could write about Andrew McKenzie. Kinsley wrote in his diary on June 23 that "Ed. Saul, a fine old Irishman, of our Co., was drowned in the Mississippi."[39] Kinsley's brief record is warm and noteworthy for its inclusiveness, making Saul not just "fine" but "of our Co." But then, Kinsley's attitudes toward the war, and deaths caused by it, differed dramatically from Spalding's often cynical approach to events around him. Kinsley could be open about Saul's death, perhaps, because he was more Christian and more familiar with ways of approaching death. Kinsley also believed—he *knew*—that Saul had died on the right side of the war, and as part of God's plan. While he believed that God had a harsh fate in store for the South, Kinsley thought that all Americans bore responsibility for slavery's sins and would have to pay a price. "The Nation is gathering in her harvest," he wrote on August 31, 1862. "Thank God for the harvest time: Yes, thank God; notwithstanding the terrible harvest we gather;—a nation of graves, and rivers of blood. But it is the legitimate fruit of the seed we have sown. There is in physical and social life, and in moral and political life as well, a law of compensation, so accurately adjusted by Infinite wisdom, that no action or purpose can fail to receive its reward."[40] Saul died, then, as part of God's plan, and Kinsley approached that death with more equanimity than the younger, less thoughtful Spalding could muster.

Other men besides Kinsley also reacted in mature ways to the deaths occurring around them that summer. In late July, about two weeks after Spalding's letter, Justus Gale wrote, "It is with somewhat sober thoughts and feelings that I attempt to write a few lines to you this morning, since I last wrote home to you there has been considerable sickness in our regiment and a number of verry sudden deaths." Others, like Jonathan Allen, chose a straightforward, factual tone in reporting the string of deaths to his parents. The day before Gale wrote home, Allen remarked, "Deaths are occurring in the hospital almost daily and some days three or four."[41] The difference in tone between all of the men's letters tells us that soldiers' reactions to mortality varied widely.

Andrew McKenzie's death seems to have brought out a nasty side of Stephen Spalding, one born, I think, of vulnerability. Considered alongside the possibility that Spalding's men may have pressured him during the court-martial, we can see him sliding into a new and less certain world as 1862 slipped away. As the Eighth Vermont moved closer to combat, Spalding would face more responsibilities. How would he react to the stresses of adulthood? Would his previous experiences of privilege—his wealth, his masculinity, his race—help him or hurt him when he and his company finally went into battle?

7

SPALDING'S PREMONITION

For Eight long weary months we have been ready to offer up
our lives on the alters of liberty.
—Stephen Spalding

Lt. Stephen Spalding comes close to disappearing from the historical record for almost a year after he wrote to James Peck. He surfaces briefly to serve on a court-martial, but we know little else about him until June 1863. All we know is what his "Compiled Service Record" at the National Archives tells us: every two months Spalding showed up "present" and healthy to collect his pay. But this does not mean that he was idle. His unit participated in several campaigns in Louisiana and interacted with elements of Louisiana society. But of Spalding the individual we know little.

In June 1863, however, Spalding makes his largest appearance in George Carpenter's history of the Eighth Vermont. As part of Gen. Nathaniel Banks's Union force laying siege to Port Hudson, a fortified Louisiana town on the Mississippi River, Spalding engaged in the most serious combat in his regiment's history so far. Banks's army had already tried to storm the Confederate lines, only to be sharply repulsed on May 27. The opposing forces then settled in for two more weeks of siege warfare, after which Banks again issued orders to carry the Confederate defenses. Orders went out on June 13 for an attack the next day, and soldiers had the night to steel themselves for what was to come.

Stephen Spalding reenters the historical record at this moment. Carpenter's regimental history relates two snippets of conversations that Spalding had that night. "I shall be at the head of my regiment to-morrow," he tells one friend. Later, to his buddy Captain Barstow, he said, "I shall not spend another night with you."[1] What did he mean?

Carpenter speculates that it was "as if some premonition of fate had come to him."[2] Certainly other Civil War soldiers had such premonitions; they show up often in Civil War books. They always seem to turn out to be true. What do we make of this phenomenon: the accurate premonitions of death? Were they real? Did false premonitions of death happen but go unrecorded because they were too embarrassing to bring up? Or is there a nonsuperstitious way of explaining the odd episode of Spalding accurately predicting his own demise?

In Spalding's case, one never gets the sense that he would have believed in mystical foreshadowings of his own death. Religion plays no apparent role in his letter, and his one recorded entrance into a church was to abuse black congregants at worship. Spalding also has been seen mocking spiritualism, another repudiation of the idea that people could blur the boundary between life and death. So did Spalding just have an attack of superstition? We cannot know, but my guess is that other matters explain his extraordinary announcements.

I think we can also rule out the idea that Stephen Spalding regarded the pending assault as likely to be a general massacre of the Eighth Vermont. It is possible, of course, that he thought this. The general assault on May 27 had gone very badly, costing the Union forces almost two thousand casualties while inflicting fewer than three hundred killed and wounded among the rebel garrison.[3] Losses in the Eighth Vermont had been relatively high on that day, but the percentage of soldiers killed in the Eighth Vermont and the rest of the Union army had been pretty low compared to casualty rates suffered by other units at other battles. In addition, the land between the Union lines and the Confederate trenches, which featured deep ravines, thickets, and fallen timber, afforded Union troops places to hide and wait out the rebel hailstorm until nightfall allowed for a retreat to the relative safety of Union trenches. Looking at the overall situation, then, Spalding would not logically have assumed that he and everyone else in his command was *likely* to be killed on the following day, especially if he chose to utilize the ample cover afforded by the topography and vegetation.

Indeed, most soldiers in the Eighth Vermont seem to have taken advantage of these hiding places during the assault on June 14, 1863. The regiment made its attack at dawn, but it did not press it with vigor.

After seeing the failures of May 27, soldiers may have thought that making only a reasonably good show of valor was the wisest course of action. A hard-pressed attack with displays of heroism would probably have produced only a much longer Union casualty list. So most Union troops that day seem not to have made the kind of suicidal dash at rebel lines that would have rendered a statement like Spalding's necessary. This was not Cold Harbor, Virginia, in 1864, where U. S. Grant's attacking soldiers pinned paper with their names on the back of their uniforms to help comrades later identify what seemed almost surely to be their corpse.

The most reasonable way to think about Spalding's premonition is to put together his two different conversations in the early morning of June 14. Spalding predicted his early death not out of superstition but from his plan to place himself "at the head of my regiment to-morrow."[4] Spalding, then, did not envision his role as just being part of the crowd; he did not plan to go forward a bit before finding a safe haven in a convenient hollow or behind a fallen tree. He planned, instead, to take the lead, to be reckless and daring. He planned to risk his life, I think, to an extent that made his survival—or at least his survival intact—unlikely. His prediction to Captain Barstow, after all, was not of his own death, as Carpenter suggests by calling it a "premonition," but only that he would not spend another night with Barstow. This would include the chance that he would be wounded severely enough to be sent home. This chapter examines why he planned to behave so recklessly.

What follows here is speculation about how a man like Stephen Spalding would have reacted to his life between the writing of his letter and the second attack on Port Hudson. There are two salient aspects of his life in that eleven-month span. First, Spalding almost certainly suffered from boredom. Even in July 1862, he had complained to Peck that "For Eight long weary months we have been ready to offer up our lives on the alters of liberty."[5] His "Eight long weary months" of inactivity then continued for almost another full year. While occasionally active, the U.S. Department of the Gulf offered few chances for action, and virtually no glory. Second, Spalding received no promotions. Other officers around him moved up the military ladder, but Spalding remained a first lieutenant. There was, however, the beginning of a chance for advancement when Spalding approached Port Hudson. What he did on June 14 might determine the future of this young man from Vermont.

Spalding was already itching for action in July 1862. "If the Vermont Eighth ever get into a fight—," he wrote with impatience, "they will be annihilated before they run." The next year must have tried his nerves. The war did not end; he did not even get to "wipe out all the various geurilla parties between here & the Texan Capital."[6] Instead, Spalding and Company B continued to miss just about every chance for combat that came along. To read the history of the Eighth Vermont is to see other companies, and other officers, get the lion's share of the action and praise. As we have seen, parts of the Eighth had skirmished with the enemy in late June, before Spalding's letter. Serving under the soon-to-be-everywhere Capt. Henry Dutton, Company H had fought at Raceland, and three companies had gone to their support: A, C, and I. Company B's exclusion from combat would continue. A foraging party in late August into St. Charles Parish was successful, but only Companies A and C took part.[7]

Early September 1862 brought more combat to the regiment but not to Spalding. On September 4, Confederate partisan rangers attacked an outpost at Boutte Station, Louisiana. The Confederates seem to have deployed a white flag dishonestly, but in any event they wreaked havoc on parts of the Eighth Vermont. They took the outpost, ambushed a trainload of troops sent to help the garrison, and forced Capt. Edward Hall to surrender 141 officers and men from Companies E, G, and K. Col. Stephen Thomas could only be thankful that a soldier had dashed ahead to throw a switch in the track, thus "thwarting the design of the enemy to run the train into the ditch."[8] Union attempts to capture the Confederates the next day literally ran into trouble when a train bearing Thomas's men struck an ox on the track and derailed. Alonzo Silver from Company A was killed, and some other members of his company were wounded. Throughout this series of "disasters," Company B was absent.[9] Thomas also did not include it among the three companies dispatched later in September to break up a Confederate force at Thibodeaux.[10]

Captain Hall's surrender of three companies at Des Allemands led to one of the more gruesome events of the war in Louisiana. Seven of

Hall's men had enlisted in New Orleans earlier that summer, and they had served in the Confederate military before deserting to the Union cause. That they were not alone in doing so made the Confederate authorities all the more eager to make an example of them. Unfortunately for the seven men, the Confederates learned of their identity soon after their capture. The men were immediately forced to dig their own graves, and the Confederates shot the prisoners to death. Later, Confederate authorities executed three more men from the Eighth Vermont captured at Des Allemands when their identity was ascertained.[11] We do not know how Spalding reacted to these shootings, but Union writers throughout the Department of the Gulf expressed outrage. Homer Sprague, a Connecticut Volunteer, asked: "Will not the great republic some day rear a monument to mark the last resting place of the seven martyrs who died for her at Bayou des Allemands in the summer of '62?"[12] If Spalding felt any of the indignation expressed by his colleagues, he would have had all the more reason to be aggrieved at being left out of the fighting as the fall of 1862 continued. If he longed for revenge, he would have to wait still longer.

Any feelings of isolation from the war's main events would have continued for Spalding during the rest of 1862. In late October, General Godfrey Weitzel took most of his brigade on an expedition toward Labadieville in hopes of clashing with local Confederate forces. His force captured some 250 prisoners and won acclaim. But Weitzel had left the Eighth Vermont behind. Instead, he had sent the Vermonters with a regiment of black troops toward Brashear City, west of Algiers. They faced Confederate resistance at Bayou des Allemands near the start of the march, and Colonel Thomas deployed his men in line of battle, threw out skirmishers, and made a patriotic speech to prepare his men for a fight. Everyone took Thomas's speech as proof that battle was imminent, but it was not. The enemy soon fled, leaving behind only charred property.

Instead of battle, Thomas's two regiments spent the next six weeks rebuilding the Opelousas and Great Western Railroad all the way to Brashear City. It was, as the regimental historian put it, "manual labor." "The men had to straighten and spike down rails, cut timber in the woods for sleepers to replace those that were missing, remove trees and other obstructions which had been put upon the track, and, for a change, pull up grass" that had grown up over the track. They also spent five days building a bridge across Bayou Boeuf, a span of 675 feet. A second bridge went up that was 475 feet long. They finally reached Brashear City on December 8. Could Spalding possibly have enjoyed this, especially with the added indignation he would have felt at working alongside a black regiment?[13]

The new year brought with it Spalding's first time under fire. We must pause here and remember that this combat occurred about *twenty months* after Spalding first enlisted in the Seventh New York State Militia. For almost two years, Spalding had read about the war, talked with combat veterans, and received the attentions paid to men going off to war, but he had not actually participated in a fight. If what we have read about the anxiety of Civil War soldiers preceding their first combat experience is true—one thinks about Henry Fleming in *The Red Badge of Courage* just for starters—then Spalding had been going through an underlying anxiety about his own bravery for an amazingly long time. Given his state of mind in the summer of 1862, when he complained about the "Eight long weary months" he had gone without a battle, he probably entered 1863 itching for a fight.

And now that fight was imminent. And, again, it would prove to be anticlimactic. His regiment, along with the rest of Weitzel's brigade, moved north from Brashear City in an effort to chase the Confederate gunboat *J. A. Cotton* so far up the Bayou Teche that it would have to be destroyed by its crew to prevent its capture. General Weitzel's force encountered the enemy, and he later reported that the Eighth Vermont performed well in its "first time in action as a regiment."[14] The regiment's success serves as a backdrop for Spalding's experiences that day, a day in which he watched other officers get the chance to distinguish themselves while he languished in the second tier. After a brief skirmish on January 13 that may have been Spalding's first time under fire, Weitzel's brigade and an accompanying Union fleet came up against the *J. A. Cotton,* supported on both sides of the river by Confederate infantry. With the rest of the Union brigade deployed on the west bank of the river, the Eighth Vermont deployed on the eastern side to clear rebel infantry out of rifle pits. The situation had marks of urgency all around it, because the Confederate troops were firing effectively on Union ships that had moved ahead faster than the infantry could march in their support.

Needing a crisply efficient officer to command a picked force of sixty men to move ahead as sharpshooters, Colonel Thomas chose Capt. Henry Dutton of Company H. When Colonel Thomas needed a messenger to run to the fleet in its hour of greatest peril, he chose Adjt. John L. Barstow. Acting on his own initiative, Barstow later found Lt. Moses McFarland and Company A nearing the Confederate positions and gave the warning. The regimental history picks up the story: "The moment had come for a brilliant dash; with the brave McFarland on the right and the gallant Dutton on the left, the entire regiment swooped down on the surprised riflemen, and literally wiped them out in an instant." Confederate losses were seven killed, twenty-seven wounded, and fifty-seven captured. The Eighth Vermont suffered no casualties.[15]

The rest of the day brought no more fighting, but the Eighth remained on alert and in the presence of enemy troops. Dutton's Company H and Capt. Luman Grout's Company A again went to the front, with Adjutant Barstow carrying vital orders. After the Confederates finally withdrew, praise for the regiment's officers followed hard on the heels of the Eighth's victory. George Carpenter's history makes the issue of who should get credit explicit: "Where so much was due to individual courage and prudence, it would be difficult to decide who of Col. Thomas's officers and men were most deserving of credit." But then Carpenter makes his selections, and the task does not seem difficult at all given what he had written so far: "Nothing could exceed the spirited dash of Capt. Dutton and his picked sixty, or Lieut. McFarland and his thirty-five." Then a Sergeant Howard (of Dutton's Company H), a courier between the fleet and the Vermonters, is seen as "equally brave." Adjutant Barstow receives special mention, since "his care for the men will be gratefully remembered by every survivor of the regiment." Only then does a second group of officers receive distinction, including two captains and Lieutenant Spalding, who was "also very efficient."[16] Being "efficient" is a virtue, and that is not Carpenter damning with faint praise. But one suspects that Spalding would have much preferred to have been listed with the "brave" and "gallant," especially when his brigade commander praised only Thomas, Dutton, McFarland, Barstow, and Grout in his report.[17]

Stephen Spalding's road to Port Hudson, where he was to have his premonition, then led him north past the burnt hulk of the *J. A. Cotton*.

But the march brought him only small skirmishes with no honors. If anything, Spalding's status in the regimental hierarchy suffered a serious blow on February 20, 1863. On that day, Spalding apparently "turned over co. to Capt. Childs [*sic*]," the man who had left Company B to become provost marshal of Algiers in the spring of 1862.[18] Capt. Charles Child's return meant that Spalding now served again as a first lieutenant in function as well as in rank. Serving at the lower rank lessened his ability to distinguish himself and placed another barrier between him and advancement.

In April 1863, the Eighth Vermont's path continued north toward Alexandria, Louisiana. Along the way, the Vermonters and much of the Army of the Gulf entered into four days of skirmishing with Confederate forces around Bisland. On April 11, Captain Dutton and Company H (again) started the fighting when they were deployed as skirmishers. The next day, Company K and Captain Barstow (again), who had been promoted to command of Company K, had a "sharp encounter with the enemy." By 3:00 p.m., the whole regiment was under artillery fire.[19] On April 13, Spalding and the Eighth spent the whole day lying on the ground under artillery fire but did not receive orders to close with the enemy. After two days of being under fire, the Vermonters had suffered a single fatality and two men wounded. None was in Spalding's company.[20] By the fourth day of combat at Bisland, the rebels were in retreat, and Colonel Thomas trusted Captain Dutton and Company H (again) to deploy in the regiment's front as they "pursued the flying [Confederate] army."[21] Company H was so used to taking the fore that one of its privates wrote home that "when we started[,] our Co., as usual. Was thrown out as skirmishers."[22] Historian Donald Frazier writes that "the speed and success of the federal invasion had blindsided the Confederates."[23] By May 6, the Union force had captured Alexandria, and Nathaniel Banks decided to follow up his advantage by striking eastward at Port Hudson on the Mississippi River.

The Union success was good news, of course, but Spalding's own role in the triumphant campaign may well have disappointed him. Colonel Thomas had not entrusted him with critical tasks. Nor was Spalding part of the regimental brain trust that sat down to write letters of condolence to the families of Capts. Samuel Craig and J. S. Clark, both of whom had died of disease. The authors of these letters, who added a series of resolutions of sorrow, included five officers whose names are mostly familiar by now: Capts. Edward Hall, Henry Dutton, and John Barstow; and Lts. George Carpenter and J. B. Mead.[24] The small world of the Eighth Vermont's officers seems to have included a clique who held disproportionate power and responsibility. This can be seen most plainly after the fighting at Port Hudson, when officers from Henry Dutton's Company H won promotion at an astonishing pace. Not only did Dutton and Alvin Franklin, original officers in the company, each rise to the rank of lieutenant colonel of the regiment, but four of the company's original NCOs went on to become officers in *other* companies, especially Companies C and F. (This group of officers also went on to dominate the regiment's postwar veterans association.) There is a chance, of course, that Dutton and his company earned the distinctions they received; even a Massachusetts soldier wrote to his newspaper after a battle that "Dutton pushed boldly ahead and the enemy retired. The Captain did so well all day, often under very gallant fire, that he needs especial praise."[25]

What is perhaps most amazing is that even the officers *within* the clique grumbled about the pace of promotion. John L. Barstow, an ambitious man who rose to be governor of Vermont, complained to his father in December 1862 that the Eighth was operating independently of its brigade. This meant that "we have been apart from the *direct* observance of a general, which has been very unfortunate for the other officers, who perhaps in other circumstances might have attracted attention + received merited promotion." Barstow followed this statement with *seven* lines of prose that were very heavily blacked out, only to conclude, not quite plausibly, that "I am perfectly satisfied as I am." Like the men in the Seventh New York State Militia, the officers of the Eighth Vermont regarded promotion as a serious matter that brought with it higher pay, more honor, and the promise of future success.[26]

Lieutenant Spalding failed to crack the inner circle and secure the recognition that he wanted, and perhaps needed. Whatever his fellow officers may have thought about his pranks and his July Fourth debauchery, his own command worked against him in Alexandria. The regiment stayed there for about a week, and during this rest period a man in his company killed a wagoner by the name of Jason H. Hill. The murderer was Pvt. John O'Mere, who had been found guilty by Spalding and the others the previous summer for "getting drunk on duty." Spalding had gotten him off that time with a fine of only one month's pay. What happened to him after he murdered Jason Hill is unknown. People told different stories about O'Mere. Some people said that he took flight and was never found; at least one officer reported that he was confined as a lunatic. All agreed to blame the attack on "temporary insanity," but this incident may have sparked negative gossip about Company B.[27] It was with this dark event hanging over his unit that Spalding began his march to Port Hudson.

But a small window seemed to be opening up for Stephen Spalding, though the records are vague as to the extent of his opportunity and even when it might have occurred. Given the vagaries of the evidence, it is best to start at the beginning of his possible advancement. On March 20, 1863, Capt. John Clark of Company K died of disease at the Hotel Dieu in New Orleans. At some point, Adjt. John Barstow, who had distinguished himself repeatedly, was appointed captain and given Clark's command. Regimental records date his promotion to the day after Clark's death, but that is probably a postdated event.[28] Whatever the exact date of Barstow's promotion, Spalding gained Barstow's old job as the adjutant of the Eighth Vermont. But he held it only temporarily, since he was listed as the "Acting Adjt." on his service return at the end of April 1863.[29] Though he was only filling in, Spalding probably saw this as his chance to move into the unit's command staff. As a role model, he could look to John Barstow, who had parleyed the position into recognition in battlefield reports and promotion to captain. Better still, when the brigade adjutant was killed at Port Hudson in late May, Colonel Thomas (who now headed the brigade) named Barstow the acting adjutant of the brigade, certainly a step up.

Why Spalding received this temporary appointment is not clear. Perhaps Colonel Thomas felt that Company B could spare Spalding's services now that Captain Clark had returned from his detached duty in Algiers. But a second factor may have influenced the colonel as well. Spalding may have been Barstow's friend and protégé. As we have seen, Spalding followed Barstow into the adjutant job. Barstow had been Spalding's accomplice when the two fell off their horses in the unfortunate prank described in chapter 1. Also, it was Barstow to whom Spalding made his dire statement on the night before the second charge at

Port Hudson. If he was to predict his own courageous end, why not make it to an officer who was his friend and who had helped to secure his recent acting appointment? Spalding's statements, in fact, may have been less a premonition than a declaration that he was going to try to earn his way into the regiment's hierarchy through bravery on the next day, regardless of the consequences. If that is what Spalding meant, then he foreshadowed a Confederate officer, Abner Perrin, who declared shortly before his 1864 death, "I shall come out of this fight a live major general or a dead brigadier general." More famously, Theodore Roosevelt made a similar statement prior to landing in Cuba during the Spanish-American War. While still on board ship, Roosevelt and his officers drank the following toast: "May we be killed, wounded, or promoted."[30]

But first, Spalding and the rest of the Eighth Vermont had to endure over two weeks of what became known as the siege of Port Hudson. A town of about two hundred people before the war, Port Hudson had assumed strategic importance as one of the two Confederate posts remaining on the Mississippi—the other being the much more famous Vicksburg, located upstream. General Banks moved two forces to converge on Port Hudson late in May 1863. Spalding was with the northern wing moving from Alexandria via Simmesport, while another Union column approached from Baton Rouge to the south. The Confederates under Maj. Gen. Franklin Gardner had a chance to escape before Banks's pincers enclosed his garrison, but he remained in Port Hudson, intent on holding the town and its eighty-foot-high bluffs along the river. His heavy artillery, placed on this commanding site, had stopped nearly all Union ships from ascending the river toward Vicksburg and the important west-east supply route tying the Trans-Mississippi Department to the remainder of the Confederacy.[31] As such, Port Hudson represented a rich prize, and for Spalding it promised a bigger fight than anything he had seen so far.

Spalding did not have to wait long. He reached Simmesport on May 24 and probably spent the next two days listening to advance units of the army skirmishing with Confederates on the road to Port Hudson. By nightfall on May 26, Banks had Port Hudson surrounded, and orders went out for an attack on the Confederate entrenchments the next day. Historians agree that the May 27 assault failed miserably, gaining little ground, inflicting few casualties on the Confederates and resulting in high losses for the Union army. Much of the blame has fallen on Banks for the severe reverse, since he failed to coordinate the attacks, allowing the Confederates to shift troops to meet each assault in turn.[32] But historians do not agree about everything, and one controversy relates directly to the story of Stephen Spalding. At issue is just how hard the Eighth Vermont fought on May 27.

Did the Eighth Vermont attack that day with determination and courage, or was it lackluster in pressing its assault? The answer matters because how the regiment was perceived among the army's officers and men could have influenced how Spalding approached the next attack on June 14. If men in and out of the Eighth Vermont faulted the regiment for how it behaved on May 27, then Spalding may have felt compelled to inspire a fiercer attack two and a half weeks later. On the other hand, a courageous but failed attack on the 27th may have convinced Spalding and his men that no amount of reckless bravery would be sufficient for the task at hand, and thus he kept the men close to the ground and safety.

George Carpenter's regimental history predictably says that the Eighth Vermont acted heroically in the May attack. The regiment lined up on the north side of Port Hudson in Godfrey Weitzel's division, in a brigade temporarily commanded by their former colonel, Stephen Thomas. Laying the groundwork for his unit's inability to win the day, Carpenter introduces the Confederate position as having "a series of works of remarkable strength. . . . Every adjacent hill was a redoubt."[33] Photographs held at the National Archives in Washington show extensive Confederate fortifications and thus seem to back up this claim, though the rebels had almost six additional weeks between the initial attack on May 27 and their surrender on July 9 to strengthen the fortifications before the pictures were taken. Almost certainly, the entrenchments that Spalding and his men encountered in late May were not as formidable as those in the photographs. Whatever the strength of the enemy's line, Carpenter describes the day's action as almost a victory.

Deployed in Weitzel's third line of attackers, the Eighth watched as the first Union soldiers went into combat against a rebel line holding an advance position on the north bank of Little Sandy Creek. The

Union soldiers progressed slowly, and Thomas's brigade eventually went forward to strengthen the attack. As Carpenter tells the story, the arrival of the Eighth Vermont sparked a successful advance that drove the Confederates across Little Sandy Creek and into their main line of entrenchments at Commissary Hill: "In a few moments [after receiving the order to charge] they passed the broken lines of the other brigades, fell upon the enemy with a rush, drove them from their position, captured many of them, and hurried the rest from point to point, until they were sent back in disorder behind their main fortifications."[34] So far so good.

But the Eighth Vermont soon faltered. Carpenter notes that Colonel Thomas "halted his line after his brilliant sally," the end of which found them "within fifty or seventy-five yards of the main earthworks, and exposed to a murderous fire which the Confederates instantly opened upon them. To remain there or attempt to scale the works was wholesale butchery, and, not having orders to thus sacrifice his men, Thomas fell back to the cover of a ravine, and reported to Gen. Weitzel what he had done." For his part, Weitzel seems to have been satisfied with the Vermonters' accomplishments, and he apparently told Thomas to "hold his position if possible."[35] Carpenter claims that Weitzel's division could have carried the day if the Union command had coordinated its attack with assaults by troops from the center and southern wings of the army.[36] Summing up the day, Carpenter writes that "nothing can detract from the credit due Col. Thomas and his gallant brigade on that eventful day; and let it be recorded that they took up and sustained the charge at a critical moment, led by the colonel in front of his troops." John Winter's history of Civil War Louisiana agrees, noting that Weitzel's command engaged in "furious fighting" and that it meet "a withering fusillade" that caused "fearsome loss" among the attackers.[37] Presented in this light, Spalding and his comrades would have had nothing to be embarrassed about over the next few weeks.

Letters written at the time by members of the Eighth Vermont agree with this positive assessment of their unit's performance. Only two days after the fight, Justus Gale wrote that "we drove them through a piece of woods over two hills" and then held their advanced ground for two days. Jonathan Allen likewise said that he had seen a "hard fight. We charged on them and drove them from their first works back to their main fortifications. We could drive them no farther and so were placed in position in the most advantagous places." The two correspondents estimated the regiment's losses—killed and wounded—at between fifty and sixty men, a total that Allen found "pretty severe." He speculated that this was about one in every eight men who had gone into the battle.[38] From the officers down to the men in the ranks, the Eighth Vermont seems to have felt that it acquitted itself well during its toughest fight of the war so far.

But not everyone agrees with the valorous portrayal handed down to us by Carpenter and the others, and perhaps with good reason. The fullest history of the May 27 attack is by Lawrence Lee Hewitt, and he concludes that the Eighth Vermont and many of the other Union infantrymen who struck Port Hudson's northern flank had little reason to boast about their conduct. Hewitt places Thomas's brigade in the second wave of the attack, immediately behind Jacob Van Zandt's brigade. He notes that Van Zandt's men were "exhausted and widely dispersed" by the time they cleared the first rebel line out of the woods north of Little Sandy Creek.[39] Thomas's brigade then pushed through Van Zandt's men, but here the story diverges from the narrative offered in Carpenter's history. In Hewitt's less flattering version of the attack, topography conspired against the Vermonters. Dense woods, ridges, ravines, and gullies made it hard for officers to keep troops together and under effective control. The Eighth Vermont also experienced its first heavy fighting during this assault. So perhaps it is not surprising that Thomas's brigade was not as successful or as resolute as it might have been. Hewitt remarks that even while still north of the Little Sandy, the Union soldiers had already lost "any sense of organization above the regimental level" and that "scores of blue-clad infantrymen, confused and separated from their officers, advanced no further."[40] Hewitt acknowledges that diverse companies of several regiments pressed the attack across the Little Sandy and approached the Confederate entrenchments, but he concludes that Weitzel's assault lacked vigor.

Hewitt bases his conclusion mostly on unit casualty reports and on the failure of the numerically superior Union forces to take the Confederate trenches. Assessing Weitzel's attack, and also that of Paine's and Grover's divisions on Weitzel's immediate left, Hewitt concludes that "their failure to breach the Confederate defenses, coupled with a loss of only 8 percent of the attacking force, strongly indicates that the Federals . . . clearly lacked the determination needed to achieve victory."[41] Not all Union units were equally guilty, however, and Hewitt praises the Fourth Wisconsin, Eighth New Hampshire, and First and Third Native Guards (regiments made up of black Louisianans) for their bravery.[42] But Hewitt criticizes the rest of the Union infantry (including the Eighth Vermont) for their "widespread shirking." He concludes that "with few exceptions, Union losses indicate that the remaining twelve [regiments engaged] made no serious effort to breach the Confederate defenses. Out of more than eight thousand blue-clad infantrymen, fewer than seven hundred were killed or wounded. One-fourth of these casualties occurred in the 8th New Hampshire and the 4th Wisconsin."[43] The broken, wooded terrain gave "the more faint-hearted soldiers" places to hide from both Confederate fire and their own officers.[44] The Confederate hospital records for Port Hudson suggest that only one regiment anywhere on the Union line, the 165th New York, had wounded men fall so close to enemy lines that they became prisoners of war.[45]

Hewitt does not perform a casualty analysis of the Eighth Vermont for the assault, perhaps because it is hard to find the numbers necessary for such an analysis. Carpenter's regimental history puts the unit's losses on May 27 at eighty-eight men killed and wounded. But the truth is that statements about the regiment's casualty list vary widely. Lieutenant Colonel Dillingham's report lists only fifty-four casualties. Private Allen, however, stated that about one in every eight soldiers present was killed or wounded during the attack, probably making for a higher total.[46]

Figuring out what percentage of the regiment was killed or wounded during the assault is even more difficult because there is no reliable way to know how many men were in the regiment's ranks that day. Historian Edward Cunningham states that the Eighth Vermont went into action at Port Hudson with 940 officers and men.[47] While this figure could be right, especially given its few battle casualties and success in recruiting Louisianans, that number probably represents only its paper strength rather than being an accurate reflection of the number of men present for duty. The Eighth Vermont had just endured a strenuous march across hundreds of miles of Louisiana countryside. The regiment's newspaper (still located near the coast) reported in mid-May that "there are about 100 convalescent sick boys of the 8th Vt Reg't now in camp at this place. Others are in Hospital on the Island."[48] Vermonter Justus Gale estimated that the regiment went into the later fight on June 14, 1863, with only "some over 300 men." Jonathan Allen thought that the unit had lost 160 men during the entire campaign for Port Hudson, "about a third of our number."[49] Allen's numbers mean that they had started the siege with about 480 men. Depending on which numbers we pick, the Eighth Vermont during this first assault might have lost anywhere from 54 of 940 men up to 88 soldiers out of a bit more than 300. For our purposes, we might note that Spalding's Company B, which he very likely fought alongside as the regiment's acting adjutant, suffered no battlefield deaths that day.

It is hard, then, to know how Spalding might have felt about his performance on May 27. The men seem to have thought well of themselves, at least that was what they expressed publicly and in their correspondence home. Neither does the larger military record offer criticisms of their actions on that day. But if Hewitt is right, and men did find ways to drop out of the battle quickly, might they have experienced lingering doubts about their own conduct? Did Spalding wonder if he had been inspirational enough, especially given his company's small contribution to the regiment's casualty list?

The next two and a half weeks of Spalding's life—his last two and a half weeks—passed by in a grueling stretch of trench warfare. Stuck in the trenches for weeks during intense heat, just as he had been stuck at lieutenant rank for a year and a half, Spalding may have wanted to prove himself worthy of a promotion by the time orders came down for an assault to begin at dawn on June 14. Spalding greeted the orders by predicting that he would lead his regiment and not share another meal with them. He was right on both counts.

The attack on June 14 failed as completely as the one on May 27. Gen. Nathaniel Banks's official report puts the best face possible on the fresh slaughter of his troops, noting that none of the attacks "was successful in fully gaining its object, but our lines were advanced from a distance of 300 yards to distances of from 50 to 200 yards from the enemy's fortifications, where the troops intrenched themselves and commenced construction of new batteries."[50] But the day was a disaster for Union soldiers, who suffered severely while inflicting few casualties on their enemies.[51] For their part, the Eighth Vermont repeated their performance during the May attack. Again positioned in the second wave, they pushed forward when the first wave faltered in front of the main Confederate works. George Carpenter writes that the men of the first Union wave "all seemed about to be driven back in hopeless confusion" when the Eighth Vermont moved forward to save the situation.[52]

And this is when Lt. Stephen Spalding died. Carpenter gives Spalding a brave death: "With difficulty the lines moved over and passed the men with cotton-bags [in the first wave], who stood huddled together, a ready mark for the enemy's guns. 'Forward, Eighth Vermont!' shouted Adjt. Spalding from the head of the column; and fell dead." His heroic example, Carpenter says, inspired the men. "The men obeyed," he writes, "and instantly the line was in motion."[53] This was as good a death as a Civil War officer could hope for. Historian Frances M. Clarke's study of Civil War attitudes toward death, pain, and mutilation has found that people valued deaths that transformed those who had been killed into "heroic martyrs." Such men did more than die bravely; they fell conspicuously, and their deaths moved other men to acts of courage. Their deaths could even improve other men's characters. More broadly, their deaths inspired the nation as a whole to perform noble deeds.[54] By dying at the head of his men and by moving the attack forward, Spalding died purposefully and bravely.

Accounts written by or for Vermont newspapers in the aftermath of Stephen Spalding's death celebrate his battlefield performance. That they make a few unexpected comments about his life indicates that their words, which were at least partially obituaries, were not entirely formulaic tropes of mourning. An early editorial notice of his death, based only on a telegraph that gave "no details," expressed confidence that Spalding had died "in the faithful discharge of his duty." Once details of his death were known, there was agreement that he had been "shot through the head," with one report adding that he had been hit "by a Minie ball while in the act of discharging a musket he had borrowed from a soldier."[55] An anonymous officer from the Eighth Vermont assured readers that Spalding had "met his death as a brave man would wish, while in front of his command."[56]

For the writers who commented on Spalding right after his death, his life was a commendable model for others to follow. But their accounts stress different aspects of Spalding's character, and they convey an honesty in their depictions of the young man that more polished or impersonal accounts might not carry. The first of these accounts, written by a Montpelier editor, mourned Spalding's death as that of a "Montpelier boy" because his "father, mother, and god-father" had all been born in the capital city. He wrote that Spalding "was a good officer, attached to the service, ambitious of distinction, and anxious to make arms his profession by entering the regular army." This is the only hint anywhere that Spalding wanted to become a professional soldier, and it is written by someone who probably did not know him well, but his description of Spalding as "ambitious of distinction" sounds right. A later journalist summarized the young man's life in familiar ways. He recorded Spalding's career as a law student in New York City and noted that he had "promptly enlisted in the battery of the 7th New York regiment." This account, with its statement of Spalding's "prompt" enlistment in the Seventh New York, suggests that the story of his joining up right after Fort Sumter had gained currency before his death, most likely based on Spalding's own accounts. It is notably accurate in placing Spalding in the artillery battery of the Seventh New York, a part of the regiment not everyone would have known about or remembered. Interestingly, the editor, like others before him, believed that Spalding's time with the New Yorkers was spent "acquiring a high degree of proficiency in the practical duties of a soldier."[57] One can almost hear Spalding telling people in Montpelier and Derby Line about his "proficiency" during the whole summer of 1861.

But perhaps the most candid comment slipped into a eulogistic letter written about Spalding by his anonymous brother officer from the Eighth Vermont. Much of this letter reads like a set of well-rehearsed military clichés: "As a military man, he had but few superiors. His career was a successful one." The officer continued, generically: "He had the fullest confidence of his superior officers and the admiration of his subordinates." Near the end, the writer reaches for a nice-sounding but vague platitude: "He was as brave an officer as he was a courteous gentleman." But the anonymous writer buried in the middle of these drab sentences a single detail that is, perhaps, authentic. It is certainly an odd detail to highlight in an otherwise vague letter: "As a disciplinarian he stood among the first."[58] Here, perhaps, is a hint that Spalding's sense of privilege, so evident when he interacted with women and freedmen, extended into his interactions with men beneath him in social status. Perhaps he brought so many men up on charges before the court-martial because he enjoyed, at some level, all the "talking and punishing."

It is unfortunate to have to qualify the stories of Stephen Spalding's purposeful death. But we must ask whether the deaths of even some of the best of soldiers serve any purpose at all. In Spalding's case, we have to wonder whether seeing him die so well at the front of his command inspired any of his fellow soldiers to press their attack with additional determination. During this attack on Port Hudson, seven Union regiments pressed far enough toward the Confederate entrenchments that some of their wounded fell into rebel hands over the next few days; Spalding's inspirational conduct aside, no one from the Eighth Vermont got that close.[59] Testimony from within Spalding's Company B offers little evidence that Spalding's death inspired men to attack with greater fury than they had two weeks before. Pvt. Edward Belville of Spalding's company wrote home that "Our Co. lost Lieut. Spaulding who was killed instantly in the fore part of the day."[60] One cannot help but notice that Belville writes nothing else about Spalding's death, and little about the rest of the attack. Nor does he mourn Spalding's death in any way. Maybe Spalding's love of discipline, noted by the anonymous officer after Spalding's death, explains Belville's brief, noncommittal notice.

The list of killed and wounded from Spalding's Company B sheds only faint light on whether Spalding's bravery added determination to the attack. Company B lost three men killed and nineteen wounded, significantly more than the nine wounded they had suffered in the May assault. But Belville admitted that of the nineteen wounded, "only three or four" were wounded "very badly," and that six of the wounded, including himself, were back in the ranks two days later. A similar review of Company B's losses on June 14, written by its captain, lists four killed, twenty wounded, and one missing from a total of forty men. This is a very much higher total percentage of losses, even if Captain Child also conceded that the men's wounds were "mostly slight in arm, foot and head." Child added that the regiment lost 107 men out of 350.

Jonathan Allen, by contrast, noted regimental losses at 85 men and said it was only that high because the enemy had used buckshot against them. The extent of buckshot wounds, he said, meant that many of the men on the casualty list had been wounded only "slightly."[61] So the effect of Spalding's possibly very brave death must remain in doubt.

If Carpenter is telling the truth about Spalding's last moments, we can also say that the young Vermonter was spared from the horrible miseries that so many Union soldiers had to endure on June 14. Spalding and the rest of his command moved forward at about 7:00 a.m., and almost all of the fighting in his part of the battlefield ended by noon at the latest. But the suffering of wounded men did not end at that hour. The summer sun baked the wounded as they lay between the lines, and no Union officer called for a cease-fire to care for the fallen. Wounded men endured terrible conditions, with Confederates sniping at anyone who sought to relieve their suffering and Union troops returning a steady fire on Confederate lines. Gen. Halbert Paine of Wisconsin, who fell wounded between the lines that day, later wrote that the "fourteenth of June was a long day for us. It seemed an age. The experience of the survivors lying on an open field in the burning sun, tortured with pain and thirst, waiting and hoping for rescue was that of hundreds of others who did not survive but gave their lives to their country on that bloody battlefield." Paine also had to endure the knowledge that two men died trying to rescue him. By the time men carried Paine from the field that night, doctors judged him too weak to endure the amputation that they knew he would have to undergo.[62] Spalding would have been lucky if he died as quickly as Carpenter says he did.

Having tried to give Spalding a brave death, Carpenter took considerable time to reassure his postwar readers that Spalding's corpse was looked after with care. He writes that Lt. F. E. Smith recovered Spalding's body and then sent it to New Orleans. All along the way, his body was accompanied by friends, the men who had served with him over the past year and a half. It was escorted to New Orleans by "George W. Fairfield, of Company F, who delivered it to Lieut. Butterfield." Carpenter's history bears Spalding's body out of Louisiana; it is dispatched from New Orleans, "sent to his friends" in Vermont to be buried. It is sardonically appropriate that the paragraph about his mortal remains concludes with this sentence, written by George N. Carpenter: "After

[Spalding's] death, Lieut. Geo. N. Carpenter became acting adjutant of the regiment."[63]

We can travel with Stephen Spalding's body to its final resting place in Derby Line. Several Vermont newspapers carried stories about the young man's death, and there is a lengthy report on his funeral. From these accounts, we learn that Spalding had been concerned that his mortal remains be returned to the Green Mountain State. One newspaper reported soon after his death that his body was being "sent to Vermont in compliance with his wishes, expressed the night before the battle, in case of his death."[64] Thus it would appear that Spalding made plans for his own death, whether or not he had had an actual premonition. But we might not read too much into Spalding's request early on June 14; he had earlier made a "mutual promise" with Company B's second lieutenant Frederick Butterfield that, "in case one should fall, the one left should take the body to Vermont." Since Lieutenant Butterfield seems to have remained on detached service with the Signal Corps, this agreement could not have been made during Spalding's final night.[65] As he had promised to do, Lieutenant Butterfield escorted his friend's body back to their hometown of Derby Line. When he did so, he was about twenty-four years old, a year older than Stephen Spalding had been.

It took Frederick Butterfield and his late friend's remains about two months to get back to northern Vermont. However delayed it was, Stephen Spalding's funeral shows us how many people cared about him and lamented his death. Four ministers performed the funeral service. The Newport Cornet Band traveled to Derby Line to play "at the Church and to and from the grave." His casket was placed into the grave by ten men. Then, according to the otherwise restrained account, "hundreds of mothers and sisters came forward with garlands and boquets to deposit their memorials of friendship and tokens of prowess in the soldier's grave."[66] The young Stephen's funeral must have involved virtually the entire town. The family's sadness can be seen from Reverend R. V. Hall's decision to skip over "all attempts at patriotic sermonizing," choosing instead to focus on "such remarks as he deemed most suitable for solacing the bereavement of the afflicted family."[67]

Spalding's burial in Derby Line halts this history. Judging by his remarks during the night before the battle, Spalding meant to expose himself at the head of his troops. It is possible, of course, that he just had a superstitious sense that his time was up. But Spalding's words, combined with his frustratingly uncertain place in his regiment's leadership circle, suggest that he intended to earn his superiors' notice during the coming battle. He may also have felt the need to shore up his reputation with the men in his command. These men (perhaps like his fellow officers) may not have been as impressed with the young lieutenant as he thought they should be. Stuck at the same rank that he had been given when the regiment was formed more than a year and a half earlier, Spalding had a chance to be made adjutant on a permanent basis if he played his cards right. The pending attack also opened up the chance to go home, wounded badly enough to resume his civilian career. The law certainly may have seemed more promising than marching around Louisiana, one of the war's true backwaters. Confronted with subordinates who disobeyed his orders and superiors who did not promote him, Spalding may have been seizing a chance to either earn respect or depart from the army as a wounded man and a hero. In a very small way, he did win hero status: in 1894 or 1895, the veterans in the Grand Army of the Republic in Derby Line named their post after him. Like so many others, however, they misspelled his name.[68]

But it is speculation to try to say what was on Stephen Spalding's mind during the night before the attack. What we do know is that he died on June 14, 1863. I cannot help but view his death as a tragedy, even if his political viewpoints are, to me, regrettable even when seen in the context of his times. At times his actions—his personal conduct—seem unthinking and unfortunate. But he was also young and smart, and it would be intriguing to see how he matured and reacted to the social and political changes of postwar America. I regret that he was not given the chance to write more. Spalding could have become a substantial writer. But then, he could have become so many different things, many of them valuable or wonderful. That the war robbed him of the chance to develop as a person—that it robbed him of his life— was a horrible crime, one committed all too often over the course of these four years and during all wars before and since.

CONCLUSION
Spalding and the Other Letters

Comfortable Homes are made desolate.

—Stephen Spalding

There is one more surprise in store for us. We have parts of two more letters written by Stephen Spalding. They come to us courtesy of a newspaper published by Stephen's cousin, C. C. Spalding, who started a paper in 1863 in Newport, Vermont, the next town over from Spalding's hometown of Derby Line. The name of the paper is further proof of how much Civil War Americans loved a joke; C. C. Spalding called his paper the *Newport News*, which is both a fine name for a paper and the name of a town in Virginia. Indeed, C. C. Spalding had marched through Newport News while serving in the Peninsula Campaign in 1862. (He had originally thought to name his paper the *Monitor*, presumably after the famous Union ironclad that had fought in the waters off Newport News.) Sadly, only two issues of the *Newport News* have survived, but one of them contains two full columns related to Stephen Spalding and his death in faraway Louisiana. The editor included excerpts from two of Spalding's letters to his family, one to his father and a shorter clipping from one to his sister. The contrast between Spalding's voice in his letter to his friend James Peck and how he wrote to his family could not be more jarring. Writing to his father and sister, he sounds stiff and serious, even stodgy. We will think about what to make of these letters soon, but first the passages C. C. Spalding lifted from Stephen's letter to his father, Levi. It was written, he notes, "a few weeks before his death":

> It is more than a year since I enlisted, and I must confess that this war has been protracted beyond all of my expectations. I little

thought when I left Derby that I should be gone a year; but it is even so, and the prospects are that two more years will hardly suffice to put down this rebellion. While I regret the loss of time, which is most precious to young men of my age, I am resolved to see an end to this war, and to give my life, if necessary, for my country. If I should be fortunate enough to escape and return home, it will be pleasant for me and my folks to know, that when the first alarm was sounded that the Union was in danger, I was among the first to volunteer; and when a second time a call was made for young men to come forward and sustain the "Stars and Stripes," I was among the first to step forward. No one in future years shall ever point his finger at me and say that I did not dare to go forth and fight for my country. No one shall say that I waited until a draft was threatened.—No one shall accuse me of enlisting because public feeling was so strong that I was obliged to go. Fort Sumter fell the 18th of April, and I was on my way to Washington to avenge the insult in less than 24 hours after. A great many of our officers have gone to the war with no intention of remaining any length of time. They resign and go home and people look upon them with adoration, and praise them for their courage and valor. I am going to remain until the company I came out with goes home, and redeem my promise that I made them when I left the Line. In the mean time, while we are fighting and suffering, God only knows what you at home can pay the taxes with, and you may think yourselves well off if you have anything worth paying taxes on. You can form no idea of the ravages made by an invading army. Comfortable homes are made desolate—the accumulations of years are destroyed, and the rich man made a beggar.

The editor followed this clipping with three brief passages from a letter to "a sister he loved most tenderly":

We suffer a good deal, and we expected to when we enlisted, but I would not accept an honorable discharge if it were offered to me to-day. I am happy and contented, and intend to stay until the war closes.

. . . I enlisted out of pure patriotism, and my conscience will not permit me to desert the cause at this trying hour. Out of 30 officers in our regiment who came out with us, but 11 of them remain.

. . . After the rebellion is suppressed, let the government call for troops to settle accounts with England, and every man in Weitzel's brigade will step forward.[1]

He sounds like a completely different person from the one who took up his pen to write to James Peck, his friend and former roommate. There are obvious contradictions between what Spalding professes in these letters and what he has written to Peck. Here, he speaks of "pure patriotism," while to his friend he sarcastically states that "were it not for the simple fact that we are "Patriots" and fighting in a "Glorious Cause" our courage I fear would give way." To his father, he lies about having joined up right after Fort Sumter. His claim that his regiment had lost nineteen of its thirty officers would appear to be an exaggeration (though we cannot be precise about this, because it is undated). How would his father like his jingoistic talk about invading Canada, where the family had extensive landholdings and business ties, especially in Stanstead? Would Peck have thought that his friend could seriously write that sentence?

More than just his insistent talk of patriotism, Spalding's selection of subjects for his familial letters seems to have changed almost entirely. He worries about his future reputation. He talks of his determination to serve out the war. He mourns the passing of time. Gone is his drinking, his napping, his fit of the blues. Of course, there are times when Spalding, even to Peck, boasts of the Eighth Vermont's valor and promises a good performance on the battlefield. But in his familial letters, service to his country is almost his only topic, one apparently so overwhelming that it drives out any talk of New Orleans, slavery, discipline, or promotions. Was he angling to have his letters used in public to lobby the politicians at home for promotion? Was he familiar with the advice manuals that told young men how to write letters to their parents, complete with stiff, formal examples that sound vaguely like the ones reprinted in the *Newport News*? Without more information, these questions must go unanswered.

Most of all, Spalding's sense of humor vanishes without a trace. Nothing in Spalding's letters to his family is funny. There is a point toward the end of his letter to his father which sounds a bit lively, but it turns only to depressing things. "God only knows what you at home can pay the taxes with," he writes, adding, "and you may think your-selves well off if you have anything worth paying taxes on." This could be a comically exaggerated critique of the Republicans and their high taxes, but instead it turns instantly sober. His warning about not being left with anything at all is not a joke about high tax rates, but a black comment about the destruction and chaos of war as he has seen it. This is a grim letter, closing with the horrors of impoverishment and beg-ging. Sincerity and sentiment have replaced sarcasm and cynicism.

What are we, as historians, to make of the differences between Spal-ding's letters? Is this the difference between Spalding in July 1862 and what he had become after an additional year of being at war? Had he become more serious, sober, and patriotic? Or can we explain his al-tered tone and topics in the fact that people often tell different things to different people? We cannot really know.

There is a temptation to try to decide which of these letters rep-resents the true, or authentic, Stephen Spalding. I suspect, though, that all of the letters contain some true element of Spalding's multifac-eted character. Spalding's letter to his friend is probably truer to what he thought most of the time—one chooses one's friends and writes to them accordingly. But that is not to say his letter to his father is some-how false. If nothing else, Spalding's familial letters demonstrate his fixation on what others think of him. That seems to have been a preoc-cupation of his.

The real question is not which letter reflects the true Spalding, but which one stands out in a sea of Civil War letters. Families and friends have tended to preserve the letters that sound like the ones Spalding wrote to his family. In time, those family letters were the ones deemed respectable and worthy of being given to libraries and historical soci-eties when the time came. Our history, our understanding of who fought the Civil War and how they thought about their experiences, has been tainted by the fact that letters about drinking and self-interest, let alone ones about fear or sexual misadventures, have tended to find their way into people's fireplaces. There is no way that I would have written a book about Spalding's familial letters; they tell us little that is new about soldiers even if they are genuine expressions of some of the things he thought. Spalding's letter to Peck, however, is different enough to warrant deep examination. By reading an especially candid letter, we can see into newer, more intimate parts of Civil War soldiers' lives.

Stephen Spalding did not leave us much in the way of documentation. Spalding's perspective, as that of a young lieutenant who was not destined to write his memoirs, is often left out of a historical record occupied mostly, even now, by accounts of generals and presidents. Professional historians are increasingly writing biographies of common people, even in the face of the substantial challenges caused by sparse evidence.[2] Such biographies are worth the dangers inherent in studying poorly documented subjects because they help to flesh out the history of a time period. Sometimes we study common people because their very averageness puts them in the mainstream of historical events and ideas, helping us to complete an imperfect understanding of their times. Other studies focus on groups of people who have been underrepresented in our histories, such as people of color, women of all races, and working-class people. History gains usefulness and complexity when these groups blend into, and then change, our national narratives.

Spalding, privileged as he was, does not fit into these parameters. He was not, perhaps, a very normal or average man. Nor was he a member of a disenfranchised group. Instead, he was one of the many white American men who looked down on those kinds of people. His life and his words nevertheless lead us into parts of nineteenth-century America that have been largely unexplored. Spalding was a well-educated young man, and his exuberant, expressive writing makes him a spokesman for viewpoints that tend to get excluded from Civil War studies. He wrote sarcasm, not sentiment. He joked when others were serious. He drank in the midst of sobering circumstances. He was a Democrat and a conservative in a time and place historians have peopled with Republicans and reformers. He angled for promotions in an army we have filled with idealists and patriots. He lied, I think, when we imagine that Americans told the truth, and by doing so he endangered others who did not know the extent of his military inexperience. He did not, I think, serve as a completely impartial judge on a court-martial panel, thereby helping some soldiers while harshly punishing others.

Does any of this necessarily make for a better and truer vision of the past than what we had before? Certainly Spalding serves as a kind of reality check for people who would have Civil War Americans be too pure, too simple, or too noble. Civil War America, too, had its share of dishonesty, striving, and loutishness.

But mostly, I think, examining Stephen Spalding reminds us of how many Americans, even from the very northern border of the North, understood the world in hierarchical terms. Not all Americans did, of course. Historians have recently found many abolitionists who sought to end racial inequality during Spalding's lifetime, as well as women's rights activists who campaigned for gender equality. But equality cannot be said to have always been an American ideal. For much of the American electorate, even in the North, which had rid itself of slavery (starting in Spalding's own Vermont), belief in inequality was often the order of the day.

Spalding's life and letter give us the rare opportunity to see inside the minds of people who enjoyed social, economic, and political privileges. Spalding's letter gives us a personal, unburnished look at how people at the top of the social pyramid talked about their world and their place in it among themselves. Mostly, Spalding simply made unquestioning assumptions about his superior status in society—and his superiority as a person. His place was so secure that he and Peck could make fun of the people they saw as their inferiors—without apparently giving it any thought at all. Blacks entered their life stories only to be cowed. Women existed to offer sexual release as prostitutes. To think too long about Stephen Spalding is to become convinced that equality is less of an American value than an American dream. To study Stephen Spalding is to know that anyone who values equality must fight for it, because the people at the top are not even thinking about their privileges. They just accept their superiority—their comforts and pleasures—as givens. The inferiority of others is only a laughing matter.

Spalding's and Peck's unthinking acceptance of their own privilege has serious repercussions, I think, for the study of egalitarian movements such as feminism and civil rights. We need to recognize that conservatives who opposed these campaigns did not seek to defend only their economic security or their way of life. Spalding did not oppose emancipation or spiritualism because they threatened his livelihood or family fortune. Spalding and Peck had internalized their superiority to such an extent that it became part of who they were: it made them laugh; it helped them make friends. Carpenter's history, with its subservient, apolitical Louisiana women and its murderous, dialect-ridden, looting African Americans, shows how little these men were able to change their ways of thought even in the 1880s. Change would not be easy, just as it is not today.

None of this is to say that Stephen Spalding should be thrown entirely in the dustbin of history. His wit and his ability to make Peck laugh and, yes, perhaps to get us laughing make him a writer with whom we can happily spend time. It was this quality, his talent with a pen, that first made me curious about his letter. But his humanity also fascinates. Spalding's thirst for promotion can make us think about other twenty-two-year-olds, then and now, and the awful mix of uncertainty and ambition that animates so many of them. His reaction to living among wartime death reminds us that the war brought men—and their families—into contact with their own mortality. For readers and writers of Civil War histories, the extent of Spalding's emotional discomfort in the face of deaths teaches that men in these armies faced extremely upsetting times. All historians of war can become inured to the long casualty lists that fill battle accounts, but this is all wrong. Getting to know Stephen Spalding offers us more than a window into hierarchical thinking; he offers us a complex person full of humanity, occasionally obnoxious but also often afraid, funny, and even self-deprecating. Everyone in Civil War America, North and South, was a complex individual, and earning that realization alone makes creating a plausible biography of a junior officer a worthy, even if hazardous, endeavor. This book is a starting point for such an attempt to understand Stephen Spalding. It is up to each of us, however, to come to an understanding of the young Vermont lieutenant, and to explore what his life tells us about the war and how we should see the United States of America, then and now.

ACKNOWLEDGMENTS

Many people have been of great help to me while I have been working on this book. This is true about every stage of the process, from research to writing to publication. It is a pleasure to be able to acknowledge their important contributions at this point.

During the research stage, I was helped by librarians at several institutions. Marjorie Strong at the Vermont Historical Society has a superb knowledge of the collections under her care, and I have benefited from several of her suggestions about where to look for further information. She also produced an initial transcript of Spalding's letter that has served as an important guide for me as I worked through the letter. While at the Special Collections Department at the Bailey/Howe Library of the University of Vermont, I received important help from Sylvia Bugbee and Jeffrey D. Marshall. I also would like to thank the staff of the New-York Historical Society Museum and Library for their help during my visit with the Seventh New York State Militia collection. Janet Bloom at the Clements Library of the University of Michigan also provided timely answers to my long-distance inquiries about their holdings.

Several scholars have read significant portions of the book manuscript. Their ideas have informed major interpretive points, and they made suggestions for further readings that have improved the book in ways large and small. Frank Towers and Andrew Slap read multiple drafts of what became the chapter about Spalding's masculinity, and they had very useful input each time; the breadth and depth of their learning is amazing. The editor, Lesley J. Gordon, and assistant editor, Kevin Adams, of *Civil War History* read drafts of what became the chapter on Spalding and race relations. It is good to be able to thank them for their support and hard work on that piece. Most important, they secured two great anonymous readers, one of whom made especially important interpretive leaps that I had not yet seen—and may never have without that prodding.

I would also like to thank *Civil War History* for granting me permission to reprint my 2015 article in their journal as chapter 3 of this book. Likewise, I appreciate the permission from the University of Chicago Press to reprint my essay for their anthology, Andrew L. Slap and Frank Towers, *Confederate Cities: The Urban South during the Civil War*, as chapter 4 here.

Joseph Lipchitz was my Department Chair at the University of Massachusetts, Lowell, during most of the years I was working on this book. In addition to fulfilling all of the regular duties of the Chair with expertise and apparent ease, he also provided humane leadership and support during an alarming period of my life. It is a great pleasure to thank him here for everything he has done. More recently, Lisa Edwards has stepped into the job of Department Chair, and she, too, has helped this project move ahead in many ways. I have enjoyed and benefited from talking with Professor Melissa Pennell about this project over the past few years. I would also like to thank Professor Mary Kramer for giving this manuscript one last reading before it went to press.

I have had the pleasure of talking about Stephen Spalding with several groups of students. Each time, students have asked new questions that pushed my thinking along new paths. I'd especially like to thank Tim Houlihan, Provost of St. Francis College, for inviting me to speak to the Francis J. Greene Honors College freshman seminars in 2012. I have also explored the Spalding letter with the History Club at the University of Massachusetts, Lowell, on two occasions. They're always a great group of students, and it has been a pleasure to sit with them every two weeks or so as advisor over the last dozen (and more) years.

During the publication process at Louisiana State University Press, Executive Editor Rand Dotson has been a helpful guide. Susan Murray has done fine work as the manuscript's copy editor, saving me from errors large and small. Most of all, I am grateful to the anonymous reader for detailed, supportive, and very encouraging reviews of the entire manuscript.

I would also like to thank my mom, Jane Pierson, for moving up to Nashua, New Hampshire, so that we can hang out together more often. And lastly, thanks to my wife, Laura Barefield, for her gifts of love and kindness over the past years—given even though she does not particularly like Stephen Spalding.

NOTES

Preface

1. Ivor Noël Hume, *Martin's Hundred* (New York: Knopf, 1982), xv.

2. Ingrid D. Rowland, *From Pompeii: The Afterlife of a Roman Town* (Cambridge: Harvard University Press, 2014), 88. The thrill of discovery also keeps readers hard at work reading archaeology stories in their armchairs. Readers pick up on the sense of discovery—of newness—that marks archaeological writing. Here's the way one online reviewer wrote about *Martin's Hundred:* "As the author and his team uncover the existence of an early Virginia colony and utilize an astounding range of techniques and research to slowly piece together the lives of the inhabitants you will be drawn into the past. More than that you will be excited to read on and discover with these archaeologists what really happened." Uncover. Discover. Unearthing something lost to all; it is a step into a new, old world. Another reviewer put it this way: "This book leads you through the discovery of Wolstenhome step by step, and as each new artifact is discovered, the story of this forgotten town unfolds in vivid detail" (R. J. Marsala, "An Outstanding Book for the Non-Archaeologist," www.amazon.com/Martins-Hundred-Ivor-No%C3%ABl-Hume/product-reviews/0813913233/ref=dp_top_cm_cr_acr_txt?ie=UTF8&showViewpoints=1).

3. Alexander S. Webb, *The Peninsula: McClellan's Campaign of 1862* (New York: Scribner's Sons, 1881), 113. Another handwritten note talks about being left on picket while the army retreated without him, which suggests that he read the book to understand what had happened to him that day and why (notation on 140).

4. David Blight, *Race and Reunion: The American Civil War in Memory* (Cambridge: Harvard University Press, 2001). Union and Confederate soldiers did not, however, always maintain harmonious relations in the postwar period (see Barbara A. Gannon, *The Won Cause: Black and White Comradeship in the Grand Army of the Republic* [Chapel Hill: University of North Carolina Press, 2011]; Caroline E. Janney, *Remembering the Civil War: Reunion and the Limits of Reconciliation* [Chapel Hill: University of North Carolina Press, 2013]; and Carol Reardon, *Pickett's Charge in History and Memory* [Chapel Hill: University of North Carolina Press, 1997], 96, 104–5, 108–10, 114–15, 119–20).

5. http://catalog.vermonthistory.org/vhsweb2/tramp2.exe/authority_hits/A08f59tt.002?server=1home&item=1.

6. Andrew Carroll, ed., *War Letters: Extraordinary Correspondence from American Wars* (New York: Scribner, 2001), 31, quotation on 36. See also the Legacy Project website at www.warletters.com, which includes notations on other books

drawn from the project. Other examples of this genre include David H. Lowenherz, ed., *The 50 Greatest Letters from America's Wars* (New York: Crown, 2002); Bill Adler, ed., *World War II Letters: A Glimpse into the Heart of the Second World War through Those Who Were Fighting It*, with Tracy Quinn McLennan (New York: St. Martin's, 2002); and Jon E. Lewis, ed., *The Mammoth Book of War Diaries and Letters: Life on the Battlefield in the Words of the Ordinary Soldier* (1998; repr., New York: Carroll and Graf, 1999).

7. Robert Brent Toplin notes the film's technical artistry and innovations, the movie's use of music and ambient sounds, and its solid grasp of the emotional roots of good storytelling to explain its success. Burns also employed superb actors to read from diaries and letters written by the people in the midst of the war. The eloquence of soldiers like Sullivan Ballou and Elisha Hunt Rhodes made these long-dead men into something approaching "stars," talked about at work and in people's homes (Toplin, *Ken Burns's The Civil War: Historians Respond* [New York: Oxford University Press, 1996], xix–xxiv; letters, xxi–xxii; ratings, xvi).

8. Wilder Dwight to Mother, September 17, 1862, Wilder Dwight Papers, Massachusetts Historical Society, Boston. See also Eliza Amelia White Dwight, ed., *Life and Letters of Wilder Dwight, Lieut.-Col. Second Mass. Inf. Vols.* (Boston: Ticknor and Fields, 1868), 292–304, which includes Dwight's letter as well as considerably more information about the circumstances of his death. The account of his death in this volume, which is as moving as his letter, reads very much like the "stories" of martyrdom and suffering in Frances Clarke, *War Stories: Suffering and Sacrifice in the Civil War North* (Chicago: University of Chicago Press, 2011), 28–83.

9. *The Purchase by Blood: Massachusetts in the Civil War*, exhibit, Massachusetts Historical Society, October 7, 2011, to January 13, 2012. The exhibit also included a wonderful handwritten draft of Louisa May Alcott's *Hospital Sketches*.

10. Melvan Tibbetts to Dear Parents Brothers & Sisters, June 8, 1862, Melvan Tibbetts Letters, MSS 284, Williams Research Center, Historic New Orleans Collection. Punctuation has been added for clarity. Other letters by Melvan Tibbetts are housed at the Maine Historical Society.

11. Melvan Tibbetts, April 12, 1864, Melvan Tibbetts Letters, MSS 284, Williams Research Center, Historic New Orleans Collection, punctuation added for clarity; Pension Records, Melvan Tibbetts, National Archives and Records Administration (hereafter cited as NARA).

12. Melvan Tibbetts, May 27, 1864, Melvan Tibbetts Letters, MSS 284, Williams Research Center, Historic New Orleans Collection, punctuation added for clarity.

13. William Marvel, *Lee's Last Retreat: The Flight to Appomattox* (Chapel Hill: University of North Carolina Press, 2002), 182–99, esp. 184–85, 198; Michael D. Pierson, *Mutiny at Fort Jackson: The Untold Story of the Fall of New Orleans* (Chapel Hill: University of North Carolina Press, 2008), 135–36. For more on Appomattox, see Elizabeth R. Varon, *Appomattox: Victory, Defeat, and Freedom at the End of the Civil War* (New York: Oxford University Press, 2014), 79–112.

14. Mike Parker Pearson, and the Stonehenge Riverside Project, *Stonehenge: Exploring the Greatest Stone Age Mystery* (New York: Simon and Schuster, 2012), 211.

15. Jill Lepore, "Historians Who Love Too Much: Reflections on Microhistory and Biography," *Journal of American History* 88 (June 2001): 129–44.

16. Careful readers of one of my earlier books will find one or two places where I employed Spalding's words to build a case that my current, more informed interpretation undercuts.

Chapter One

1. How the letter managed to get to the Vermont Historical Society is not known. The letter, officially, is Stephen Spalding to James Peck, July 8, 1862 (hereafter cited as Stephen F. Spalding Letter), Vermont Historical Society (hereafter cited as VtHS), Barre. My citations to the Spalding Letter silently correct the misspelling "Spaulding" in the Vermont Historical Society records.

2. See, for example, many of the letters included in Jeffrey D. Marshall, ed., *A War of the People: Vermont Civil War Letters* (Hanover, NH: University Press of New England, 1999); and Nina Silber and Mary Beth Sievens, eds., *Yankee Correspondence: Civil War Letters between New England Soldiers and the Home Front* (Charlottesville: University Press of Virginia, 1996).

3. Letter from anonymous soldier dated February 10, 1863, *Vermont Watchman and State Journal* (Montpelier), February 27, 1863; Howard Coffin, *Nine Months to Gettysburg: Stannard's Vermonters and the Repulse of Pickett's Charge* (Woodstock, VT: Countryman, 1997), 130–31.

4. *Vanity Fair,* April 27, 1861.

5. George N. Carpenter, *History of the Eighth Regiment Vermont Volunteers, 1861–1865* (Boston: Deland and Barta, 1886), 47.

6. This slip of paper is missing; there is no evidence that the Vermont Historical Society ever received it. A reading of the *New Orleans Daily True Delta* shows several possibilities for what Spalding *may* have included with his letter, but there is of course no way to be sure what he sent to Peck. If Spalding clipped from the July 6 edition, he might have sent along a story about two or three Union soldiers, including Eugene Rogers (there was a private by that name in Company E of the Eighth Vermont), illegally posting themselves at the entrances of Jackson Square and charging citizens five cents to enter. Two of the men were sent to jail for a month for their offense. Or he might have chosen to include the regular column that offered synopses of cases heard by Maj. J. M. Bell, the judge of the Provost Court. One story reads: "A number who had been arrested for drunkenness were discharged, the court considering it no great crime to get tight on the Fourth of July." Not everyone got off so lightly, but another drunk was excused by the judge because he claimed to have gotten "drunk on Confederate whisky" (*New Orleans Daily True Delta,* July 6, 1862; Eugene Rogers's service record, Compiled Service Records, M557, roll 11, NARA).

7. A correspondent noted that the regiment's officers lived in the "side rooms, sleeping about on their camp-cots, and the privates using the open station" (see letter by "W," dated June 14, 1862, published in *Brattleboro Phoenix,* June 26, 1862).

8. These sentences are written across the top of page 5 of the manuscript.

9. "Big" is Lucius Bigelow, who graduated from UVM in the class of 1861, a year after Spalding.

10. These two sentences are written across the top of page 6 of the manuscript.

11. These sentences are written across the top of page 7, the final page of the manuscript.

12. Charles Warren Spalding, *The Spalding Memorial: A Genealogical History of Edward Spalding of Virginia and Massachusetts Bay. And His Descendants . . . Revised and Enlarged* (1897; repr., Chelmsford, MA: Spalding Documentation Services, 1996), 61–68.

13. First quotation in William H. Jeffrey, *Successful Vermonters: A Modern Gazetteer of Caledonia, Essex, and Orleans Counties* (East Burke, VT: Historical Publishing, 1904), 233; second quotation in Spalding, *The Spalding Memorial*, 446. For Levi's business career, see also Hamilton Child, *Gazetteer and Business Directory of Lamoille and Orleans Counties, Vermont, for 1883–84* (Syracuse, NY: Journal Office, 1883), 261–62.

14. *A Catalogue of the Officers and Students of the University of Vermont, for the Academical Year 1856-7* (Burlington: Free Press Print, 1856), 17–18; *A Catalogue of the Officers and Students of the University of Vermont, for the Academical Year 1859-60* (Burlington: Sentinel Print, 1859), 12.

15. The invitation is inserted into *Catalogues Etc VT. University, 1860–1869*, at the Vermont Historical Society. The binding call number is 378.743VHf. Also included is the "Bill of Fare" for the sumptuous meal. In addition to the dinner, held at 9:00 p.m. on August 1, 1859, guests listened to an oration and a poem.

16. Spalding, *The Spalding Memorial*, 446; Carpenter, *History of the Eighth Regiment Vermont Volunteers*, 126.

17. For junior year, see *A Catalogue of the Officers and Students of the University of Vermont, for the Academical Year 1858-9* (Burlington: Sentinel Print, 1858), 14; for senior year, see *A Catalogue of the Officers and Students of the University of Vermont, for . . . 1859–60*, 12.

18. For the history of the Thirteenth Vermont, see Coffin, *Nine Months to Gettysburg*, which also covers the creation of the Seventeenth Vermont from its ranks (277). For the Thirteenth Vermont and its role repulsing Pickett's Charge, see Earl J. Hess, *Pickett's Charge: The Last Attack at Gettysburg* (Chapel Hill: University of North Carolina Press, 2001), 234–41, 276–77, 294. For Peck's service record, see Ralph Orson Sturtevant, *Pictorial History: The Thirteenth Regiment Vermont Volunteers, 1861–1865* (Burlington, VT, 1913), 672; and Peck's personnel records, Compiled Service Records, microfilm roll M557, roll 10, NARA. Peck received a monthly invalid pension of $8.50 starting on July 15, 1865, and saw it increased to $17.00 in April 1879 ("Pension File of James S. Peck," Pension Records, Union Veterans, NARA).

19. See E. Anthony Rotundo, "Romantic Friendship: Male Intimacy and Middle-Class Youth in the Northern United States, 1800–1900," *Journal of Social History* 23 (October 1989): 1–25; quotation from Caleb Crain, *American Sympathy: Men, Friendship, and Literature in the New Nation* (New Haven: Yale University Press, 2001), 33. For young southern men's friendships, see Lorri Glover, *Southern Sons: Becoming Men in the New Nation* (Baltimore: Johns Hopkins University Press,

2007); and Anya Jabour, "Male Friendship and Masculinity in the Early National South: William Wirt and His Friends," *Journal of the Early Republic* 20 (Spring 2000): 83–111.

20. For photographs, see David Deitcher, *Dear Friends: American Photographs of Men Together, 1840–1918* (New York: Abrams, 2001).

21. Ibid., 34.

22. Thomas J. Balcerski, "'Under These Classic Shades Together': Intimate Male Friendship at the Antebellum College of New Jersey," *Pennsylvania History: A Journal of Mid-Atlantic Studies* 80 (Spring 2013): 182, 184.

23. Both quotations from Frederick J. Blue, "The Poet and the Reformer: Longfellow, Sumner, and the Bonds of Male Friendship, 1837–1874," *Journal of the Early Republic* 15 (Summer 1995): 292.

Chapter Two

1. Carpenter, *History of the Eighth Regiment Vermont Volunteers,* 126.

2. No one named "Spalding" or "Spaulding" matches the parameters defined by Carpenter (Soldiers and Sailors website, NARA). In Montpelier, Spalding was recruiting for a unit to be commanded by a "Col. Ramsey." The unit seems never to have been mustered in, but Spalding is identified as "a graduate of the University of Vermont, and lately of the N.Y. Seventh Regiment" (*Vermont Watchman and State Journal* [Montpelier], June 21, 1861).

3. The National Archives contains two documents that list a private in Company I named Spaulding, one with the initials T. S. and one with the initials P. J. The regiment's early records at the New-York Historical Society list an F. F. Spaulding. All of them are twenty years old, the correct age, and later records for the regiment list Stephen F. Spalding (see Compiled Service Records, Seventh New York State Militia, NARA; and "Muster Rolls, 1861–1863," bound volume, Seventh Regiment Records, 1767–1983, New-York Historical Society).

4. Civil War Recruits, Donors, 1861, Seventh Regiment Records, 1767–1983, Box 9, folder 14, New-York Historical Society. Zeph Spaulding was twenty-four years old and served in Company D (see "Muster Rolls, 1861–1863," bound volume, Seventh Regiment Records, 1767–1983, New-York Historical Society; see also Spalding, *The Spalding Memorial,* 463–64).

5. Theodore Winthrop, *Life in the Open Air, and Other Papers* (Boston: Ticknor and Fields, 1862), 221–22.

6. Civil War Recruits, Donors, 1861, Seventh Regiment Records, 1767–1983, Box 9, folder 14, New-York Historical Society.

7. For Thomas Nast's depictions of the Seventh New York State Militia parading down Broadway, including a preliminary sketch, see Harold Holzer and Mark E. Neely Jr., *Mine Eyes Have Seen the Glory: The Civil War in Art* (New York: Orion, 1993), xvi–5.

8. In addition to the Thomas Nast painting, the Museum of Fine Arts in Boston has a less famous rendition of the parade on Broadway (see James M. McPherson, *The Illustrated Battle Cry of Freedom: The Civil War Era* [New York: Oxford University Press, 2003], 227). The famous *Battles and Leaders* features four

depictions of the Seventh New York, all of them illustrating an article by someone from a different regiment (Robert Underwood Johnson and Clarence Clough Buel, eds., *Battles and Leaders of the Civil War*, vol. 1 [New York: Century, 1887], 150, 154, 155, 159).

9. Winthrop, *Life in the Open Air*, 243; shoes on 243–44.

10. Robert Gould Shaw to Dearest Mother, April 26, 1861, in Russell Duncan, ed., *Blue-Eyed Child of Fortune: The Civil War Letters of Colonel Robert Gould Shaw* (Athens: University of Georgia Press, 1992), 82. In addition to the record left by Theodore Winthrop, the details of the march can be found in John Lockwood and Charles Lockwood, *The Siege of Washington: The Untold Story of the Twelve Days That Shook the Union* (New York: Oxford University Press, 2011); and David Detzer, *Dissonance: The Turbulent Days between Fort Sumter and Bull Run* (New York: Harcourt, 2006).

11. Winthrop, *Life in the Open Air*, 261.

12. Their term of service eventually stretched from four to six weeks. It started once they were formally mustered in by Maj. Irwin McDowell in Washington on April 26, not on the date they left New York.

13. On photographers and the Seventh, see Jeff L. Rosenheim, *Photography and the American Civil War* (New Haven: Yale University Press, 2013), 58–61, 63–64; gymnastics photograph on 64. As an example of the number of photographs of the Seventh that can appear in illustrated histories of the war, see eight photographs in William C. Davis and Bell I. Wiley, eds., *Photographic History of the Civil War: Fort Sumter to Gettysburg* (1981; repr., New York: Black Dog and Leventhal, 1994), 135, 147, 157–58, 161, 170.

14. Dignitaries at parades listed in William Swinton, *History of the Seventh Regiment, National Guard, State of New York* (Boston: Fields, Osgood and Co., 1870), 175; quartermaster's appeal and eight hundred to nine hundred boxes and packages on 174. Statement about Sybarites from Winthrop, *Life in the Open Air*, 269. For provisions sent from New York, see R[obert] M. Weed to My Dear Comrades, April 29, 1861, and a letter to Colonel Lefferts, April 23, 1861, accompanying "a cask of good brandy," both in Correspondence, 1860–1869, Seventh Regiment Records, 1767–1983, Box 4, folder 7, New-York Historical Society. For artillery, see Swinton, *History of the Seventh Regiment*, 183.

15. Jasper to *New York Times*, dated May 24, 1861, published in *New York Times*, May 28, 1861.

16. Men in the Seventh received pay based on service of "one month + 17 days." For privates, this equaled $23.21. Corporals received a bit more, $26.32, and sergeants, $32.61. The big jump in pay came between NCOs and officers. The first lieutenant received $173.63, and the captain $202. Notice on pay in General Order No. 29, August 7, 1861, in Regimental Orders, 1855–1861, Seventh Regiment Records, 1767–1983, Box 1, folder 10, New-York Historical Society.

17. Change in branch of service in "Co. I: Roster, 1838–1913," bound volume, Seventh Regiment Records, 1767–1983, New-York Historical Society; howitzers in Claude Leland, *The First Hundred Years: Records and Reminiscences of a Century of Company I, Seventh Regiment N.G.N.Y., 1838–1938* (n.p., 1938), 24.

18. Enlistment totals in Board and Council of Officers—Meeting Minutes, 1860–1861, Box 7, folder 13, Seventh Regiment Records, 1767–1983, New-York Historical Society.

19. "Muster Rolls, 1861–1863," bound volume, Seventh Regiment Records, 1767–1983, New-York Historical Society. Swinton places the company's strength at thirty-two as late as May 3, 1861 (see Swinton, *History of the Seventh Regiment*, 177; see also Leland, *The First Hundred Years*, 29).

20. "Muster Rolls, 1861–1863," bound volume, Seventh Regiment Records, 1767–1983, New-York Historical Society. See also Leland, *The First Hundred Years*, 31. Leland estimates the number of new recruits at sixty-eight.

21. Swinton, *History of the Seventh Regiment*, 178.

22. Ibid., 182.

23. "Muster Rolls, 1861–1863," bound volume, Seventh Regiment Records, 1767–1983, New-York Historical Society. Leffert's April 29 plea to halt the flow of enlistments is in Swinton, *History of the Seventh Regiment*, 178.

24. Swinton, *History of the Seventh Regiment*, 178.

25. Colonel Lefferts to Sir, May 11, 1861, Correspondence, 1860–1869, Seventh Regiment Records, 1767–1983, Box 4, folder 7, New-York Historical Society.

26. Leland, *The First Hundred Years*, 34; quartering in outbuildings on 30.

27. For the French cook, see *New York Times*, May 5, 1861. A member of the Seventh wrote on May 6, 1861, that "we are about indulging in an article of luxury in the shape of a matting to cover the floor, and are getting things in shape to make us more comfortable." He complained that the tent, only nine feet square, had to house seven men, though he added that usually some men were out keeping guard, which opened up space (*New York Evangelist*, May 16, 1861).

28. Robert Gould Shaw to Dear Father, May 4, 1861, in Duncan, ed., *Blue-Eyed Child of Fortune*, 93.

29. Davis and Wiley, eds., *Photographic History of the Civil War*, 157.

30. Holzer and Neely Jr., *Mine Eyes Have Seen the Glory*, 8–9. For analysis and reproductions of Gifford's Civil War paintings, see Eleanor Jones Harvey, *The Civil War and American Art* (Washington, DC: Smithsonian American Art Museum in association with Yale University Press, 2012), 114–23; and Kevin J. Avery and Franklin Kelly, eds., *Hudson River School Visions: The Landscapes of Sanford R. Gifford* (New Haven: Yale University Press, 2003), illustrations pertaining to the Seventh on 38, 39, 158, 159, and 161.

31. Sanford Gifford's second 1861 painting, *Bivouac of the Seventh Regiment, Arlington Heights, Virginia*, demonstrates the pride felt by members of the unit. It also shows Gifford's sense that a painting of the Seventh would be marketable. Again, the scene is bucolic, a landscape at peace with itself. Guns are present in this painting, as befits a force newly arrived in Virginia, but they are stacked except for one picket at right center. Two prominent knapsacks are shown adorned with the regiment's "7." Perhaps not coincidentally, there are seven fires burning, illuminating the darkness that has fallen over the Old Dominion. While Spalding missed the chance to set foot on the "sacred soil of Virginia," he could, and did, live the rest of his life in the limelight cast by the pride and fame earned by his comrades during

their short stay in Virginia. Whether it was Theodore Winthrop's letters to the *Atlantic Monthly* or Sanford Gifford's paintings on display in New York, the Seventh continued to play an overly large part in the North's vision of the war.

32. That Spalding served as an artilleryman while in the Seventh is confirmed by the family genealogist, who wrote in 1897 that Stephen had served in the "Seventh N.Y. Battery" (see Charles Warren Spalding, *The Spalding Memorial*, 446).

33. See illustration in ibid., 32.

34. Swinton, *History of the Seventh Regiment*, 183. Shaw wrote that the regiment had four howitzers while at Annapolis (see Robert Gould Shaw to Dearest Mother, April 26, 1861, in Duncan, ed., *Blue-Eyed Child of Fortune*, 79).

35. Robert Gould Shaw to Dearest Mother, May 10, 1861, in Duncan, ed., *Blue-Eyed Child of Fortune*, 97. Estimated distance to Willard's in Leland, *The First Hundred Years*, 30.

36. "Guard Book, Camp Cameron, 1861," bound volume, Seventh Regiment Records, 1767–1983, New-York Historical Society; quotation from Leland, *The First Hundred Years*, 31.

37. Sanford Robinson Gifford, "Military Correspondence. Washington, May 17, 1861," *Crayon* 8 (June 1861), 134; Jasper to *New York Times*, dated May 24, 1861, published May 28, 1861. Spalding's company-mate Theodore Winthrop managed to talk his way into accompanying most of the regiment into Virginia. The fact that he was known to be writing accounts of the regiment's actions for the *Atlantic* gave officers some incentive to allow him to cross the Potomac.

38. Lt. Kemp to Col. Lefferts, May 10, 1861, in Swinton, *History of the Seventh Regiment*, 182.

39. Leland, *The First Hundred Years*, 34.

40. "Muster Rolls, 1861–1863," bound volume, Seventh Regiment Records, 1767–1983, New-York Historical Society.

41. Swinton, *History of the Seventh Regiment*, 186; McDowell quotation in ibid.

42. Robert Gould Shaw to Dear Father, May 12, 1861, in Duncan, ed., *Blue-Eyed Child of Fortune*, 98–99.

43. Swinton, *History of the Seventh Regiment*, 193; for the "Roll of Honor" of officers, see ibid., 385–490.

44. *Newport News*, July 8, 1863.

45. The regiment's economic status underlay a complaint by "H" that the Seventh was a group of "carpet knights" who were too "Fifth Avenueish." "H" drew a classical allusion that predicted that the Seventh might fly from any foe in order "to save their handsome faces" (see *Christian Advocate and Journal*, May 23, 1861). On May 18, the *New York Times* noticed that "there is considerable feeling expressed against the regiment, on account of the short time of service for which they serve. Hundreds of letters are daily received, intimating that the regiment will be hissed through Broadway if it returns at the time stated." One of the soldiers, Jasper, wrote to the *Times* to say that "every man among them feels that these attacks are entirely uncalled for and untrue in every particular." Despite pressing business commitments in the city, the men of the Seventh overstayed their term, and their service in Virginia seems to have quieted the animosity against them. The *Times* reported that "the reception accorded to these fine fellows was sufficiently hearty.

People were evidently glad to see them, and clapped their hands, shouted and waved their handkerchiefs with real delight" (Jasper to *New York Times*, dated May 16, 1861, published May 20, 1861; *New York Times*, June 2, 1861; see also a defense of the regiment by "C," *New York Times*, May 24, 1861).

46. Karen Halttunen, *Confidence Men and Painted Women: A Study of Middle-Class Culture in America, 1830-1870* (New Haven: Yale University Press, 1982), 1–55, quotation on 2.

47. Joe B. Fulton, *The Reconstruction of Mark Twain: How a Confederate Bushwhacker Became the Lincoln of Our Literature* (Baton Rouge: Louisiana State University Press, 2010).

48. Mark M. Boatner III, *The Civil War Dictionary* (New York: McKay, 1959), 624. Pay continued to climb, sometimes steeply, from rank to rank. Union colonels, for example, received $212 every month.

49. Stephen F. Spalding Letter, VtHS.

50. Jane Kamensky, *The Exchange Artist: A Tale of High-Flying Speculation and America's First Banking Collapse* (New York: Viking, 2008), 5; Mary Babson Fuhrer, *A Crisis of Community: The Trials and Transformation of a New England Town, 1815-1848* (Chapel Hill: University of North Carolina Press, 2014), 103; Edward A. Longacre, *The Early Morning of the War: Bull Run, 1861* (Norman: University of Oklahoma Press, 2014), 98. For a historical overview of attitudes toward ambition, see William Casey King, *Ambition, A History: From Vice to Virtue* (New Haven: Yale University Press, 2013).

Chapter Three

1. Winthrop D. Jordan, *White over Black: American Attitudes toward the Negro, 1550-1812* (New York: Norton, 1968), 3–43.

2. David A. Cecere, "Carrying the Home Front to War: Soldiers, Race, and New England Culture during the Civil War," in *Union Soldiers and the Northern Home Front: Wartime Experiences, Postwar Adjustments*, ed. Paul A. Cimbala and Randall M. Miller, 293–323 (New York: Fordham University Press, 2002). For New England soldiers and racial issues, see also Silber and Sievens, eds., *Yankee Correspondence*, 13–17. For white Union soldiers and their early encounters with southern blacks, see Glenn David Brasher, *The Peninsula Campaign and the Necessity of Emancipation* (Chapel Hill: University of North Carolina Press, 2012); John H. Matsui, "War in Earnest: The Army of Virginia and the Radicalization of the Union War Effort, 1862" *Civil War History* 58 (June 2012): 180–223; and Leon F. Litwack, *Been in the Storm So Long: The Aftermath of Slavery* (New York: Knopf, 1979), 117–35. For racial humor during the Civil War, see Marc Simpson, "The Bright Side: 'Humorously Conceived and Truthfully Executed,'" in *Winslow Homer: Paintings of the Civil War*, ed. Simpson, 47–64 (San Francisco: Bedford Arts, 1988).

3. Donald S. Frazier, *Fire in the Cane Field: The Federal Invasion of Louisiana and Texas, January 1861-January 1863* (Buffalo Gap, TX: State House, 2009), 49–50.

4. John William De Forest, *A Volunteer's Adventures: A Union Captain's Record of the Civil War* (Baton Rouge: Louisiana State University Press, 1996), 26.

5. The most thorough work on the Confederate leadership's reluctance to enlist black men is Bruce Levine, *Confederate Emancipation: Southern Plans to Free and Arm Slaves during the Civil War* (New York: Oxford University Press, 2006). For a recent review of the controversy, see Kevin M. Levin, "Black Confederates out of the Attic and into the Mainstream," *Journal of the Civil War Era* 4 (December 2014): 627–36.

6. James G. Hollandsworth, *The Louisiana Native Guards: The Black Military Experience during the Civil War* (Baton Rouge: Louisiana State University Press, 1995), 1–11.

7. Contraband policy is explored in James M. McPherson, *Battle Cry of Freedom: The Civil War Era* (New York: Oxford University Press, 1988), 355–56; Kate Masur, "'A Rare Phenomenon of Philological Vegetation': The Word 'Contraband' and the Meanings of Emancipation in the United States," *Journal of American History* 93 (March 2007): 1050–84; Benjamin F. Butler, *Butler's Book: Autobiography and Personal Reminiscences of Maj.-Gen. Benjamin F. Butler* (Boston: A. M. Thayer, 1892), 256–64; and Adam Goodyear, *1861: The Civil War Awakening* (New York: Knopf, 2011), 293–347.

8. Edwin Hergesheimer, *Map Showing the Distribution of the Slave Population of the Southern United States. Compiled from the Census of 1860* (Washington, DC., 1861).

9. Thomas and the organization of the Eighth in Carpenter, *History of the Eighth Regiment Vermont Volunteers*, 1–17.

10. In Connecticut, Butler arranged for a former mayor of Hartford, Henry Deming, to be appointed to command a regiment. According to Butler, Deming had also been a delegate to the Charleston convention. New Hampshire's colonel was to be John H. George, "one of the most reliable Democrats." George F. Shepley, also a delegate to Charleston, assumed the colonelcy of a Maine regiment (Butler, *Butler's Book*, 299–314, quotation on 303).

11. Ibid., 307.

12. *Newport News*, May 20, 1863. The paper's owner had served in a Vermont regiment during the Peninsula campaign and eventually chose the name "Newport News" because of his fondness for the town of the same name. As further proof that the Spaldings liked jokes, he said he chose that name over his second choice, "The Monitor." The famous Union ship *Monitor* had served near Newport News, Virginia. Regrettably, only two issues of this weekly have survived.

13. Jean H. Baker, *Affairs of Party: The Political Culture of Northern Democrats in the Mid-Nineteenth Century* (Ithaca: Cornell University Press, 1983), 177–258, Douglas quotation on 185. There is extensive scholarship about the Democratic Party before and during the war, including Martin H. Quitt, *Stephen A. Douglas and Antebellum Democracy* (New York: Cambridge University Press, 2012); Elise Lemire, *"Miscegenation": Making Race in America* (Philadelphia: University of Pennsylvania Press, 2002); Joel H. Silbey, *A Respectable Minority: The Democratic Party in the Civil War Era, 1860–1868* (New York: Norton, 1977), 81–83; and John Ashworth, *The Coming of the Civil War, 1850–1861*, vol. 2 of *Slavery, Capitalism, and Politics in the Antebellum Republic* (New York: Cambridge University Press,

2007), 354–69. Two recent books have uncompromisingly emphasized the Democratic Party's racial positions to the exclusion of other matters: Michael Todd Landis, *Northern Men with Southern Loyalties* (Ithaca: Cornell University Press, 2014); and Jennifer L. Weber, *Copperheads: The Rise and Fall of Lincoln's Opponents in the North* (New York: Oxford University Press, 2006). Joel H. Silbey reminds us, however, that the Democrats stood for other things besides white supremacy in "'There Are Other Questions Besides That of Slavery Merely': The Democratic Party and Antislavery Politics," in *Crusaders and Compromisers: Essays on the Relationship of the Antislavery Struggle to the Antebellum Party System*, ed. Alan M. Kraut (Westport, CT: Greenwood, 1983), 143–75.

14. The distinction between slavery and white supremacy as issues is developed in a southern context in Charles B. Dew, *Apostles of Disunion: Southern Secession Commissioners and the Causes of the Civil War* (Charlottesville: University Press of Virginia, 2001).

15. Michael D. Pierson, "'He Helped the Poor and Snubbed the Rich': Benjamin F. Butler and Class Politics in Lowell and New Orleans," *Massachusetts Historical Review* 7 (2005): 36–68.

16. *Burlington Weekly Sentinel,* January 10, 1862. They again blamed abolitionists for starting the war on February, 21, 1862.

17. Ibid., March 7, 1862; Confiscation Act opposed, ibid., May 9, 1862.

18. William Haskins to My Dear Wife + children, April 17, 1862, Williams Haskins Papers, Special Collections, Bailey/Howe Library, University of Vermont (hereafter cited as UVM); Benjamin F. Morse to Rosina, June 7, 1862, in Silber and Sievens, eds., *Yankee Correspondence,* 157.

19. John L. Barstow to Dear Laura, November 23, 1862; John L. Barstow to Laura, May 11, 1862, both in John Lester Barstow Civil War Letters and Misc. 1862-65, Special Collections, Bailey/Howe Library, UVM. The editor of the Eighth Vermont's regimental newspaper also listed the prizes won during a long march, ending his catalogue with "pullets, pigs, and picaninnies" (*Soldier's News-Letter* [Brashear City, LA], May 16, 1863).

20. Carpenter, *History of the Eighth Regiment Vermont Volunteers,* 41.

21. Ibid., first quotation, 41; subsequent quotations, 42.

22. L. S. Thompson, *The Story of Mattie J. Jackson: Her Parentage—Experience of Eighteen Years in Slavery—Incidents during the War—Her Escape from Slavery. A True Story* (Lawrence, MA.: The Sentinel Office, 1866), 16.

23. Carpenter, *History of the Eighth Regiment Vermont Volunteers,* 42.

24. Ibid., 42–43.

25. Rufus Kinsley Diary, June 22, 1862, in David C. Rankin, ed., *Diary of a Christian Soldier: Rufus Kinsley and the Civil War* (New York: Cambridge University Press, 2004), 98.

26. Carpenter, *History of the Eighth Regiment Vermont Volunteers,* Stamps case, 73–74; overseer's murder, 58–59.

27. Ibid., 59–61, quotation on 59.

28. The growing literature about reconciliation started with two studies that highlight much of what Spalding's comrades did in the 1880s (see Blight, *Race and*

Reunion; and Nina Silber, *The Romance of Reunion: Northerners and the South, 1865–1900* [Chapel Hill: University of North Carolina Press, 1993]). Subsequent studies have found northerners defending emancipation and black civil rights. That George Carpenter and his fellow officers emphasized white unity over black valor indicates where their political allegiances lay (see Janney, *Remembering the Civil War;* and Gannon, *The Won Cause*). Other works that highlight the difficulties of reunion include James Alan Marten, *Sing Not War: The Lives of Union and Confederate Veterans in Gilded Age America* (Chapel Hill: University of North Carolina Press, 2011); and John R. Neff, *Honoring the Civil War Dead: Commemoration and the Problem of Reconciliation* (Lawrence: University Press of Kansas, 2005).

29. Carpenter, *History of the Eighth Regiment Vermont Volunteers,* 105, 93.

30. Ibid., 92, 95.

31. Moses McFarland, *Some Experiences of the Eighth Vermont West of the Mississippi* (Morrisville, VT.: News and Citizen, 1896), fugitive slaves incident, 8; quotations, 9.

32. Ibid., 10, both quotations. For similar descriptions of escaping slaves weighted down with belongings from ransacked plantation houses, including one from an anonymous member of the Eighth Vermont, see Barnes F. Lathrop, ed., "Federals 'Sweep the Coast': An Expedition into St. Charles Parish, August 1862," *Louisiana History* 9 (Winter 1968): 62–68.

33. Jonathan V. Allen to Dear Sister, February 6, 1863, Allen Family Papers, 1856–1884, VtHS. For recruitment of officers, see Joseph T. Glatthaar, *Forged in Battle: The Civil War Alliance of Black Soldiers and White Officers* (New York: Meridian, 1991), 35–59. Glatthaar notes that officer candidates had to pass exams, but it seems likely that Spalding could have done so if he pleased.

34. The official paperwork about this large departure is borne out by Roger Hovey of Company A, who complained that "we have lost some of our best officers and men" to the USCT (Roger Hovey to Dear Sister, November 20, 1862, Roger Hovey Civil War Letters, Special Collections, Bailey/Howe Library, UVM). Union soldiers often joined the USCT in groups, a way, Glatthaar writes, of avoiding "the sense of guilt over leaving the boys and to insulate themselves from negative reactions on racist grounds" (Glatthaar, *Forged in Battle,* 58).

35. Chris Pena, ed., "Dr. Charles S. Cooper's 'Reminiscences,'" *Louisiana History* 41 (Winter 2000): 72–73.

36. C. Peter Ripley, *Slaves and Freedmen in Civil War Louisiana* (Baton Rouge: Louisiana State University Press, 1976), 22–39.

37. Ibid., 22.

38. Cecere, "Carrying the Home Front to War," 297–98.

39. For some examples of this kind of racial description, see Mark Twain, *Roughing It* (1872; repr., Berkeley: University of California Press, 1995), 501–5; Mark Twain, *The Innocents Abroad, or the New Pilgrim's Progress* (1869; repr., Ware, UK: Wordsworth Classics, 2010), 321–22, 350–52; and Sam R. Watkins, *Co. Aytch: A Confederate Memoir of the Civil War* (1962; repr., New York: Touchstone, 1997), 136–37, 225.

40. For minstrel shows, see especially Baker, *Affairs of Party*, 212–58; and Eric Lott, *Love and Theft: Blackface Minstrelsy and the American Working Class* (New York: Oxford University Press, 1993).

41. Carpenter, *History of the Eighth Regiment Vermont Volunteers*, 47, all quotations.

42. Ibid., 47–48.

43. Sigmund Freud, *Jokes and Their Relation to the Unconscious*, trans. James Strachey (New York: Norton, 1989), 114, 121, 122, 125 (last two quotations).

44. Jonathan W. White finds that many Democrats in the army censored themselves when writing about the Emancipation Proclamation, having seen a number of their fellow officers disciplined or dismissed for opposing government policy (White, *Emancipation, the Union Army, and the Reelection of Abraham Lincoln* [Baton Rouge: Louisiana State University Press, 2014], 38–68).

45. Crandall Shifflett, ed., *John Washington's Civil War: A Slave Narrative* (Baton Rouge: Louisiana State University Press, 2008), 49.

46. For newspapers, see Justus Gale to Dear Sister, May 22, 1862, and Justus Gale, July 18, 1862, Gale–Morse Family Papers, 1861–1876, VtHS. For reports of abused slaves, see Justus Gale to Dear Father, June 14, 1862, ibid.

47. Justus Gale to his sister Almeida, August 26, 1862, in Silber and Sievens, eds., *Yankee Correspondence*, 92; Pena, ed., "Dr. Charles S. Cooper's 'Reminiscences,'" quotations on 73, 86.

48. Letter from W, dated Algiers, Louisiana, June 2, 1862, in *Brattleboro Phoenix*, June 26, 1862.

49. Letter from W, dated Algiers, Louisiana, August 8, 1862, in *Brattleboro Phoenix*, August 21, 1862. For recruitment, see letter from W, dated Algiers, Louisiana, August 31, 1862, in *Brattleboro Phoenix*, September 18, 1862.

50. *Soldier's News-Letter* (Brashear City, LA), May 16, 1863.

51. Rufus Kinsley Diary, August 25 and 26, 1862, in Rankin, ed., *Diary of a Christian Soldier*, 102, 104, quotation on 104.

52. Kinsley Diary, June 19, 1862, in Rankin, ed., *Diary of a Christian Soldier*, 98; Camp population in Rufus Kinsley to Daniel, September 19, 1862, Rufus Kinsley Papers, VtHS; higher estimate of 6,000 in Kinsley Diary, September 25, 1862, in Rankin, ed., *Diary of a Christian Soldier*, 109.

53. School promised in Kinsley Diary, September 21, 1862; church services in September 21 and 28, 1862, June 7, 1863, in Rankin, ed., *Diary of a Christian Soldier*, 109, 130.

54. Kinsley Diary, September 7, 1862, in Rankin, ed., *Diary of a Christian Soldier*, 107.

Chapter Four

1. More than one-quarter of the population of New Orleans in 1860 had been born in Ireland or the German States. At that time, the city's overall population was about 168,000 (see Ella Lonn, *Foreigners in the Confederacy* [Chapel Hill: University of North Carolina Press, 1940], 417). For New Orleans compared to

Philadelphia, see Dell Upton, *Another City: Urban Life and Urban Spaces in the New American Republic* (New Haven: Yale University Press, 2008).

2. For the history of southern cities behind Union lines, see especially Stephen V. Ash, *When the Yankees Came: Conflict and Chaos in the Occupied South, 1861–1865* (Chapel Hill: University of North Carolina Press, 1995), 76–92; Walter T. Durham, *Nashville, the Occupied City, 1862–1863* (1985; repr., Knoxville: University of Tennessee Press, 2008); and Walter T. Durham, *Reluctant Partners: Nashville and the Union, July 1, 1863 to June 30, 1865* (1987; repr., Knoxville: University of Tennessee Press, 2008).

3. Lorien Foote, *The Gentlemen and the Roughs: Violence, Honor, and Manliness in the Union Army* (New York: New York University Press, 2010), 1–66.

4. For Democrats and the politicization of sexual issues in the 1850s, see Michael D. Pierson, *Free Hearts and Free Homes: Gender and American Antislavery Politics* (Chapel Hill: University of North Carolina Press, 2003), 97–114.

5. Stephen Spalding to James Peck, July 8, 1862, Stephen F. Spalding Letter, VtHS.

6. Frank Towers, *The Urban South and the Coming of the Civil War* (Charlottesville: University Press of Virginia, 2004), 196–98; John D. Winters, *The Civil War in Louisiana* (Baton Rouge: Louisiana State University Press, 1963), 3–13; Jefferson Davis Bragg, *Louisiana in the Confederacy* (Baton Rouge: Louisiana State University Press, 1941), 1–33.

7. Jonathan Allen to Dear Sister, July 9, 1862, Allen Family Papers, 1856–1884, VtHS; Justus F. Gale to Dear Brother, July 4, 1862, Gale–Morse Family Papers, 1861–1876, VtHS.

8. Pierson, *Mutiny at Fort Jackson*, 129–84.

9. Michael Kimmel, *Manhood in America: A Cultural History* (New York: Free Press, 1996), 43–50; Charles E. Rosenberg, "Sexuality, Class and Role in 19th-Century America," in *The American Man*, ed. Elizabeth H. Pleck and Joseph H. Pleck (Englewood Cliffs, NJ: Prentice-Hall, 1980), 223–29; E. Anthony Rotundo, "Learning about Manhood: Gender Ideals and the Middle-Class Family in Nineteenth-Century America," in *Manliness and Morality: Middle-Class Masculinity in Britain and America*, ed. J. A. Mangan and James Walvin (New York: St. Martin's, 1987): 35–51. On southern masculinity, see Glover, *Southern Sons*.

10. "Daniel S. Foster," Compiled Service Records, Eighth Vermont Infantry, NARA. Foster was twenty-two years old when he joined the regiment on February 18, 1862. He was elected first lieutenant immediately. He made captain in the summer of 1863 and was mustered out in June 1864.

11. *Burlington Weekly Sentinel*, February 7, 1862.

12. Judkin Browning, "'I Am Not So Patriotic as I Once Was': The Effects of Military Occupation on the Occupying Union Soldiers during the Civil War," *Civil War History* 55 (June 2009): 234.

13. Silber and Sievens, eds., *Yankee Correspondence*, 99.

14. Pena, ed., "Dr. Charles S. Cooper's 'Reminiscences,'" 85–86.

15. Ibid., 86.

16. McFarland, *Some Experiences of the Eighth Vermont*, first two quotations on 4; final quotation on 5.

17. Ibid., 8, 9.

18. Ibid., 17, final quotation, 18.

19. Silber, *The Romance of Reunion*, 159–96.

20. McFarland, *Some Experiences of the Eighth Vermont*, 7.

21. Ibid., 8.

22. Ibid.

23. Stephen F. Spalding Letter, VtHS.

24. On alcohol, see W. J. Rorabaugh, *The Alcoholic Republic: An American Tradition* (New York: Oxford University Press, 1979).

25. *Ouachita Telegraph* (Monroe, LA), October 18, 1866; see also *New York Times*, October 9, 1866. The ill-fated ship was traveling from New York to New Orleans.

26. Case of Mrs. M. Johnson v. Succession of B. Robbins, in J. Hawkins, ed., *Reports of Cases Argued and Determined in the Supreme Court of Louisiana, Volume XX, for the Year 1868* (New Orleans: Caxton, 1868), 569–71.

27. Ann Braude, *Radical Spirits: Spiritualism and Women's Rights in Nineteenth-Century America* (Boston: Beacon, 1989).

28. Timothy J. Gilfoyle, *City of Eros: New York City, Prostitution, and the Commercialization of Sex, 1790–1920* (New York: Norton, 1992), 130, 232–34.

29. Judith Kelleher Schafer, *Brothels, Depravity, and Abandoned Women: Illegal Sex in Antebellum New Orleans* (Baton Rouge: Louisiana State University Press, 2009), esp. 140–55, quotation on 155. For the postwar period, see Alecia P. Long, *The Great Southern Babylon: Sex, Race, and Respectability in New Orleans, 1865–1920* (Baton Rouge: Louisiana State University Press, 2004). See also Dell Upton, *Madaline: Love and Survival in Antebellum New Orleans* (Athens: University of Georgia Press, 1996).

30. Steven J. Ramold, *Baring the Iron Hand: Discipline in the Union Army* (DeKalb: Northern Illinois University Press, 2010), 79–80, 110–18, quotation on 118; Joy J. Jackson, "Keeping Law and Order in New Orleans under General Butler, 1862," *Louisiana History* 34, no. 1 (1993): 51–67.

31. Catherine Clinton, *Public Women and the Confederacy* (Milwaukee: Marquette University Press, 1999), 9.

32. Patricia Cline Cohen, *The Murder of Helen Jewett* (New York: Vintage, 1998); Amy Gilman Srebnick, *The Mysterious Death of Mary Rogers: Sex and Culture in Nineteenth-Century New York* (New York: Oxford University Press, 1995); Daniel Stashower, *The Beautiful Cigar Girl: Mary Rogers, Edgar Allen Poe, and the Invention of Murder* (New York: Dutton, 2006).

33. Srebnick, *Mysterious Death of Mary Rogers*, 53. For sporting culture, see also Richard Stott, *Jolly Fellows: Male Milieus in Nineteenth-Century America* (Baltimore: Johns Hopkins University Press, 2009), 97–128, 214–24.

34. Patricia Cline Cohen, Timothy J. Gilfoyle, and Helen Lefkowitz Horowitz, *The Flash Press: Sporting Male Weeklies in 1840s New York* (Chicago: University of Chicago Press, 2008).

35. Ibid., 10, 23–25.

36. Helen Lefkowitz Horowitz, *Rereading Sex: Battles over Sexual Knowledge and Suppression in Nineteenth-Century America* (New York: Knopf, 2002), 11. For examples of this dialogue, see Helen Lefkowitz Horowitz, ed., *Attitudes toward Sex in Antebellum America: A Brief History with Documents* (Boston: Bedford/St. Martin's, 2006). See also Donna Dennis, *Licentious Gotham: Erotic Publishing and Its Prosecution in Nineteenth-Century New York* (Cambridge: Harvard University Press, 2009).

37. Carroll Smith-Rosenberg, "Beauty, the Beast and the Militant Woman," *American Quarterly* 23 (October 1971): 562–84; Daniel S. Wright, *The First of Causes to Our Sex: The Female Moral Reform Movement in the Antebellum Northeast, 1834-1848* (New York: Routledge, 2006).

38. Spalding wrote that "'Liber XXI' was the first thing that met my eyes" when he opened Peck's letter. The practice of numbering letters was a common way of knowing which letters arrived and which went astray (Stephen F. Spalding Letter, VtHS).

39. George W. Matsell, *Vocabulum: or, the Rogue's Lexicon* (New York: George W. Matsell, 1859); Ned Buntline, *The Mysteries and Miseries of New York: A Story of Real Life* (New York: Bedford, 1847), glossary on 113–16.

40. Ted Cohen, *Jokes: Philosophical Thoughts on Joking Matters* (Chicago: University of Chicago Press, 1999), 25. Cohen adds that jokes "can work only with certain audiences. The audience must supply something in order to either get the joke or to be amused by it" (ibid., 12).

41. William T. Church to friend Ed, May 14, 1863, William T. Church Civil War Letters, Special Collections, Bailey/Howe Library, UVM.

42. Deming Fairbanks to Mary Spencer Fairbanks, May 12, 1862, Deming Dexter Fairbanks Letters, VtHS.

43. Gilfoyle, *City of Eros*, 59, 60; for juvenile sex workers, see 63–70. For New York City prostitution, see also Marilyn Wood Hill, *Their Sisters' Keepers: Prostitution in New York City, 1830-1870* (Berkeley: University of California Press, 1993).

44. Christine Stansell, *City of Women: Sex and Class in New York, 1789-1860* (New York: Knopf, 1982), 176, 179.

45. Rufus Kinsley to Charlie Bingham, July 23, 1863, Rufus Kinsley Papers, VtHS.

Chapter Five

1. Foote, *The Gentlemen and the Roughs*, on double standard, 37; on courts, 10–11.

2. For example, the most recent court-martial had been held on May 7, 1862, and had included Lieutenant Colonel Brown, Captain Childs, and Lt. C. Nason (see Regimental Books, Eighth Vermont Infantry, vol. 3, NARA).

3. De Forest, *A Volunteer's Adventures*, 29.

4. Ibid., 29; drinking, 29–30.

5. General Order no. 13: court-martial transcript, dated July 25, 1862, Algiers, Louisiana, Regimental Books, Eighth Vermont Infantry, vol. 3, NARA.

6. Foote, *The Gentlemen and the Roughs,* 129, 133.

7. See ibid., 145–70, for tensions between officers and privates, including examples of officers shooting men in the ranks, usually without punishment, and of ordinary soldiers' hostility against officers who put on airs, enforced regulations too tightly, or questioned the equality and masculinity of their men. For anti-officer humor, see Cameron Nickels, *Civil War Humor* (Jackson: University Press of Mississippi, 2010), 99–100.

8. General Order no. 10, dated June 19, 1862, Algiers, Louisiana, Regimental Books, Eighth Vermont Infantry, vol. 3, NARA.

9. General Order no. 13: court-martial transcript, dated July 25, 1862, Algiers, Louisiana, Regimental Books, Eighth Vermont Infantry, vol. 3, NARA.

10. For court record, see ibid. Smith's age is recorded in Regimental Books, Eighth Vermont Infantry, vol. 2, NARA.

11. General Order no. 13: court-martial transcript, dated July 25, 1862, Algiers, Louisiana, Regimental Books, Eighth Vermont Infantry, vol. 3, NARA.

12. Ramold, *Baring the Iron Hand,* 61–66; quotation on 61.

13. Ibid., liquor, 150; drunken officers and authority, 170–71, 210–11.

14. Ibid., 342; see also 315.

15. General Order no. 13: court-martial transcript, dated July 25, 1862, Algiers, Louisiana, Regimental Books, Eighth Vermont Infantry, vol. 3, NARA.

16. Coffin, *Nine Months to Gettysburg,* 27.

17. General Order no. 13: court-martial transcript, dated July 25, 1862, Algiers, Louisiana, Regimental Books, Eighth Vermont Infantry, vol. 1, NARA.

18. For the disproportionate influence of attorneys on American government, see Charles Sellers, *The Market Revolution: Jacksonian America, 1815–1846* (New York: Oxford University Press, 1991), 47–50.

Chapter Six

1. Stephen F. Spalding Letter, VtHS. Curiously, fellow Vermonter Rufus Kinsley also refers to a grave as a "long home" (Rankin, ed., *Diary of a Christian Soldier,* 117).

2. Stephen F. Spalding Letter, VtHS.

3. Child's assignment in Regimental Books, Eighth Vermont Infantry, vol. 1, NARA, by order of General George Shepley; Carpenter, *History of the Eighth Regiment Vermont Volunteers,* 40; Butterfield detailed, Regimental Books, Eighth Vermont Infantry, vol. 3, Special Order No. 30, June 27, 1862, NARA.

4. Stephen F. Spalding Letter, VtHS; Roger Hovey to Dear Sisters, July 16, 1862, Roger Hovey Civil War Letters, Special Collections, Bailey/Howe Library, UVM; Justus Gale to Dear Sister, July 18, 1862, Gale–Morse Family Papers, 1861–1876, VtHS; Horace Morse to mother and sister, September 23, 1862, Frank Morse Papers, Massachusetts Historical Society, Boston; Pena, ed., "Dr. Charles S. Cooper's 'Reminiscences,'" all quotations on 81; Kathryn S. Meier, "'No Place for the Sick':

Nature's War on Civil War Soldier Mental and Physical Health in the 1862 Peninsula and Shenandoah Valley Campaigns," *Journal of the Civil War Era* 1 (June 2011): 178–79.

5. Rankin, ed., *Diary of a Christian Soldier*, 97 (June 1, 1862). Rankin notes that Kinsley crossed this passage out of the diary with "a thick line" (ibid.).

6. Justus Gale to Dear Father, June 6, 1862, Gale–Morse Family Papers, 1861–1876, VtHS.

7. Stephen F. Spalding Letter, VtHS; Browning, "I Am Not So Patriotic as I Once Was," 217–43.

8. "W," dated July 15, 1862, Algiers, in *Brattleboro Phoenix*, August 7, 1862; Roger Hovey to Dear and ever beloved sister, July 2, 1862, Roger Hovey Civil War Letters, Special Collections, Bailey/Howe Library, UVM; Justus Gale to Dear Father, June 6, 1862, Gale–Morse Family Papers, 1861–1876, VtHS. Not everyone in the regiment felt this way. At least one private was able to keep himself entertained, though his letter reveals him to be witty enough to amuse himself under most circumstances. Jonathan Allen noted: "We can find plenty to do and to amuse us. shooting alligators (I shot one yesterday measuring fourteen feet long as the 'western school marm' measured, viz. seven feet from the end of the nose to the tip of his tail and seven back again) riding on the handcars, picking berries etc." All in all, he thought he was enjoying himself "as well as I ever did a summer" (Jonathan V. Allen to Dear Sister, June 20, 1862, Allen Family Papers, 1856–1884, VtHS).

9. Benjamin Morse to Rosina Morse, October 22, 1862 and July 30, 1862, in Silber and Sievens, eds., *Yankee Correspondence*, 161, 159; Dexter Deming Fairbanks to Mary Spencer Fairbanks, September 16, 1862, Dexter Deming Fairbanks Letters, VtHS. Benjamin Morse also wrote his wife: "what a good sound there is to the word *home* I think that we shall all know how to value it if we ever get there" (Benjamin Morse to Rosina Morse, June 7, 1862, Gale–Morse Family Papers, 1861–1876, VtHS).

10. Carpenter, *History of the Eighth Regiment Vermont Volunteers*, v.

11. Ibid., 46.

12. Ibid. 46, 47.

13. Casualties listed in Regimental Books, Eighth Vermont Infantry, vol. 1, NARA.

14. Jonathan V. Allen to Dear Parents, June 23, 1862, Allen Family Papers, 1856–1884, VtHS.

15. The trauma of combat and its aftermath is emphasized in Reid Mitchell, *Civil War Soldiers: Their Expectations and Their Experiences* (New York: Simon and Schuster, 1988), 62–64; Eric T. Dean Jr., *Shook over Hell: Post-Traumatic Stress, Vietnam, and the Civil War* (Cambridge: Harvard University Press, 1997); and Joseph Allan Frank and George A. Reaves, *"Seeing the Elephant": Raw Recruits at the Battle of Shiloh* (New York: Greenwood , 1989), 87–128, especially the witnessing of casualties and battlefield fatalities, 105–8. Earl J. Hess does not diminish the horrors of Civil War battles, writing that "the northern soldier was deeply impressed by the sights and sounds associated with death and injury on the battlefield," but he emphasizes the ability of most soldiers to deploy various ideologies to minimize the psychological damage they suffered (see Hess, *The Union Soldier in Battle:*

Enduring the Ordeal of Combat [Lawrence: University of Kansas, 1997], quotation on 29).

16. Details of Victory Rotary's death from William Haskins to Dear Wife, May 14, 1862, William Haskins Papers, Special Collections, Bailey/Howe Library, UVM. Haskins also noted that Rotary was Chilean. All mortality statistics from Regimental Books, Eighth Vermont Infantry, vol. 1, Unit Roster, NARA.

17. Meier, "No Place for the Sick," 179–80, 184–86, 197–98; Drew Gilpin Faust, *This Republic of Suffering: Death and the American Civil War* (New York: Vintage, 2008): xi–101; on the absence of women, 9–10. The absence of loved ones, especially women, is noted in Hess, *The Union Soldier in Battle*, 133–42; and Reid Mitchell, *The Vacant Chair: The Northern Soldier Leaves Home* (New York: Oxford University Press, 1993), 71–87.

18. Nickels, *Civil War Humor*, 84–87, quotation on 83; Alice Fahs, *The Imagined Civil War: Popular Literature of the North and South* (Chapel Hill: University of North Carolina Press, 2001), 205–9. Union soldier James Abraham agreed, writing that "To die for one's country is glorious and honorable . . . but quite a different phrase when analyzed amid screeching shells, plunging shot and singing, zipping, thugging bullets, with charging, yelling masses all around, mingled with the cries of wounded comrades and the agony of dying friends. . . . I conclude much of the battlefield poetry is written on a distant hill and the scenes gathered through a long range field glass" (Ramold, *Baring the Iron Hand*, 193).

19. Robert E. Bonner, *The Soldier's Pen: Firsthand Impressions of the Civil War* (New York: Hill and Wang, 2006), 50.

20. Jon Grinspan, "'Sorrowfully Amused': The Popular Comedy of the Civil War" *Journal of the Civil War Era* 1 (September 2011): 313–38, quotation on 314.

21. Pierson, *Mutiny at Fort Jackson*, 148–50, quotation on 149. For recent work on white southern Unionists during the Civil War, start with Victoria E. Bynum, *The Free State of Jones: Mississippi's Longest Civil War* (Chapel Hill: University of North Carolina Press, 2001); Richard Nelson Current, *Lincoln's Loyalists: Union Soldiers from the Confederacy* (New York: Oxford University Press, 1992); William W. Freehling, *The South Versus the South: How Anti-Confederate Southerners Shaped the Course of the Civil War* (New York: Oxford University Press, 2001); Margaret M. Storey, *Loyalty and Loss: Alabama's Unionists in the Civil War and Reconstruction* (Baton Rouge: Louisiana State University Press, 2004); Daniel E. Sutherland, ed., *Guerillas, Unionists, and Violence on the Confederate Home Front* (Fayetteville: University of Arkansas Press, 1999); and John C. Inscoe and Robert C. Kenzer, eds., *Enemies of the Country: New Perspectives on Unionists in the Civil War South* (Athens: University of Georgia Press, 2001).

22. Pierson, *Mutiny at Fort Jackson*, 45–51.

23. Stephen F. Spalding Letter, VtHS.

24. For the mutiny at Fort Jackson and desertion from Confederate units across southeastern Louisiana in its aftermath, see Pierson, *Mutiny at Fort Jackson*, 97–128.

25. Quotation from Bruce Catton, *Mr. Lincoln's Army* (1951; repr., New York: Anchor, 1990), 177. See also Fahs, *Imagined Civil War*, 202.

26. Regimental Books, Eighth Vermont Infantry, vol. 3, NARA. The regimental order was published in accordance with Departmental Headquarters Special Order No. 173, which called for twenty-five other corporals to be detailed from other regiments.

27. The rumor that the Ninth Connecticut recruited successfully in New Orleans was also picked up by John W. De Forest, who wrote (six days after Spalding's letter) that "three regiments of white troops are to be recruited here, and no one expects any difficulty in finding the men. Probably half the fellows who defended the forts [Jackson and St. Phillip] against us are already wearing our uniform; some of them, I know, are in the twelfth Connecticut, and many more in the Ninth" (De Forest, *A Volunteer's Adventures*, 31).

28. Thomas Hamilton Murray, *History of the Ninth Regiment, Connecticut Volunteer Infantry, "The Irish Regiment," in the War of the Rebellion, 1861–65* (New Haven: Price, Lee and Adkins, 1903), 241–300.

29. G. Howard Hunter, "The Politics of Resentment: Unionist Regiments and the New Orleans Immigrant Community, 1862–1864" *Louisiana History* 44 (Spring 2003): 185–210.

30. Murray, *History of the Ninth Regiment, Connecticut Volunteer Infantry*, 47–51. Of interest is Murray's comment that the Ninth was, even at its start, surrounded by rumors of its notorious conduct; of its train ride north, he wrote that "the wildest and most ridiculous yarns were circulated about the command at this stage" (see ibid., 48).

31. Regimental Books, Eighth Vermont Infantry, vol. 1, NARA.

32. Private Andrew McKenzie, Compiled Service Records, Eighth Vermont Infantry, NARA.

33. "Casualty Sheet," Private Andrew McKenzie, Compiled Service Records, Eighth Vermont Infantry, NARA. Hospital steward William Haskins noted that McKenzie's only personal effects were an "Overcoat & Blanket," which was not unusual but was more spare than most (William Haskins, "Hospital Memorandum Book," William Haskins Papers, Special Collections, Bailey/Howe Library, UVM).

34. Carpenter, *History of the Eighth Regiment Vermont Volunteers*, 66.

35. Ibid., 23.

36. Historians have begun to plumb the psychological stresses under which Civil War soldiers labored. Unlike the soldiers studied by these historians, however, Spalding used humor to get through the difficult summer of 1862 (see Carol Reardon, *With a Sword in One Hand and Jomini in the Other: The Problem of Military Thought in the Civil War North* [Chapel Hill: University of North Carolina Press, 2012], 89–123; and Dean, *Shook over Hell*).

37. Croteau, also spelled Croto, drowned when "he attempted to jump into a boat after it had started from the wharf" but failed to reach it (Roger Hovey to unknown, June 20, 1862, Roger Hovey Civil War Letters, Special Collections, Bailey/Howe Library, UVM).

38. Regimental Books, Eighth Vermont Infantry, vol. 1, NARA,

39. Rankin, ed., *Diary of a Christian Soldier*, 100.

40. Ibid., 106. Kinsley especially believed that Confederates deserved the ruin

visited upon them (see entries for January 1 and 21, 1863, ibid., 116, 119).

41. Justus Gale to Dear Mother + all the rest, July 24, 1862, Gale–Morse Family Papers, 1861–1876, VtHS; Jonathan V. Allen to Parents, July 23, 1862, Allen Family Papers, 1856–1884, VtHS.

Chapter Seven

1. Carpenter, *History of the Eighth Regiment Vermont Volunteers*, 127.

2. Ibid.

3. Edward Cunningham, *The Port Hudson Campaign, 1862–1863* (Baton Rouge: Louisiana State University Press, 1963), 66.

4. Ibid.

5. Stephen F. Spalding Letter, VtHS.

6. Ibid.

7. Carpenter, *History of the Eighth Regiment Vermont Volunteers*, 51; *Official Records of the War of the Rebellion*, 30 vols. (Washington, DC: Government Printing Office, 1894–1922), ser. 1, 15:132.

8. Col. Stephen Thomas, report dated September 6, 1862, in *Official Records of the War of the Rebellion*, ser. 1, 15:134. For addition details about the flag of truce incident, see Carpenter, *History of the Eighth Regiment Vermont Volunteers*, 53–55; Rufus Kinsley to Daniel, September 19, 1862, Rufus Kinsley Papers, VtHS; and Dexter Deming Fairbanks to Unknown, September 16, 1862, Dexter Deming Fairbanks Letters, VtHS. For an overview of this small campaign, see Frazier, *Fire in the Cane Field*, 114–22; Winters, *The Civil War in Louisiana*, 155–56; and Holman D. Jordan Jr., "The Eighth Regiment of Vermont Volunteers in the Lafourche Country, 1862–1863," *Vermont History* 31 (April 1963): 106–16. For a veteran's recollections of the incident, see McFarland, *Some Experiences of the Eighth Vermont*, 6, 10–12.

9. Carpenter, *History of the Eighth Regiment Vermont Volunteers*, 56; *Official Records of the War of the Rebellion*, ser. 1, 15:134. "Disasters" is used by Carpenter to describe the events of "Raceland, Des Allemands, and Boutte Station" (Carpenter, *History of the Eighth Regiment Vermont Volunteers*, 57–58). The cow incident is in McFarland, *Some Experiences of the Eighth Vermont*, 14.

10. Carpenter, *History of the Eighth Regiment Vermont Volunteers*, 57.

11. The seven men were Bernard Hurst, Deidrich Bahne, John and Michael Leichleiver, Michael Masman, Frank Paul, and Gustave C. Becher. The three men from Hall's command who were executed after more formal proceedings in Mississippi were Thomas Graham, Dennis Kean, and William Brown (Carpenter, *History of the Eighth Regiment Vermont Volunteers*, 63–66, 72–73). Of the ten men, only Deidrich Bahne's Confederate service can be traced. He served as a private in the Thirtieth Louisiana Volunteers as late as March 20, 1862 (see Andrew B. Booth, *Records of Louisiana Confederate Soldiers and Louisiana Confederate Commands* [New Orleans, 1920]). For the massacre, see also McFarland, *Some Experiences of the Eighth Vermont*, 12–13, 18.

12. Homer B. Sprague, *History of the Thirteenth Infantry Regiment of Connecticut Volunteers, during the Great Rebellion* (Hartford: Case, Lockwood and

Co. 1867), 56. Gen. Benjamin Butler also expressed outrage, alluding to the soldiers who were "in cold blood murdered" (*Official Records of the War of the Rebellion*, ser. 1, 15:165).

13. Carpenter, *History of the Eighth Regiment Vermont Volunteers*, 68–71, 74–75, quotations from 69; see also *Official Records of the War of the Rebellion*, ser. 1, 15:161–63. For an overview of the campaign, see Barnes F. Lathrop, "The Lafourche District in 1862: Invasion," *Louisiana History* 2 (Spring 1961): 175–201.

14. Report of Brig. Gen. Godfrey Weitzel, January 18, 1863, *Official Records of the War of the Rebellion*, ser. 1, 15:236. Brief summaries of this campaign can be found in Winters, *Civil War in Louisiana*, 212–14; and Frazier, *Fire in the Cane Field*, 315–24.

15. Carpenter, *History of the Eighth Regiment Vermont Volunteers*, 83–86, quotation on 85. Captain Dutton appears to have been popular with his men as well as with his colonel; in May 1862, his men presented him with a watch valued at fifty-five dollars (*Brattleboro Phoenix*, May 29, 1862). Other accounts at the time of the battle put the number of Confederate prisoners between thirty and forty, with seven or eight men killed (see *Vermont Watchman and State Journal* [Montpelier], February 6 and 13, 1863).

16. Carpenter, *History of the Eighth Regiment Vermont Volunteers*, 91. There is a description of this battle told by Rufus Kinsley of Company F, who served as one of the sixty sharpshooters (see Rankin, ed., *Diary of a Christian Soldier*, 117–18).

17. *Official Records of the War of the Rebellion*, ser. 1, 15:236.

18. 1st Lieutenant Stephen Spalding, February 28, 1863, entry, Compiled Service Records, Eighth Vermont Infantry, NARA. It should be said that Captain Child's return to front-line service is not mentioned in other places, hence it is stated only tentatively here. The appearance of it in the compiled service record, a bureaucratic document created at the time, seems credible. How long he stayed with Company B is not known. The presence of Child and Spalding in the same company may have made it easier for Colonel Thomas to make Spalding acting adjutant.

19. Carpenter, *History of the Eighth Regiment Vermont Volunteers*, 97–101, quotation on 98.

20. Ibid., 102–4.

21. Ibid., 105. The Battle of Bisland and the related Battle of Irish Bend are detailed in Donald S. Frazier, *Thunder across the Swamp: The Fight for the Lower Mississippi, February 1863-May 1863* (Buffalo Gap, TX: State House, 2011), 147–3312. For a larger perspective of the campaign to Alexandria, see Winters, *Civil War in Louisiana*, 230–41; and Frazier, *Thunder across the Swamp*, 313–469.

22. Jonathan V. Allen to Dear Sister Mary, April 30, 1863, Allen Family Papers, 1856–1884, VtHS.

23. Frazier, *Thunder across the Swamp*, 352.

24. Carpenter, *History of the Eighth Regiment Vermont Volunteers*, 108–9. The patriotic, sentimental resolutions were later printed in at least one Vermont newspaper (see *Vermont Watchman and State Journal* [Montpelier], June 13, 1863).

25. The officers were Henry Dutton and Alvin Franklin. The NCOs promoted

into other companies were S. E. Howard, William Smith, Joseph Dunton, and Merrill Hodgkins (Carpenter, *History of the Eighth Regiment Vermont Volunteers*, 266, 268–70, 272). The "8th Vermont Volunteers Associational Records, 1871–1924" are housed at the Vermont Historical Society. The names of Colonel Thomas and his most prominent subordinates, including Barstow, Mead, Dutton, and Carpenter, recur there with great frequency. Quotation from anonymous correspondent in the *Boston Traveller*, qtd. in *Vermont Watchman and State Journal* (Montpelier), May 8, 1863.

26. John Barstow to Dear Father, December 28, 1862, John Lester Barstow Civil War Letters and Misc. 1862–1865, Special Collections, Bailey/Howe Library, UVM. For the extent to which interpersonal conflicts over promotion could dominate brigade life and damage morale, see Robert J. Wynstra, *The Rashness of That Hour: Politics, Gettysburg, and the Downfall of Confederate Brigadier General Alfred Iverson* (New York: Savas Beatie, 2010).

27. Carpenter, *History of the Eighth Regiment Vermont Volunteers*, 108. Spalding's friend John Barstow, however, noted (perhaps in Spalding's defense) that "the murderer had shown signs of insanity for a few days and is now confined as a lunatic. (John Barstow to My Dear Laura, May 16, 1863, John Lester Barstow Civil War Letters and Misc. 1862–1865, Special Collections, Bailey/Howe Library, UVM). Quotation and information about O'Mere's court-martial from General Order no. 13: court-martial transcript, dated July 25, 1862, Algiers, Louisiana, Regimental Books, Eighth Vermont Infantry, vol. 3, NARA.

28. Regimental Books, Eighth Vermont Infantry, vol. 1, NARA.

29. Someone, perhaps Spalding himself, cared enough to spread the word about his promotion to adjutant. His promotion is noted, without the word "Acting," in the *Manchester (NH) Daily Mirror*, May 30, 1863. His status as "Acting Adjutant," however, is confirmed in a letter written by a fellow officer at the time of Spalding's death (see *Vermont Watchman and State Journal* [Montpelier], July 3, 1863).

30. Perrin qtd. in Ezra J. Warner, *Generals in Gray* (Baton Rouge: Louisiana State University Press, 1959), 235; Sarah Watts, *Rough Rider in the White House: Theodore Roosevelt and the Politics of Desire* (Chicago: University of Chicago Press, 2003), 225.

31. The first half of the Port Hudson campaign is detailed in Lawrence Lee Hewitt, *Port Hudson: Confederate Bastion on the Mississippi* (Baton Rouge: Louisiana State University Press, 1987); Winters, *Civil War in Louisiana*, 242–67; and the more dated Cunningham, *The Port Hudson Campaign*.

32. See esp. Cunningham, *The Port Hudson Campaign*, 49, 66–67.

33. Carpenter, *History of the Eighth Regiment Vermont Volunteers*, 113.

34. Ibid., 114.

35. First quotation, ibid., 114–15; second quotation, 115.

36. Ibid., 115.

37. Winters, *Civil War in Louisiana*, 251.

38. Justus Gale to unknown, May 29, 1863, Gale–Morse Family Papers, 1861–1876, VtHS; Jonathan V. Allen to Dear Sister, June 6, 1863, Allen Family Papers, 1856–1884, VtHS.

39. Hewitt, *Port Hudson,* 142.

40. Ibid.

41. Ibid., 155; see also 147.

42. For African Americans at Port Hudson, see Hollandsworth, *The Louisiana Native Guard;* Lawrence Lee Hewitt, "An Ironic Route to Glory: Louisiana's Native Guards at Port Hudson," in *Black Soldiers in Blue: African American Troops in the Civil War Era,* ed. John David Smith (Chapel Hill: University of North Carolina Press, 2002), 78–106; and Hewitt, *Port Hudson,* 147–50.

43. Hewitt, *Port Hudson,* 154, 153.

44. Ibid, 153.

45. Lawrence L. Hewitt and Arthur W. Bergeron Jr., eds., *Post Hospital Ledger: Port Hudson, Louisiana, 1862–1863* (Baton Rouge: Le Comite des Archives de la Louisiane, 1981), 95.

46. Jonathan Allen to Miss Mary Allen, June 6, 1863, Jonathan V. Allen Letters, Allen Family Papers, 1856–1884, VtHS. Lieutenant Colonel Dillingham's regimental report listed nine killed and forty-five wounded for the day, a total of fifty-four casualties (see report by Lieutenant Colonel Dillingham in *Burlington Weekly Sentinel,* June 26, 1863).

47. Cunningham, *Port Hudson Campaign,* 122, 157n62.

48. *Soldier's News-Letter* (Brashear City, LA), May 16, 1863.

49. Justus F. Gale to sister Almeda, June 19, 1863, in Marshall, *A War of the People,* 158; Jonathan V. Allen to Dear Sister Elsie, June 15, 1863, VtHS.

50. *Official Records of the War of the Rebellion,* ser. 1, 26:14.

51. For overviews of June 14, see Cunningham, *Port Hudson Campaign,* 82–93; and Winters, *Civil War in Louisiana,* 267–73.

52. Carpenter, *History of the Eighth Regiment Vermont Volunteers,* 123.

53. Ibid., 124.

54. Clarke, *War Stories,* 28–50.

55. St. Johnsbury *Caledonian,* July 10, 1863, http://vermontcivilwar.org/units/8/obits.php?input=5557; longer quotation from Montpelier *Vermont Watchman and State Journal* (Montpelier), July 3, 1863, copied from "Times."

56. *Vermont Watchman and State Journal* (Montpelier), July 3, 1863, copied from "Times."

57. Ibid.

58. Ibid.

59. Hewitt and Bergeron, eds., *Post Hospital Ledger,* 98–100.

60. Edward Belville to Dear friends at home, June 16, 1863, Joseph Rutherford Collection, Special Collections, Bailey/Howe Library, UVM.

61. Ibid.; *Vermont Watchmen and State Journal* (Montpelier), July 10, 1863, copied from the *Newport News;* Jonathan Allen to Dear Sister Elsie, June 15, 1863, Allen Family Papers, 1856–1884, VtHS. For other descriptions of the June 14 attack, see Justus F. Gale to sister Almeda, June 19, 1863, in Marshall, *A War of the People,* 157–58; letter by W, June 20, 1863, published in *Brattleboro Phoenix,* July 23, 1863; William Haskins to Dear Sarah, June 28, 1863, William Haskins Papers, Special Collections, Bailey/Howe Library, UVM; and John R. Dawson to Dear friend

Elmira, November 12, 1863, Cargill Family Collection, Special Collections, Bailey/ Howe Library, UVM. One historian, in a postwar speech celebrating Vermont soldiers, claimed that the Eighth Vermont lost "nearly a third of its number" on June 14, including Adjutant Spalding (George Grenville Benedict, *An Oration before the Re-Union Society of Vermont Officers, in the Representatives' Hall, Montpelier, VT, November 2, 1882* [Montpelier: Watchman and Journal Press, 1882], 16).

62. Samuel C. Hyde Jr., *A Wisconsin Yankee in Confederate Bayou Country: The Civil War Reminiscences of a Union General* (Baton Rouge: Louisiana State University Press, 2009), 150. Death of rescuers and Paine's subsequent medical care, 151–53.

63. Carpenter, *History of the Eighth Regiment Vermont Volunteers,* 127.

64. *Vermont Watchman and State Journal* (Montpelier), July 3, 1863, copied from "Times."

65. *Vermont Watchman and State Journal* (Montpelier), August 28, 1863, copied from *Newport News.*

66. Ibid.

67. Ibid.

68. The Derby Line, Vermont, chapter of the Grand Army of the Republic (Post 115 of Vermont's 116 Posts) was the Stephen F. Spaulding post (see http://suvcw. org/garposts/vt.pdf.; and *Boston Herald,* January 30, 1895, which reports on the founding of the Spaulding post within the last year).

Conclusion

1. *Newport News,* July 8, 1863.

2. Examples that have influenced this study, at least indirectly, include Carlo Ginzburg, *The Cheese and the Worms: The Cosmos of a Sixteenth-Century Miller* (1976; repr., Baltimore: Johns Hopkins University Press, 2013); Paul E. Johnson, *Sam Patch: The Famous Jumper* (New York: Hill and Wang, 2003); Catherine Clinton, *Harriet Tubman: The Road to Freedom* (Boston: Little, Brown, 2004); Timothy J. Gilfoyle, *A Pickpocket's Tale: The Underworld of Nineteenth-Century New York* (New York: Norton, 2006); Rhys Isaac, *Landon Carter's Uneasy Kingdom: Revolution and Rebellion on a Virginia Plantation* (New York: Oxford University Press, 2004); Nick Salvatore, *We All Got History: The Memory Books of Amos Webber* (1996; repr., New York: Vintage, 1997); Jon F. Sensbach, *Rebecca's Revival: Creating Black Christianity in the Atlantic World* (Cambridge: Harvard University Press, 2005); Laurel Thatcher Ulrich, *A Midwife's Tale: The Life of Martha Ballard, Based on Her Diary, 1785–1812* (New York: Knopf, 1990); Jean Fagan Yellin, *Harriet Jacobs: A Life; The Remarkable Adventures of the Woman Who Wrote "Incidents in the Life of a Slave Girl"* (New York: Basic, 2004); and Alfred F. Young, *The Shoemaker and the Tea Party: Memory and the American Revolution* (Boston: Beacon, 1999). For a theoretical consideration of these kinds of biographies, see Lepore, "Historians Who Love Too Much," 129–44.

BIBLIOGRAPHY

Primary Sources

Manuscript Collections

Barre, Vermont

Vermont Historical Society (VtHS)
    Allen Family Papers, 1856–1884
    Deming Dexter Fairbanks Letters
    Gale–Morse Family Papers, 1861–1876
    Rufus Kinsley Diary and Papers
    Stephen F. Spalding Letter

Boston, Massachusetts

Massachusetts Historical Society
    Wilder Dwight Papers
    Frank Morse Papers

Burlington, Vermont

Special Collections, Bailey/Howe Library, University of Vermont (UVM)
    John Lester Barstow Civil War Letters and Misc. 1862–1865
    Cargill Family Collection
    William T. Church Civil War Letters
    Williams Haskins Papers
    Roger Hovey Civil War Letters
    Joseph Rutherford Collection

New Orleans

Williams Research Center, Historic New Orleans Collection
    Melvan Tibbetts Letters

NEW YORK CITY

New-York Historical Society
    Seventh Regiment Records, 1767–1983
        Board and Council of Officers—Meeting Minutes, 1860–1861
        Civil War Recruits, Donors, 1861
        "Co. I: Roster, 1838–1913" (bound volume)
        Correspondence, 1860–1869
        "Guard Book, Camp Cameron, 1861" (bound volume)
        "Muster Rolls, 1861–1863" (bound volume)
        Regimental Orders, 1855–1861

WASHINGTON, D. C.

National Archives and Records Administration (NARA)
    Compiled Service Records
        Eighth Vermont Infantry
        Seventh New York State Militia, M557
    Pension Records, Union Veterans.
    Regimental Books, Record Group 94
        Eighth Vermont Infantry, Books 1–4

Newspapers and Magazines

Boston Herald (1895)
Brattleboro (VT) Phoenix (1862–1863)
Burlington (VT) Weekly Sentinel (1862)
Christian Advocate and Journal (1861)
Manchester (NH) Daily Mirror (1863)
Ouchita Telegraph (Monroe, LA) (1866)
New Orleans Daily True Delta (1862)
Newport (VT) News (1863)
New York Evangelist (1861)
New York Daily Times (1861, 1866)
Soldier's News-Letter (Brashear City, LA) (1863)
St. Johnsbury (VT) Caledonian (1863)
Vanity Fair (1861)
Vermont Watchman and State Journal (Montpelier) (1861–63)

Books, Articles, and Microfilm Collections

Buntline, Ned. *The Mysteries and Miseries of New York: A Story of Real Life.*
    New York: Bedford, 1847.

Butler, Benjamin F. *Butler's Book: Autobiography and Personal Reminiscences of Maj.-Gen. Benjamin F. Butler.* Boston: A. M. Thayer, 1892.

———. *Character and Results of the War: How to Prosecute and How to End It.* New York: Wm. C. Bryant and Co., 1863.

———. *Miscellaneous Papers, 1835–1858.* Washington, D.C.: Library of Congress, 1959. Microfilm.

———. *Private and Official Correspondence of General Benjamin F. Butler during the Period of the Civil War.* Vol. 1, *April 1860–June 1862.* Norwood, MA: Plimpton, 1917.

Carpenter, George N. *History of the Eighth Regiment Vermont Volunteers, 1861–1865.* Boston: Deland and Barta, 1886.

A Catalogue of the Officers and Students of the University of Vermont, for the Academical Year 1856–7. Burlington: Free Press Print, 1856.

A Catalogue of the Officers and Students of the University of Vermont, for the Academical Year 1858–9. Burlington: Sentinel Print, 1858.

A Catalogue of the Officers and Students of the University of Vermont, for the Academical Year 1859–60. Burlington: Sentinel Print, 1859.

De Forest, John William. *A Volunteer's Adventures: A Union Captain's Record of the Civil War.* Baton Rouge: Louisiana State University Press, 1996.

Duncan, Russell, ed. *Blue-Eyed Child of Fortune: The Civil War Letters of Colonel Robert Gould Shaw.* Athens: University of Georgia Press, 1992.

Gifford, Sanford Robinson. "Military Correspondence. Washington, May 17, 1861." *Crayon* 8 (June 1861).

Hawkins, J., ed. *Reports of Cases Argued and Determined in the Supreme Court of Louisiana, Volume XX, for the Year 1868.* New Orleans: Caxton, 1868.

Hergesheimer, Edwin. *Map Showing the Distribution of the Slave Population of the Southern United States. Compiled from the Census of 1860.* Washington, D.C., 1861.

Hyde, Samuel C., Jr. *A Wisconsin Yankee in Confederate Bayou Country: The Civil War Reminiscences of a Union General.* Baton Rouge: Louisiana State University Press, 2009.

Kamphoefner, Walter D., and Wolfgang Helbich, eds. *Germans in the Civil War: The Letters They Wrote Home.* Translated by Susan Carter Vogel. Chapel Hill: University of North Carolina Press, 2006.

Marshall, Jeffrey D., ed. *A War of the People: Vermont Civil War Letters.* Hanover, NH: University Press of New England, 1999.

Matsell, George W. *Vocabulum: or, the Rogue's Lexicon.* New York: George W. Matsell, 1859.

McFarland, Moses. *Some Experiences of the Eighth Vermont West of the Mississippi.* Morrisville and Hyde Park, VT: News and Citizen, 1896.

Murray, Hamilton. *History of the Ninth Regiment, Connecticut Volunteer Infantry, "The Irish Regiment," in the War of the Rebellion, 1861–1865.* New Haven: Price, Lee and Adkins, 1903.

Official Records of the Union and Confederate Navies in the War of the Rebellion. 30 vols. Washington, DC: Government Printing Office, 1894–1922.

Pena, Chris, ed. "Dr. Charles S. Cooper's 'Reminiscences.'" *Louisiana History* 41 (Winter 2000): 71–91.

Rankin, David C., ed. *Diary of a Christian Soldier: Rufus Kinsley and the Civil War.* New York: Cambridge University Press, 2004.

Rowland, Kate Mason, and Mrs. Morris L. Croxall, eds. *The Journal of Julia Le Grand: New Orleans, 1862–1863.* Richmond: Everett Waddey, 1911.

Shifflett, Crandall, ed. *John Washington's Civil War: A Slave Narrative.* Baton Rouge: Louisiana State University Press, 2008.

Silber, Nina, and Mary Beth Sievens, eds. *Yankee Correspondence: Civil War Letters between New England Soldiers and the Home Front.* Charlottesville: University Press of Virginia, 1996.

Smith, George G. *Leaves from a Soldier's Diary.* Putnam, CT: George G. Smith, 1906.

Sons of Union Veterans of the Civil War. http://suvcw.org/garposts/vt.pdf.

Sprague, Homer B. *History of the 13th Infantry Regiment of Connecticut Volunteers, during the Great Rebellion.* Hartford: Case, Lockwood and Co., 1867.

Sturtevant, Ralph Orson. *Pictorial History: The Thirteenth Regiment Vermont Volunteers, 1861–1865.* Burlington, VT, 1913.

Thompson, L. S. *The Story of Mattie J. Jackson: Her Parentage—Experience of Eighteen Years in Slavery—Incidents during the War—Her Escape from Slavery. A True Story.* Lawrence, MA: The Sentinel Office, 1866.

Twain, Mark. *The Innocents Abroad, or the New Pilgrim's Progress.* 1869. Reprint, Ware, UK: Wordsworth Classics, 2010.

———. *Roughing It.* 1872. Reprint, Berkeley: University of California Press, 1995.

The War of the Rebellion: A Compilation of the Official Records of the Union and Confederate Armies. 128 vols. Washington, D.C.: Government Printing Office, 1880–1901.

Watkins, Sam R. *Co. Aytch: A Confederate Memoir of the Civil War.* 1962. Reprint, New York: Touchstone, 1997.

Webb, Alexander S. *The Peninsula: McClellan's Campaign of 1862.* (New York: Scribner's Sons, 1881.

Winthrop, Theodore. *Life in the Open Air, and Other Papers.* Boston: Ticknor and Fields, 1862.

Secondary Sources

Books and Articles

Ash, Stephen V. *When the Yankees Came: Conflict and Chaos in the Occupied South, 1861–1865*. Chapel Hill: University of North Carolina Press, 1995.

Ashworth, John. *The Coming of the Civil War, 1850–1861*. Vol. 2 of *Slavery, Capitalism, and Politics in the Antebellum Republic*. New York: Cambridge University Press, 2007.

Avery, Kevin J., and Franklin Kelly, eds. *Hudson River School Visions: The Landscapes of Sanford R. Gifford*. New Haven: Yale University Press, 2003.

Baker, Jean H. *Affairs of Party: The Political Culture of Northern Democrats in the Mid-Nineteenth Century*. Ithaca: Cornell University Press, 1983.

Balcerski, Thomas J. "'Under These Classic Shades Together': Intimate Male Friendship at the Antebellum College of New Jersey." *Pennsylvania History: A Journal of Mid-Atlantic Studies* 80 (Spring 2013): 169–203.

Benedict, George Grenville. *An Oration before the Re-Union Society of Vermont Officers, in the Representatives' Hall, Montpelier, VT, November 2, 1882*. Montpelier: Watchman and Journal Press, 1882.

Benson, Lee. *The Concept of Jacksonian Democracy: New York as a Test Case*. Princeton: Princeton University Press, 1961.

Blight, David W. *Race and Reunion: The Civil War in American Memory*. Cambridge: Harvard University Press, 2001.

Blue, Frederick J. "The Poet and the Reformer: Longfellow, Sumner, and the Bonds of Male Friendship, 1837–1874." *Journal of the Early Republic* 15 (Summer 1995): 273–97.

Boatner, Mark M. *The Civil War Dictionary*. New York: McKay, 1959.

Bonner, Robert E. *The Soldier's Pen: Firsthand Impressions of the Civil War*. New York: Hill and Wang, 2006.

Booth, Andrew B. *Records of Louisiana Confederate Soldiers and Louisiana Confederate Commands*. New Orleans, 1920.

Bragg, Jefferson Davis. *Louisiana in the Confederacy*. Baton Rouge: Louisiana State University Press, 1941.

Brasher, Glenn David. *The Peninsula Campaign and the Necessity of Emancipation*. Chapel Hill: University of North Carolina Press, 2012.

Braude, Ann. *Radical Spirits: Spiritualism and Women's Rights in Nineteenth-Century America*. Boston: Beacon, 1989.

Browning, Judkin. "'I Am Not So Patriotic as I Once Was': The Effects of Military Occupation on the Occupying Union Soldiers during the Civil War." *Civil War History* 55 (June 2009): 217–43.

———. "Removing the Mask of Nationality: Unionism, Racism, and Federal Military Occupation in North Carolina, 1862–1865." *Journal of Southern History* 71 (August 2005): 589–620.

Bynum, Victoria E. *The Free State of Jones: Mississippi's Longest Civil War.* Chapel Hill: University of North Carolina Press, 2001.

Carriere, Marius M., Jr. "Anti-Catholicism, Nativism, and Louisiana Politics in the 1850s." *Louisiana History* 35 (Fall 1994): 455–74.

Carroll, Andrew, ed. *War Letters: Extraordinary Correspondence from American Wars.* New York: Scribner, 2001.

Catton, Bruce. *Mr. Lincoln's Army.* 1951. Reprint, New York: Anchor, 1990.

Cecere, David A. "Carrying the Home Front to War: Soldiers, Race, and New England Culture during the Civil War." In *Union Soldiers and the Northern Home Front: Wartime Experiences, Postwar Adjustments,* edited by Paul A. Cimbala and Randall M. Miller, 293–323. New York: Fordham University Press, 2002.

Child, Hamilton. *Gazetteer and Business Directory of Lamoille and Orleans Counties, Vermont, for 1883–84.* Syracuse, NY: Journal Office, 1883.

Clarke, Frances M. *War Stories: Suffering and Sacrifice in the Civil War North.* Chicago: University of Chicago Press, 2011.

Clinton, Catherine. *Harriet Tubman: The Road to Freedom.* Boston: Little, Brown, 2004.

———. *Public Women and the Confederacy.* Milwaukee: Marquette University Press, 1999.

Coffin, Howard. *Nine Months to Gettysburg: Stannard's Vermonters and the Repulse of Pickett's Charge.* Woodstock, VT: Countryman, 1997.

Cohen, Patricia Cline. *The Murder of Helen Jewett.* New York: Vintage, 1998.

Cohen, Patricia Cline, Timothy J. Gilfoyle, and Helen Lefkowitz Horowitz. *The Flash Press: Sporting Male Weeklies in 1840s New York.* Chicago: University of Chicago Press, 2008.

Cohen, Ted. *Jokes: Philosophical Thoughts on Joking Matters.* Chicago: University of Chicago Press, 1999.

Crain, Caleb. *American Sympathy: Men, Friendship, and Literature in the New Nation.* New Haven: Yale University Press, 2001.

Cunningham, Edward. *The Port Hudson Campaign, 1862–1863.* Baton Rouge: Louisiana State University Press, 1963.

Current, Richard Nelson. *Lincoln's Loyalists: Union Soldiers from the Confederacy.* New York: Oxford University Press, 1992.

Davis, William C., and Bell I. Wiley, eds. *Photographic History of the Civil War: Fort Sumter to Gettysburg.* 1981. Reprint, New York: Black Dog and Leventhal, 1994.

Dean, Eric T., Jr. *Shook over Hell: Post-Traumatic Stress, Vietnam, and the Civil War*. Cambridge: Harvard University Press, 1997.

Deitcher, David. *Dear Friends: American Photographs of Men Together, 1840–1918*. New York: Abrams, 2001.

Dennis, Donna. *Licentious Gotham: Erotic Publishing and Its Prosecution in Nineteenth-Century New York*. Cambridge: Harvard University Press, 2009.

Detzer, David. *Dissonance: The Turbulent Days between Fort Sumter and Bull Run*. New York: Harcourt, 2006.

Dew, Charles B. *Apostles of Disunion: Southern Secession Commissioners and the Causes of the Civil War*. Charlottesville: University Press of Virginia, 2001.

Durham, Walter T. *Nashville, the Occupied City, 1862–1863*. 1985. Reprint, Knoxville: University of Tennessee Press, 2008.

———. *Reluctant Partners: Nashville and the Union, July 1, 1863 to June 30, 1865*. 1987. Reprint, Knoxville: University of Tennessee Press, 2008.

Fahs, Alice. *The Imagined Civil War: Popular Literature of the North and South*. Chapel Hill: University of North Carolina Press, 2001.

Faust, Drew Gilpin. *This Republic of Suffering: Death and the American Civil War*. New York: Vintage Civil War Library, 2008.

Foote, Lorien. *The Gentlemen and the Roughs: Violence, Honor, and Manliness in the Union Army*. New York: New York University Press, 2010.

Formisano, Ronald P. *The Birth of Mass Political Parties: Michigan, 1827–1861*. Princeton: Princeton University Press, 1971.

———. "The Invention of the Ethnocultural Interpretation." *American Historical Review* 99 (April 1994): 453–77.

Frank, Joseph Allan, and George A. Reaves. *"Seeing the Elephant": Raw Recruits at the Battle of Shiloh*. New York: Greenwood, 1989.

Frazier, Donald S. *Fire in the Cane Field: The Federal Invasion of Louisiana and Texas, January 1861–January 1863*. Buffalo Gap, TX: State House Press, 2009.

———. *Thunder across the Swamp: The Fight for the Lower Mississippi, February 1863–May 1863*. Buffalo Gap, TX: State House Press, 2011.

Freehling, William W. *The South Versus the South: How Anti-Confederate Southerners Shaped the Course of the Civil War*. New York: Oxford University Press, 2001.

Freud, Sigmund. *Jokes and Their Relation to the Unconscious*. Translated by James Strachey. New York: Norton, 1989.

Fuhrer, Mary Babson. *A Crisis of Community: The Trials and Transformation of a New England Town, 1815–1848*. Chapel Hill: University of North Carolina Press, 2014.

Fulton, Joe B. *The Reconstruction of Mark Twain: How a Confederate Bush-whacker Became the Lincoln of Our Literature.* Baton Rouge: Louisiana State University Press, 2010.

Gannon, Barbara A. *The Won Cause: Black and White Comradeship in the Grand Army of the Republic.* Chapel Hill: University of North Carolina Press, 2011.

Gilfoyle, Timothy J. *City of Eros: New York City, Prostitution, and the Commercialization of Sex, 1790–1920.* New York: Norton, 1992.

———. *A Pickpocket's Tale: The Underworld of Nineteenth-Century New York.* New York: Norton, 2006.

Ginzburg, Carlo. *The Cheese and the Worms: The Cosmos of a Sixteenth-Century Miller.* 1976. Reprint, Baltimore: Johns Hopkins University Press, 2013.

Glatthaar, Joseph T. *Forged in Battle: The Civil War Alliance of Black Soldiers and White Officers.* New York: Meridian, 1991.

Glover, Lorri. *Southern Sons: Becoming Men in the New Nation.* Baltimore: Johns Hopkins University Press, 2010.

Goodyear, Adam. *1861: The Civil War Awakening.* New York: Knopf, 2011.

Grinspan, Jon. "'Sorrowfully Amused': The Popular Comedy of the Civil War." *Journal of the Civil War Era* 1 (September 2011): 313–38.

Halttunen, Karen. *Confidence Men and Painted Women: A Study of Middle-Class Culture in America, 1830–1870.* New Haven: Yale University Press, 1982.

Harvey, Eleanor Jones. *The Civil War and American Art.* Washington, DC: Smithsonian American Art Museum in association with Yale University Press, 2012.

Hess, Earl J. *Pickett's Charge: The Last Attack at Gettysburg.* Chapel Hill: University of North Carolina Press, 2001.

———. *The Union Soldier in Battle: Enduring the Ordeal of Combat.* Lawrence: University of Kansas, 1997.

Hewitt, Lawrence Lee. "An Ironic Route to Glory: Louisiana's Native Guards at Port Hudson." In *Black Soldiers in Blue: African American Troops in the Civil War Era,* edited by John David Smith, 78–106. Chapel Hill: University of North Carolina Press, 2002.

———. *Port Hudson: Confederate Bastion on the Mississippi.* Baton Rouge: Louisiana State University Press, 1987.

Hewitt, Lawrence Lee, and Arthur W. Bergeron Jr., eds. *Post Hospital Ledger: Port Hudson, Louisiana, 1862–1863.* Baton Rouge: Le Comite des Archives de la Louisiane, 1981.

Hill, Marilyn Wood. *Their Sisters' Keepers: Prostitution in New York City, 1830–1870.* Berkeley: University of California Press, 1993.

Hollandsworth, James G. *The Louisiana Native Guards: The Black Military Experience during the Civil War.* Baton Rouge: Louisiana State University Press, 1995.

Holzer, Harold, and Mark E. Neely Jr. *Mine Eyes Have Seen the Glory: The Civil War in Art.* New York: Orion, 1993.

Horowitz, Helen Lefkowitz, ed. *Attitudes toward Sex in Antebellum America: A Brief History with Documents.* Boston: Bedford/St. Martin's, 2006.

———. *Rereading Sex: Battles over Sexual Knowledge and Suppression in Nineteenth-Century America.* New York: Knopf, 2002.

Hunter, G. Howard. "The Politics of Resentment: Unionist Regiments and the New Orleans Immigrant Community, 1862–1864." *Louisiana History* 44 (Spring 2003): 185–210.

Inscoe, John C., and Robert C. Kenzer, eds. *Enemies of the Country: New Perspectives on Unionists in the Civil War South.* Athens: University of Georgia Press, 2001.

Isaac, Rhys. *Landon Carter's Uneasy Kingdom: Revolution and Rebellion on a Virginia Plantation.* New York: Oxford University Press, 2004.

Jabour, Anya. "Male Friendship and Masculinity in the Early National South: William Wirt and His Friends." *Journal of the Early Republic* 20 (Spring 2000): 83–111.

Jackson, Joy J. "Keeping Law and Order in New Orleans under General Butler, 1862." *Louisiana History* 34, no. 1 (1993): 51–67.

Janney, Caroline E. *Remembering the Civil War: Reunion and the Limits of Reconciliation.* Chapel Hill: University of North Carolina Press, 2013.

Jeffrey, William H. *Successful Vermonters: A Modern Gazetteer of Caledonia, Essex, and Orleans Counties.* East Burke, VT: Historical Publishing, 1904.

Johnson, Paul E. *Sam Patch: The Famous Jumper.* New York: Hill and Wang, 2003.

Johnson, Robert Underwood, and Clarence Clough Buel, eds. *Battles and Leaders of the Civil War.* Vol. 1. New York: Century, 1887.

Jordan, Holman D., Jr. "The Eighth Regiment of Vermont Volunteers in the Lafourche Coountry, 1862–1863." *Vermont History* 31 (April 1963): 106–16.

Jordan, Winthrop D. *White over Black: American Attitudes toward the Negro, 1550–1812.* New York: Norton, 1968.

Kamensky, Jane. *The Exchange Artist: A Tale of High-Flying Speculation and America's First Banking Collapse.* New York: Viking, 2008.

Keller, Christian B. *Chancellorsville and the Germans: Nativism, Ethnicity, and Civil War Memory.* New York: Fordham University Press, 2007.

Kimmel, Michael. *Manhood in America: A Cultural History.* New York: Free Press, 1996.

King, William Casey. *Ambition, A History: From Vice to Virtue.* New Haven: Yale University Press, 2013.

Landis, Michael Todd. *Northern Men with Southern Loyalties.* Ithaca: Cornell University Press, 2014.

Lathrop, Barnes F., ed. "Federals 'Sweep the Coast': An Expedition into St. Charles Parish, August 1862." *Louisiana History* 9 (Winter 1968): 62–68.

———. "The Lafourche District in 1862: Invasion," *Louisiana History* 2 (Spring 1961): 175–201.

Leland, Claude. *The First Hundred Years: Records and Reminiscences of a Century of Company I, Seventh Regiment N.G.N.Y., 1838–1938.* N.p., 1938.

Lemire, Elise. *"Miscegenation": Making Race in America.* Philadelphia: University of Pennsylvania Press, 2002.

Lepore, Jill. "Historians Who Love Too Much: Reflections on Microhistory and Biography." *Journal of American History* 88 (June 2001): 129–44.

Levin, Kevin M. "Black Confederates Out of the Attic and Into the Mainstream." *Journal of the Civil War Era* 4 (December 2014): 627–36.

Levine, Bruce. *Confederate Emancipation: Southern Plans to Free and Arm Slaves during the Civil War.* New York: Oxford University Press, 2006.

Litwack, Leon F. *Been in the Storm So Long: The Aftermath of Slavery.* New York: Knopf, 1979.

Lockwood, John, and Charles Lockwood. *The Siege of Washington: The Untold Story of the Twelve Days That Shook the Union.* New York: Oxford University Press, 2011.

Long, Alecia P. *The Great Southern Babylon: Sex, Race, and Respectability in New Orleans, 1865–1920.* Baton Rouge: Louisiana State University Press, 2004.

Longacre, Edward A. *The Early Morning of the War: Bull Run, 1861.* Norman: University of Oklahoma Press, 2014.

Lonn, Ella. *Foreigners in the Confederacy.* Chapel Hill: University of North Carolina Press, 1940.

Lott, Eric. *Love and Theft: Blackface Minstrelsy and the American Working Class.* New York: Oxford University Press, 1993.

Manning, Chandra. *What This Cruel War Was Over: Soldiers, Slavery, and the Civil War.* New York: Vintage Civil War Library, 2007.

Marten, James Alan. *Sing Not War: The Lives of Union and Confederate Veter-*

ans in Gilded Age America. Chapel Hill: University of North Carolina Press, 2011.

Marvel, William. *Lee's Last Retreat: The Flight to Appomattox.* Chapel Hill: University of North Carolina Press, 2002.

Masur, Kate. "'A Rare Phenomenon of Philological Vegetation': The Word 'Contraband' and the Meanings of Emancipation in the United States." *Journal of American History* 93 (March 2007): 1050–84.

Matsui, John H. "War in Earnest: The Army of Virginia and the Radicalization of the Union War Effort, 1862." *Civil War History* 58 (June 2012): 180–223.

McPherson, James M. *The Illustrated Battle Cry of Freedom: The Civil War Era.* New York: Oxford University Press, 2003.

Meier, Kathryn S. "'No Place for the Sick': Nature's War on Civil War Soldier Mental and Physical Health in the 1862 Peninsula and Shenandoah Valley Campaigns." *Journal of the Civil War Era* 1 (June 2011): 176–206.

Mitchell, Reid. *Civil War Soldiers: Their Expectations and Their Experiences.* New York: Simon and Schuster, 1988.

———. *The Vacant Chair: The Northern Soldier Leaves Home.* New York: Oxford University Press, 1993.

Neff, John R. *Honoring the Civil War Dead: Commemoration and the Problem of Reconciliation.* Lawrence: University Press of Kansas, 2005.

Nickels, Cameron. *Civil War Humor.* Jackson: University Press of Mississippi, 2010.

Oakes, James. *Freedom National: The Destruction of Slavery in the United States, 1861–1865.* New York: Norton, 2012.

Pace, Robert F. "'It Was Bedlam Let Loose': The Louisiana Sugar Country and the Civil War." *Louisiana History* 39, no. 4 (1998): 389–409.

Pearson, Mike Parker, and the Stonehenge Riverside Project. *Stonehenge: Exploring the Greatest Stone Age Mystery.* New York: Simon and Schuster, 2012.

Pierson, Michael D. *Free Hearts and Free Homes: Gender and American Antislavery Politics.* Chapel Hill: University of North Carolina Press, 2003.

———. "'He Helped the Poor and Snubbed the Rich': Benjamin F. Butler and Class Politics in Lowell and New Orleans." *Massachusetts Historical Review* 7 (2005): 36–68.

———. *Mutiny at Fort Jackson: The Untold Story of the Fall of New Orleans.* Chapel Hill: University of North Carolina Press, 2008.

Quitt, Martin H. *Stephen A. Douglas and Antebellum Democracy.* New York: Cambridge University Press, 2012.

Ramold, Steven J. *Baring the Iron Hand: Discipline in the Union Army.* DeKalb: Northern Illinois University Press, 2010.

Reardon, Carol. *Pickett's Charge in History and Memory.* Chapel Hill: University of North Carolina Press, 1997.

———. *With a Sword in One Hand and Jomini in the Other: The Problem of Military Thought in the Civil War North.* Chapel Hill: University of North Carolina Press, 2012.

Ripley, C. Peter. *Slaves and Freedmen in Civil War Louisiana.* Baton Rouge: Louisiana State University Press, 1976.

Rorabaugh, W. J. *The Alcoholic Republic: An American Tradition.* New York: Oxford University Press, 1979.

Rosenberg, Charles E. "Sexuality, Class and Role in 19th-Century America." In *The American Man,* edited by Elizabeth H. Pleck and Joseph H. Pleck, 223–29. Englewood Cliffs, NJ: Prentice-Hall, 1980.

Rosenheim, Jeff L. *Photography and the American Civil War.* New Haven: Yale University Press, 2013.

Rotundo, E. Anthony. "Learning about Manhood: Gender Ideals and the Middle-Class Family in Nineteenth-Century America." In *Manliness and Morality: Middle-Class Masculinity in Britain and America,* edited by J. A. Mangan and James Walvin, 35–51. New York: St. Martin's, 1987.

———. "Romantic Friendship: Male Intimacy and Middle-Class Youth in the Northern United States, 1800–1900." *Journal of Social History* 23 (October 1989): 1–25.

Rousey, Dennis C. *Policing the Southern City: New Orleans, 1805–1889.* Baton Rouge: Louisiana State University Press, 1996.

Rowland, Ingrid D. *From Pompeii: The Afterlife of a Roman Town.* Cambridge: Harvard University Press, 2014.

Sacher, John M. *A Perfect War of Politics: Parties, Politicians, and Democracy in Louisiana, 1824–1861.* Baton Rouge: Louisiana State University Press, 2003.

Salvatore, Nick. *We All Got History: The Memory Books of Amos Webber.* 1996. Reprint, New York: Vintage, 1997.

Schafer, Judith Kelleher. *Brothels, Depravity, and Abandoned Women: Illegal Sex in Antebellum New Orleans.* Baton Rouge: Louisiana State University Press, 2009.

Sellers, Charles. *The Market Revolution: Jacksonian America, 1815–1846.* New York: Oxford University Press, 1991.

Sensbach, Jon F. *Rebecca's Revival: Creating Black Christianity in the Atlantic World.* Cambridge: Harvard University Press, 2005.

Shugg, Roger W. *Origins of Class Struggle in Louisiana: A Social History of*

White Farmers and Laborers during Slavery and After, 1840–1875. Baton Rouge: Louisiana State University Press, 1939.

Silber, Nina. *The Romance of Reunion: Northerners and the South, 1865–1900.* Chapel Hill: University of North Carolina Press, 1993.

Silbey, Joel H. "'Let the People See': Reflections on Ethnoreligious Forces in American Politics." *Journal of Libertarian Studies* 6 (Summer/Fall 1982): 333–47.

———. *A Respectable Minority: The Democratic Party in the Civil War Era, 1860–1868.* New York: Norton, 1977.

———. "'There Are Other Questions Besides That of Slavery Merely': The Democratic Party and Antislavery Politics." In *Crusaders and Compromisers: Essays on the Relationship of the Antislavery Struggle to the Antebellum Party System,* edited by Alan M. Kraut, 143–75. Westport, CT.: Greenwood, 1983.

Simpson, Marc. "The Bright Side: 'Humorously Conceived and Truthfully Executed.'" In *Winslow Homer: Paintings of the Civil War,* edited by Simpson, 47–64. San Francisco: Bedford Arts, 1988.

Smith-Rosenberg, Carroll. "Beauty, the Beast and the Militant Woman." *American Quarterly* 23 (October 1971): 562–84.

Soulé, Leon Cyprian. *The Know Nothing Party in New Orleans: A Reappraisal.* Baton Rouge: Louisiana Historical Association, 1961.

Spalding, Charles Warren. *The Spalding Memorial: A Genealogical History of Edward Spalding of Virginia and Massachusetts Bay. And His Descendants . . . Revised and Enlarged.* 1897. Reprint, Chelmsford, MA: Spalding Documentation Services, 1996.

Srebnick, Amy Gilman. *The Mysterious Death of Mary Rogers: Sex and Culture in Nineteenth-Century New York.* New York: Oxford University Press, 1995.

Stansell, Christine. *City of Women: Sex and Class in New York, 1789–1860.* New York: Knopf, 1982.

Stashower, Daniel. *The Beautiful Cigar Girl: Mary Rogers, Edgar Allen Poe, and the Invention of Murder.* New York: Dutton, 2006.

Storey, Margaret M. *Loyalty and Loss: Alabama's Unionists in the Civil War and Reconstruction* Baton Rouge: Louisiana State University Press, 2004.

Stott, Richard. *Jolly Fellows: Male Milieus in Nineteenth-Century America.* Baltimore: Johns Hopkins University Press, 2009.

Sutherland, Daniel E., ed. *Guerillas, Unionists, and Violence on the Confederate Home Front.* Fayetteville: University of Arkansas Press, 1999.

Swinton, William. *History of the Seventh Regiment, National Guard, State of New York.* Boston: Fields, Osgood and Co., 1870.

Toplin, Robert Brent. *Ken Burns's The Civil War: Historians Respond.* New York: Oxford University Press, 1996.

Towers, Frank. *The Urban South and the Coming of the Civil War.* Charlottesville: University of Virginia Press, 2004.

Ulrich, Laurel Thatcher. *A Midwife's Tale: The Life of Martha Ballard, Based on Her Diary, 1785–1812.* New York: Knopf, 1990.

Upton, Dell. *Another City: Urban Life and Urban Spaces in the New American Republic.* New Haven: Yale University Press, 2008.

———. *Madaline: Love and Survival in Antebellum New Orleans.* Athens: University of Georgia Press, 1996.

Varon, Elizabeth R. *Appomattox: Victory, Defeat, and Freedom at the End of the Civil War.* New York: Oxford University Press, 2014.

Warner, Ezra J. *Generals in Gray.* Baton Rouge: Louisiana State University Press, 1959.

Watts, Sarah. *Rough Rider in the White House: Theodore Roosevelt and the Politics of Desire.* Chicago: University of Chicago Press, 2003.

Weber, Jennifer L. *Copperheads: The Rise and Fall of Lincoln's Opponents in the North.* New York: Oxford University Press, 2006.

White, Jonathan W. *Emancipation, the Union Army, and the Reelection of Abraham Lincoln.* Baton Rouge: Louisiana State University Press, 2014.

Williams, David. *Rich Man's War: Class, Caste, and Confederate Defeat in the Lower Chattahoochie Valley.* Athens: University of Georgia Press, 1998.

Winters, John D. *The Civil War in Louisiana.* Baton Rouge: Louisiana State University Press, 1963.

Wright, Daniel S. *The First of Causes to Our Sex: The Female Moral Reform Movement in the Antebellum Northeast, 1834–1848.* New York: Routledge, 2006.

Wynstra, Robert J. *The Rashness of That Hour: Politics, Gettysburg, and the Downfall of Confederate Brigadier General Alfred Iverson.* New York: Savas Beatie, 2010.

Yellin, Jean Fagan. *Harriet Jacobs: A Life: The Remarkable Adventures of the Woman Who Wrote "Incidents in the Life of a Slave Girl."* New York: Basic, 2004.

Young, Alfred F. *The Shoemaker and the Tea Party: Memory and the American Revolution.* Boston: Beacon, 1999.

INDEX